POLITICS
REFORMED

POLITICS REFORMED

THE ERIC VOEGELIN SERIES IN POLITICAL PHILOSOPHY

America and the Political Philosophy of Common Sense, by Scott Philip Segrest
Beginning the Quest: Law and Politics in the Early Work of Eric Voegelin, by Barry Cooper
How World Politics Is Made: François Mitterand and the Reunification of Germany, by Tilo Schabert
Worldview and Mind: Religious Thought and Psychological Development, by Eugene Webb
Rethinking Rights: Historical, Political, and Philosophical Perspectives, edited by Bruce P. Frohnen and Kenneth L. Grasso
The Philosopher and the Storyteller: Eric Voegelin and Twentieth-Century Literature, by Charles R. Embry
The Constitutionalism of American States, edited by George E. Connor and Christopher W. Hammons
Voegelin Recollected: Conversations on a Life, edited by Barry Cooper and Jodi Bruhn
The American Way of Peace: An Interpretation, by Jan Prybyla
Faith and Political Philosophy: The Correspondence between Leo Strauss and Eric Voegelin, 1934–1964, edited by Peter Emberley and Barry Cooper
New Political Religions, or an Analysis of Modern Terrorism, by Barry Cooper
Art and Intellect in the Philosophy of Étienne Gilson, by Francesca Aran Murphy
Robert B. Heilman and Eric Voegelin: A Friendship in Letters, 1944–1984, edited by Charles R. Embry
Voegelin, Schelling, and the Philosophy of Historical Existence, by Jerry Day
Transcendence and History: The Search for Ultimacy from Ancient Societies to Postmodernity, by Glenn Hughes
Eros, Wisdom, and Silence: Plato's Erotic Dialogues, by James M. Rhodes
The Narrow Path of Freedom and Other Essays, by Eugene Davidson
Hans Jonas: The Integrity of Thinking, by David J. Levy
A Government of Laws: Political Theory, Religion, and the American Founding, by Ellis Sandoz
Augustine and Politics as Longing in the World, by John von Heyking
Lonergan and the Philosophy of Historical Existence, by Thomas J. McPartland

BOOKS IN THE ERIC VOEGELIN INSTITUTE SERIES IN POLITICAL PHILOSOPHY: STUDIES IN RELIGION AND POLITICS

Etty Hillesum and the Flow of Presence: A Voegelinian Analysis, by Meins G. S. Coetsier

Christian Metaphysics and Neoplatonism, by Albert Camus; translated with an introduction by Ronald D. Srigley

Voegelin and the Problem of Christian Political Order, by Jeffrey C. Herndon

Republicanism, Religion, and the Soul of America, by Ellis Sandoz

Michael Oakeshott on Religion, Aesthetics, and Politics, by Elizabeth Campbell Corey

Jesus and the Gospel Movement: Not Afraid to Be Partners, by William Thompson-Uberuaga

The Religious Foundations of Francis Bacon's Thought, by Stephen A. McKnight

Glenn A. Moots

POLITICS REFORMED

The Anglo-American Legacy of Covenant Theology

UNIVERSITY OF MISSOURI PRESS
COLUMBIA

POLITICS REFORMED

University of Missouri Press, Columbia, Missouri 65211
Printed and bound in the United States of America

First paperback printing, 2022

Library of Congress Cataloging-in-Publication Data

Moots, Glenn A.
Politics reformed : the Anglo-American legacy of covenant theology / Glenn A. Moots.
p. cm. —(Eric Voegelin Institute series in political philosophy)
Includes bibliographical references and index.
ISBN 978–0–8262–1885–8 (cloth edition : alk. paper)
ISBN 978–0–8262–2263–3 (paperback edition : alk. paper)

1. Political theology. 2. Covenant theology 3. Covenants—Religious aspects—Reformed Church 4. Reformed Church—Doctrines. I. Title.
BT83.59.M66 2010
230'.42--dc22

2010009777

™ This paper meets the requirements of the American National Standard for Permanence of Paper for Printed Library Materials, Z39.48, 1984.

Designer and Typesetter: Foley Design
Typefaces: Optima and Minion

Publication of this book has been assisted by a contribution from the Eric Voegelin Institute, which gratefully acknowledges the generous support provided for the series by the Earhart Foundation and the Sidney Richards Moore Memorial Fund.

FOR

Pastor Raymond P. Joseph, d. 2006
and
Francis John Bicsak, d. 1993
both instruments of Providence

Contents

Preface

In 1939 and 1953, Perry Miller published the two volumes of his seminal work on Puritanism, *The New England Mind.* They became landmarks of scholarship and captivated readers with a powerful and humane narrative of theological ideas moving an entire society in fascinating and consequential directions. The ideas of Reformed Protestants continue to interest scholars. Part of the attraction is obvious enough. Reformed theology plays a substantial role in the history of Europe and America. There is also something polarizing and powerful in its arguments and personalities. We are therefore not surprised to find some who are partisans in their study of Reformed Protestantism. Some praise Calvin and his colleagues, christening them the founders of modern liberty as we know it. Others cast Calvin or the Puritans as theocratic oppressors. Both friends and enemies often miss the mark, however.

The aim of this book is to enter the debate with a generous approach similar to that of Miller's *The New England Mind.* My own study of Reformed Protestantism, *Politics Reformed,* tells the story of a very powerful political and religious idea: making a covenant. Covenants were among the very first symbols and devices to be used in ancient politics, and they remain with us in various forms today. Covenants represent a powerful moral ethos unique among all forms of political and social organization.

This book is an exploration of the merits and limitations of covenantal social thinking and asks whether such ideas have relevance today. While the usual cast of characters is revisited, this study is not just about John Calvin or the English Puritans. They play a supporting role in my pursuit of a larger theological and political tradition that remains both compelling and instructive.

While it is tempting to make apologies for talking about religion and politics together, it cannot be avoided. Covenantal politics is an important part of history. But what is past is sometimes prologue. Covenants may offer an alternative to our current fascination with dichotomous ideologies: liberalism or communitarianism, capitalism or socialism, democracy or totalitarianism. If solutions come clothed in the robes of a religious tradition, we must not block our ears and wish them away. Rightly understood, covenantal thinking has the potential to move us past the kind of cynicism and expediency that characterize political life today. Learning how to approach the call of divine transcendence must remain part of our political conversation. Transcendent politics can sometimes be a very dangerous politics, but it is the only kind of politics fit for human beings. So long as we remain lower than the angels but higher than brute beasts, our nature will rightly call on us to somehow wed transcendence to our political orders. What follows shows how one particular political tradition answered that call, and how we might think about it today.

Acknowledgments

An author is a debtor. In the course of his work he has drawn on the time, trust, and resources of others. He has relied on the talents of those who have gone before him, and he owes something to those who will use his work after it is published. The details of these obligations are not spelled out in contracts. They are implicit covenants that resemble the subject of this book. I hope those who find something of themselves in this book also find something to repay their contribution.

Too often authors will thank their family last, but I don't hesitate to mention them first. The degree of indulgence necessary to enable a book defies summary and adequate acknowledgment. To her vocation as wife and mother, Michelle quickly and cheerfully added the work of editor. This was a calling she surely did not anticipate, but she still tackled it with enthusiasm and sacrifice. Rebekah and Andrew supported me by loving gestures great and small. The encouraging notes written to support Daddy possess an eloquence and beauty surpassing all the virtues of great scholarship. My parents are surely pleased to discover that all this education and hard work finally amounted to something, and I owe them my thanks for instilling a love of learning in me.

I was blessed to be mentored by scholars who demonstrated measured and respectful treatment of religious politics. Cecil Eubanks generously launched my study of Puritanism and political theology almost twenty years ago. Jim Stoner always models keen wisdom and insight coupled with an infectious enthusiasm for political ideas. Ellis Sandoz exemplifies a peerless work ethic and broad erudition coupled with a tenacious and practical love of liberty. He bore with me while I wrestled with subjects herein over a long course of time, and he did so with patience and good nature. All three of them leave something of their legacy in all of my academic and scholarly endeavors. My faults and shortcomings are my own.

Intelligent pastors encouraged an honest and thoughtful inquiry into the practical meaning of theology. The late Pastor Ray Joseph was a model of dedication to the covenant as a motif of Reformed theology. Dr. Randy Toms served as an example of how one encounters the Christian tradition with historical appreciation and a generous mind.

Authors are often short of both time and money. Thankfully, money can buy a little more time. The Intercollegiate Studies Institute and Acton Institute were early financial supporters of my research with Salvatori and Calihan Fellowships. The academic administration at Northwood, particularly John Grether and Lance Lewis in the Michigan Academic Dean's office, helped by scheduling classes so as to facilitate dedicated blocks of time for writing. The Northwood library and Rochelle Zimmerman assisted with interlibrary loans and saved me from taking even more trips to the University of Michigan library.

Colleagues provided help on many fronts. The good offices of the Jack Miller Center (especially Mike Andrews) and the Lehrman American Studies Center (led by Kelly Hanlon) continue to facilitate the kind of fellowship and community that is hard to find in academe. The fruit of their noble efforts serves to inspire and recharge. Gordon Schochet was kind enough to offer criticism of an essay that abbreviates the argument of this book and thereby provided wise insight for the study of early modern religion and politics. My Northwood colleague, Benedict Hughes, was kind enough to edit some earlier versions of this work and provide encouragement to forge ahead. Colleagues and friends, whom I cannot even begin to rank by individual mention, have critiqued papers related directly or indirectly to the subjects in this book. Every conversation, partnership, and panel that turned to academic and scholarly matters heated the furnace that produces better writing and thinking.

John Brenner at the University of Missouri Press showed exemplary dedication in keeping this book on schedule. His labors are much appreciated. I am pleased to be published by this outstanding university press and also to join the Eric Voegelin Institute Series in Political Philosophy.

Ashgate Publishing Limited allowed reuse of some material in Chapter 11 of this book that was originally contained in a chapter on Daniel Elazar written for *The Ashgate Research Companion to Federalism,* edited by Ann Ward and Lee Ward. My study of Daniel Elazar in Chapter 11 does not exactly replicate what is contained in the Ashgate volume, but Ashgate graciously allowed me to use the lengthy passages that do overlap.

Appreciation is also due to the Swiss National Museums for allowing permission of the image of the helmet and sword of Ulrich Zwingli contained in their collection in Zurich. As I explain in this book, Reformed political theology sometimes prescribes taking up the sword. Zwingli's own sword and (damaged) helmet, worn at the battle where he met his death, are symbolic of that legacy.

POLITICS REFORMED

POLITICS REFORMED

Part I

PART I

1 INTRODUCTION
Returning to Political Theology

POLITICAL THEOLOGY

This is a study of a particular political theology and its variants, a tradition found among Reformed Protestants over three centuries and one that substantially changed the direction of political thinking in the modern world. "Political theology" is a term requiring some explanation, together with a brief defense of its use instead of the term "civil religion."[1] Noting the difference between these terms gets to the heart of the whole study.

"Theology" is a Greek word that applies the scholarly tradition of logos to the study of God.[2] Translated, logos can mean both speech and investigation. The earliest Greek philosophers understood logos to be a means of studying something by speaking about it. The earliest uses of the word "theology" are found in the works of Plato and Aristotle, who wanted to apply reasonable investigation to divine things. In Christianity the word is used both in this sense (reasonable investigation) and in the sense of words about or from God—the Word of God. The logos tradition, as it has been practiced within Christianity, emphasizes justification by argument and encourages both engagement and debate with secular philosophy and theory. To take a theo-logical approach implies that religious ideas and secular ideas can exist alongside each other and maintain a respectful discussion on the common ground of reason and speech. Thus, I intend "political theology" to be a term that respects religion and politics as a relationship between equals.

The term "civil religion," by contrast, implies a hierarchical approach to religion and politics that makes religion serve political goals. "Civil religion" flirts with judging religious opinions only in terms of what is expedient for the civil or political. This is the approach of Thomas Jefferson, Benjamin Franklin, Jean-Jacques Rousseau, and Niccolo Machiavelli. Jefferson's or Franklin's approach is superior to Rousseau's or Machiavelli's because it respects the ennobling spirit of religion to encourage the habits of ordered liberty or republican virtue. Machiavelli's or Rousseau's use is more cynical and utilitarian, using religion only to instill martial virtue or to impose ideological unity. But either use is a consequentialist approach to religion. The result is a dichotomous, even adversarial, approach to the intersection of religion and politics. For many reasons, this will not do. Religion is not the handmaid of politics.

Politics and religion, at least when practiced in a community, are best understood as partners. But this is admittedly a tense partnership. Individuals may sometimes have to resolve the tension when choosing between civil and religious imperatives. This is especially true in a liberal political order where individual rights and individual conscience are considered inviolable.

If one takes a long view of the *Western* experience, particularly following the Reformation, it is the mutual respect and support between politics and biblical religion (the dominant Western religion) that have encouraged liberty. To suggest dichotomous priorities of "religion" and "politics" invites paranoia and disables respectful discussion. Both church and state begin to wonder which will be subordinated to the other. Dichotomies that seek to divorce the civil from the religious, or to subordinate one to the other, function only in the abstract. They are contrary to political reality, which is always dictated by human nature, and human nature demonstrates itself to be both political and religious. Human nature is not either political or religious; it must be both political and religious.

Furthermore, the great traditions of biblical religion are political by nature. There are three reasons this is true. First, the practice of biblical religions is essentially social and requires institutional (political) structures and offices.[3] Second, biblical religions are inherently legal and ethical. They set boundaries on individual and community behavior. Third, biblical religions share with the political a common grounding in anthropology (in the classical sense); that is, their first principles begin with human nature. The great challenge for modern legal and political practice, therefore, is not to separate the "religious" from the "political." Instead, it is to determine proper jurisdiction for the civil and the religious, particularly as they relate to civil law and practice. Determining jurisdiction is the great challenge taken up by the most prominent early modern political philosophers. As conflict within the church spilled over into the civil during the seventeenth century, famous philosophers such as Baruch Spinoza, Thomas Hobbes, and John Locke tried to determine the proper boundaries for ecclesiastical and civil authorities. But for the most part, these political philosophers were not well-known to most people. At least, philosophers were not as well-known as churchmen and theologians. Furthermore, these philosophers were often working outside the bounds of accepted orthodoxy. We err if we look to them before we look to theologians. In the history of the church-state challenge, the arguments of Spinoza, Hobbes, and

Locke were arguably too little and too late. Where they make important contributions, they usually owe something to arguments made by theologians before them.

Though the challenge of religion and politics was known to Christians during the first fifteen hundred years of church history, the Reformation forced a reorientation of religion and politics. This reorientation occurred one hundred years or more before philosophers tried their hand at solving the problem. This study focuses on one tradition of political theology within the Reformation and its attempts to reconcile the civil/political and the religious. This "Reformed" (often erroneously called "Calvinist") tradition is particularly important because so many people subscribed to its theology. Reformed theology was more familiar to Europeans and Americans than the works of Spinoza, Hobbes, or Locke, and its doctrines had enormous political import.[4] The centerpiece of Reformed theology is the "covenant." Reformed theology's attention to covenanting distinguishes it from other Christian theologies.

THE CONTEMPORARY AND HISTORICAL IMPORTANCE OF POLITICAL THEOLOGY

In our current intellectual climate, some readers may be suspicious of the assertion that "political theology" can exist within our current political thinking. But both contemporary political practice and historical record remain intransigent against efforts to purge theology from political theory. One need only look at judicial or policy controversies in America to see how religion and politics remain in tense but perennial partnership. One might also consider debates about theological language in proposed drafts of the constitution of the European Union.[5] Perhaps most urgently, while the West continues to decide what crumbs of acknowledgment or influence it will now toss to its historical political theologies, it suffers attacks by a radically *other* political theology—that of resurgent political Islam.[6] One cannot argue that "they" have a political theology while the West does not, or that the goal should be to eliminate all political theology from political study and practice. The West continues to draw on its own political theology—even if only implicitly.[7] The scholarly community, even where it cherishes distinctly Western political values, often acts as if those political values can be found only in secular texts. This only contributes to an amnesia wherein we forget the theological roots of political theory.

Political theology must be acknowledged alongside the so-called Great Books. For centuries, theology advanced the discussion of political theory more than did the Great Books. Broad discussion of political ideas in the modern age owes its roots to the church as a political institution, Christian theology and its political implications, and the Bible as a political text in its own right. Furthermore, much modern political thought was written against the background of religious controversies. Until there is a successful effort to construct contemporary political theory free from theological arguments that have contributed to the advancement of political theory (and this would essentially be a construction from "whole cloth"), we must acknowledge that what is contemporary is inextricably bound to what is theological.[8]

The old biblical theologies not only stand in contrast to most other theologies and ideologies, they may also serve to revive the liberal West's deepest values in the face of social amnesia. The West not only confronts an identity crisis in the face of a hostile political theology; its own posterity seems unable to articulate any coherent defense of Western political virtues. This is a recipe for cultural suicide. The West appears forgetful or perhaps ashamed that religious axioms mattered historically *and matter still*—in both theory and practice. No one has yet succeeded in re-founding our modern, Western political virtues apart from some degree of theological premise. Until the proponents of a-theistic ideologies can succeed in fully rearticulating the essential Western political values, we are left with our theological roots. I hope to revive an understanding of theological roots here, perhaps in a way sensitive to modern sensibilities. But whether or not political theologies can be made sensitive to modern sensibilities cannot deter one from studying the historical record and making contemporary applications where one can. The historical record is what it is. Though the merits of political theology can be debated, they cannot be dismissed out of hand or forgotten.

REVISITING THE PARTICULAR ROLE OF REFORMED POLITICAL THEOLOGY

The historical Christianity that intersects most intimately with modern political theory is self-consciously Protestant. The Reformation's political ideas admittedly did not spring forth fully formed in the sixteenth century, and owe something to the traditions that preceded it. But reformers saw themselves offering something new, *in protest of* previous shortcomings. Given the permeating and persevering political influence of Protestant theology on so many generations, and over centuries, one can only conclude that leaping from "Christian and medieval" to "secular and modern" as the high-water marks of political theory omits the role of the Reformation from the history of political theory.[9]

Reformed political thought is notably absent from many anthologies, histories, and surveys of political ideas. Too few critical studies of modern political theory take its influence seriously, let alone carefully discern its role in forming what we now call "modern" political theory. It is certainly true that many factors and philosophies came together to overcome medieval

Christianity and its Aristotelian variants. But scholars in political theory largely ignore Christianity in its Protestant formulations, particularly during the period of early modernity when it was most influential. Such omission is especially negligent given the highly political nature of the Reformation and the massive subscription to Protestant doctrine by all classes of society over three centuries between 1550 and 1850. Perhaps nowhere is this negligence more evident than in the standard "canon" of political thought, wherein one finds few explicitly Protestant Christian authors studied beyond perhaps Calvin and Luther.[10] Students reading standard histories of political theory might be led to think that modern political ideas came from philosophical whole cloth or that there was no significantly influential political theology save for the work of a couple key reformers or churchmen.

Leo Strauss (1899–1973), while in many ways a scholar of the first rank and deeply influential among modern political theorists, doomed the Reformation to obscurity in some corners of political study by essentially separating theology from philosophy.[11] Though a dedicated student of some Jewish political philosophers, Strauss had little to say about the biblical covenants other than to place them firmly within the theological tradition and use them to support his argument "that there is a radical opposition between Bible and philosophy."[12] As for the tradition of Reformed Protestantism, his minimal treatment of Calvin is only to juxtapose him with Spinoza as part of Strauss's reason-revelation dichotomy.[13] Strauss's knowledge of Protestant political theology is difficult to discern, and it is unclear whether he had much familiarity with it at all. His landmark work, *Natural Right and History,* contains no substantial treatment of any Protestants.[14] His treatment of Luther is scant.[15]

If modern political theory is fundamentally a-theistic in its roots and justifications, then how have its propositions thrived in America and Britain over the last five centuries? This must be asked in light of both the large population of self-identified believers and political clergy. John Adams, for example, cited three Reformed theologians as key to the development of Anglo-American liberty: John Milton (English Puritan), John Ponet (English reformer), and the author of the *Vindiciae, Contra Tyrannos* (thought to be Philippe Du Plessis Mornay).[16] There is simply no reason to think that many of the texts now included in the canon of political theory took priority over political theology in the thinking of most Anglo-American Protestants.

Anglo-American Protestants in the seventeenth and eighteenth centuries were learning politics largely in the doctrinal, ecclesiastical and theological milieu of "Reformed" Christianity—not just from the canonical authors of political philosophy.[17] American Protestants and their church elders were familiar with theologians who were also political activists: Theodore Beza (Calvin's successor in Geneva), or Scottish Presbyterians John Knox, George Buchanan, and Samuel

Rutherford, for example. Americans mimicked the activism of the British and European reformers when they engaged in their own church controversies over antinomianism, religious liberty, church polity, revivalism, covenant theology, and church membership. American civil leaders in the Reformed tradition also had a remarkable opportunity to experiment with systems of government derived from their theology.

As Alexis de Tocqueville observed in the case of Puritanism, American Protestantism is overtly political in both theory and practice.[18] How can it be believed that philosophical texts could take precedence over the political theory learned from participation in a Presbyterian synod, congregational controversies about baptism and membership, or debates over itinerant revivalism, for example? To focus on largely secular texts is to miss the social dynamic of Protestantism as an active force in church and civil polity.

PLAN OF THE BOOK

Now, in the chapters of this book, it is time for an attempt to address some of these omissions and failures. The first three chapters serve by way of introduction. This first chapter has presented a general definition and defense of political theology's significance. The second chapter extends this defense, with the argument that political theology is best rooted in revealed texts, and that covenant theology in particular is a revealed political theology *par excellence.* The third chapter provides a concise introduction to the biblical narrative of the covenants and the contrasting ways they are presented in Jewish and Christian traditions.

The body of the text in the following chapters is largely historical. This historical approach is central to the study because it is not enough to discuss political theology in the abstract. We must see how political theology has been applied in order to judge of its historical successes and failures. Chapter 4 provides an introduction to the theological controversies in which early modern covenant theology took root, focusing on Calvin and Bullinger as two founders of Reformed political theology. Chapter 5 provides an overview of early political prescriptions for both church and state in the sixteenth century, comparing and contrasting various approaches to regime, tyranny, and the relationship between church and state. Chapter 6 explores the trajectory of political theology in England during the late sixteenth century, demonstrating how the influences of Zurich and Geneva diverged during the various Puritan controversies. Chapter 7 addresses the role of covenant theology during the British civil wars. Chapter 8 presents political covenanting in America and explains how various persons and events contributed to the decline of covenant theology. Chapter 9 demonstrates how both natural law and natural right were used in Reformed political theology. Chapter 10 reflects on the uses made of covenant throughout the periods just described and offers some conclusions on how the covenant progressed, declined, but eventually remained in political use.

The final chapters conclude the book. Chapter 11 provides insight from contemporary scholars such as Eric Voegelin, Daniel Elazar, and David Novak on the use of the covenant. Chapter 12 offers conclusions concerning the theory and history of the covenant device in politics, taking stock of its contemporary potential and suggesting what it has to offer the modern intersection of religion and politics.

2 Defending Political Theology

POLITICAL THEOLOGY DEFINED

The brief defense of political theology in the last chapter does not imply that this study is a defense of all political theology. Important distinctions must be made. All theology, by definition, concerns God; thus any text that concerns God can be broadly categorized as a theological text. Some theological texts are explicit in their dependence upon "revealed" sources. The Bible, for example, claims to provide divine guidance in the study of God. This is an example of "revealed" theology, that is, theology based on revelation from God. One can think of this as more than just "God talk." Revealed sources are also "God's talk."[1] Nonrevealed theological texts, by contrast, claim to provide direction on the subject of God (or, more broadly, religion) but do not claim to provide divinely inspired guidance. This type of theology is sometimes called "natural" or "philosophical" theology and depends only on reason (often inductive) and experience to draw conclusions about its subjects. It should be emphasized that these two categories of revealed theology versus natural theology are not necessarily dichotomous. They have traditionally been seen as complementary in the Western tradition, particularly within humanist or nonfundamentalist biblical traditions.[2] In this chapter revealed and natural theology will sometimes be used dichotomously in cases where one appears in opposition to the other.

Political theology, as a subset of theology, consists of those texts of political theory informed to some significant degree by theological texts. "Significant" does not mean that the argument relies entirely on theological sources. "Significant" means only that at least one key turn in an argument relies on a theological text.

The point here is not to provide a precise taxonomy for the classification of texts within political theory, but, rather, to emphasize how theological texts provide key axioms or premises in familiar political arguments. Many familiar texts of political orientation are in fact hybrids of both nontheological and theological arguments, including many canonical and seminal texts in political theory, such as works by Plato, Aristotle, Augustine, Aquinas, Hobbes, and Locke. All include some elements of political theology.

THE FAILURE OF RADICAL POLITICAL SECULARISM

What should the role of theology be in the construction of political prescriptions? The role of theology can be said to exist on a continuum between two hypothetical extremes. One extreme would assert that all political thought must be rooted in revealed theology. This is a hard standard to find in historical practice. There has always existed a strain of humanism in Christian political thought, which has saved it from this kind of political fundamentalism. At the other extreme is the assertion that political thought cannot appeal to traditional theological categories at all. This standard can be charged to some atheistic totalitarian regimes in recent memory, as well as some postmodern criticisms of traditional (or at least traditional metaphysical) theological discourse.

Any effort to purge all political thought of theological content will prove unsuccessful. Such an attempted purge would require one to disentangle "theological" texts and arguments from "secular" texts and arguments.[3] The practical challenge of such an exercise speaks for itself. How would one conclusively disentangle longstanding theological axioms and premises from recognizable conclusions? There are too many complicated threads to follow. Furthermore, such a segregation implies a threat to the rights and beliefs of religious persons who consider theological texts an indispensable resource for most or all matters of life.

The argument for an exclusively secular political thought might be premised on the idea that, whereas philosophical arguments are inclusive because they depend upon a universal faculty of reason, theological arguments are exclusive because they rely for their authenticity on special experiences, particularly supernatural experiences. It is self-defeating, however, to argue that political theology cannot inform political thought because theology is controversial or lacks comprehensive agreement within the population or is not universally well-known. The same charge can certainly be made against all political or moral philosophies. There is no standard interpretation of Karl Marx, no widespread knowledge of John Stuart Mill, and no explicit popular agreement with John Rawls. Their supposed accessibility gives them no advantage whatsoever in practice. Merely appealing to the faculty of reason or to experience does not necessarily give something universal appeal or acceptance.

It also cannot be argued that theological texts impose, prima facie, an undue burden on the human conscience. This is no truer of theological texts than of any text of secular moral or political philosophy. For example, why should the

Kantian imperatives to act consistent with duty or to treat people as ends instead of means be any less of an imposition on conscience than the biblical imperative to love your neighbor as yourself?[4] One may disagree with Immanuel Kant, or find oneself unmoved by his argument. One cannot repair to claiming that Kant, for example, relies on reason whereas the author of the Gospel relies on faith. As categories of knowledge, faith and reason are not so easily dichotomized.

There are good reasons that theologically or religiously rooted imperatives are greeted with sensitivity when they seem forced on others. But sensitivity to religious arguments was originally derived from theological and religious motives. The concept of an "inviolable conscience" in Western political thought was predicated on theological arguments and a desire to protect conscience and religious practice from state imposition.[5] One of the most famous arguments for toleration is John Locke's, for example, who advocated toleration on the grounds that the imposition of a particular path to heaven might put one on the wrong path.[6] He further argued that toleration was a Christian virtue.[7] If one did not believe in Christian virtues, or rejected the authenticity of heaven's existence, then a new argument for toleration would have to be constructed. Locke's appeal, premised as it is on religious grounds and against the abuse of religious and civil authority, would fall on deaf ears if directed to an atheist. After all, the atheist believes neither in heaven nor in Christian virtue. Locke's argument for toleration should have no appeal for him.[8]

Finally, insofar as secular political ideologies offer temptations to excesses or abuses similar to the ones they accuse theologies of offering, they can claim no moral superiority. Among the most important reasons that modern political theories come into conflict with political theology is that many modern philosophers offer an eschaton which competes with the biblical eschaton. (Following Voegelin's lead, the word *eschaton* is used to mean the "last things" or the final events of history.) Some modern philosophers direct their political prescription toward some future event of ultimate significance, trying to hasten its arrival by human action. By politics, they hope to bring heaven or utopia to earth. The result is a politics of redemption.[9] Such redemptive politics stands opposed to biblical politics. In Christian theology, eschatology refers to the study of the last things and to heaven. But when understood in the traditional or Augustinian sense, these last things are not immanent such that any particular human act can accelerate their arrival. Humankind cannot bring heaven to earth.

Attempting to create a paradise on earth is especially characteristic of the so-called Left or Young Hegelians, for example. One can only guess what Marx himself would have done if he had sought and won political power—but it is well known what terrors greeted those who endured the eschaton or "heaven" of his disciples. For Mao or Stalin, for example, the paradise of communism required subordinating persons to a murderous totalitarian government.[10] It is not surprising that these regimes saw revealed religion as their mortal enemy.[11] Modern political ideologues understand the challenge posed by political theologies and are quick to offer competing visions. Ludwig Feuerbach, who preceded Marx, presents an eschaton of human progress.[12] Before Feuerbach and Marx, Rousseau presented a revolutionary narrative of fall and redemption in his famous discourses and his essay on the social contract.[13]

These modern ideologues appeal to events outside of historical experience and may rightly be criticized as hypocritical insofar as they consider themselves superior to theology. Their various eschatological visions of progress and earthly salvation may rightly be called Christian heresies. They are narratives of fall and redemption appealing to faith and promising heaven on earth. Preferring secular eschatons to theological ones still requires, in a manner of speaking, an act of faith. Insofar as both secular thinking and religious thinking rely on some measure of faith to interpret our experience toward these hoped-for future conditions, neither is more epistemologically inclusive than theology. What is sneaked into the promotion of secular thought is the implication that it alone is a *rational* politics. Political theologies are cast as parochial and mystical, in contrast to "secular" political theories, which are cast as inclusive and factual, which is not the case.

CAN POLITICAL THEOLOGY BE ELIMINATED?

Political theology's modern opponents have historically considered two routes of attack in replacing or eliminating political theology. One route attempts to make religion politically innocuous or irrelevant. In other words, take away all "revealed" content. The other route subordinates religion to political goals. Both routes of attack are substantially problematic.

To make religion politically innocuous or irrelevant attempts the articulation of religion without existential significance. If religion can be stripped of fundamental and absolute moral imperatives, usually drawn from eschatology, it will be less likely to conflict with the moral and political demands of competing political ideologies. Removing these imperatives allows "religion" to remain but disarms it of its more politically minded content. This project is impossible—short of a massive revisionist project against both theology and history.

A second alternative to robust political theology is a civil religion in the spirit of Machiavelli or Rousseau, for example. Such civil religions are designed to serve political ends by promoting loyalty, courage, or civic mindedness. This includes the more cynical kind of civil religion—the kind that creates a moral hierarchy which subordinates all religion to political goals. This alternative is guilty of massive epistemological and ontological overreach, tempts tyranny, and violates natural rights.

CHRISTIANITY: IDEA OR EXISTENTIAL IMPERATIVE?

Recall the first alternative: replacing or eliminating religion by taking away its eschaton. Is it possible to have religion without an eschaton? In other words, is it possible to have religion that is not directed toward some climactic and ultimate justifying event? Exploring that question comprehensively would require a massive project, so I will simplify it in two ways. First, I will confine the examination to one political theology. Thus rephrased, the question becomes, Can Christianity be robbed of its eschaton? Second, because the theological question of diverse biblical eschatologies can become complicated, I will again simplify the question. Can Christianity be reduced from its historically existential role, which calls for experience and action, to mere intelligibility—a set of propositions without existential significance? Can Christianity be reduced to an idea, an *eidos?*

If Christianity can be reduced merely to an *eidos,* intelligible only and not existential, then the demands of the Christian faith would no longer come into conflict with the demands of the civil polity. After all, politics is a practical science having existential significance. Robbing Christianity's existential imperatives would disable it as a potential competitor to political philosophies. But can Christianity be understood as something less demanding than politics, or at least subordinate to it? The question must be asked with a close eye to history; it cannot be asked in the abstract. For example, we cannot ask if a nonexistential Christian theology can be formulated on paper regardless of whether that formulation has anything to do with the historical tradition or Scriptures. We must examine particular historical articulations of Christianity because those particular historical articulations are what real people are adhering to. The relative merit of political theology must be evaluated based on what *is,* not on the basis of what one might wish for.

There are three main historical periods to be addressed in this inquiry. The first period does not concern Christianity as such but considers the context of early Greek thought, since Christian theology takes root in Greco-Roman cultural soil. The second period includes two high-water marks in the articulation of Christianity—the metaphysics of Saint Thomas Aquinas and the claims of the Reformation. The third period sees the rise of parochial natural theology (excluding revealed sources) together with the challenge of modern atheism beginning in the seventeenth century. This last period sought to offer *logos* about God without the use of a revealed theological text and thereby lost God altogether. By the deliberate omission of revealed theological texts, natural theology not only missed the key existential ingredient of historical Christianity, the role of the theological text as willed revelation; it also led to the development of modern atheism. The resulting "death" of God (as Nietzsche famously called it) did not lead to the loss of the eschaton, however. The loss of the biblical eschaton led to a utopian and earthly eschaton more destructive to humane politics. The biblical eschaton was largely contained in a hermeneutic capable of neutralizing its danger through self-examination or self-criticism. By contrast, the philosophical peddlers of modern secular eschatons and political redemption seek to exterminate all competitors and bring heaven to earth. They are incapable of self-examination or self-criticism.

The Classical Period

Presupposing the Hebrew tradition as the revelatory foundation, classical philosophy provided much of the philosophical milieu in which Christian theology was first articulated.[14] In this milieu one can see the tension between what might be called an existentially stillborn natural theology (a variant of natural theology in opposition to revealed theology) and the vibrant and existentially living revealed theology characterizing historic Christianity.

Contrary to the popular argument that the ancient philosophers launched a long assault on religion, it seems that they were quite religious. Those who first inquired into the cosmos did not suggest it could be reduced to "intelligible" terms. In other words, they could not think of the cosmos simply as a set of ideas, let alone the mechanical "push-pull" material of modern science. In their search for a cosmology, the pre-Socratic philosophers never confused the foundational elements (water or earth, for example) with the gods. The gods had existential qualities. The foundational elements did not. Water or earth may have provided an intelligible "how" for questions, but they failed to provide any kind of existential "why." The material elements of earth or fire do not think or decide, will or command. A person's lot in the universe was not explained by his being favored or disfavored by prime matter but, instead, by his relationship to the gods.[15] Whatever was at the back of what happened in the world had to have a will. It had to be the deliberate product of an acting (and therefore willing) being.[16] Etienne Gilson rightly argues that Greek mythology was not a stepping-stone to philosophy but, rather, a stepping-stone to religion. Ancient mythology preserved an existential nature of the *logos,* even though this meant a dualistic *logos* in the early Greek schema: nonexistential matter (water, air, fire, earth) and existential persons (the gods). Asserting the existence of existential persons was the Greek means of accounting for the existence of human will, a phenomenon not readily explained by the mere combination of nonexistential elements.[17]

Aristotle's philosophy, however, discards the separateness of the elements from the gods. To the degree that Aristotle influenced others and the existential nature of the gods was lost, the Greeks began to lose their religion. Aristotle asserts a class of divinities existing in the spheres together with his famous unmoved mover, but their existential status is unclear.[18] Aristotle's divinities are engaged in an activity, but that activity is not clearly dictated by any kind of moral deliberation according to principle. It is more necessary ("by nature") than it is chosen. So while Aristotle's divinities provide a kind of ontological benchmark for excellence, they provide no clear moral imperative.[19] We may be moved to mimic Aristotle's gods (and thereby pursue contemplation of the noblest things) or we may not. But whether we do or not has no bearing on our *relationship* to those gods. Discounting any existential significance for divinity, Aristotle stresses that the most perfect being has no apparent relationship with persons or the rest of existence, save for the way in which it puts the other spheres into motion.[20]

Aristotle's divinities are certainly excellent. They are, according to Aristotle's argument, perfect. This fact, Aristotle argues, ought to be inspirational for our human pursuit of the contemplative life. But the existential import of this fact for us is otherwise nil or unclear. Aristotle's divinities are indeed active, and we are inspired to mimic their excellent activity of contemplation.[21] But there is no deliberate relationship for these gods to us or to the world. Nor is Aristotle's god a deliberate Creator, one governing toward a revealed or willed end. Human beings would not discern anything in these "gods" that they would recognize in themselves. The Olympian gods, by contrast, were readily recognizable as persons. Perhaps they were too much like humans, but at least they were paying attention. They possessed a will. They had virtues and vices. Their attributes had more existential import for the average person, and also for politics. So while Aristotle may have advanced the theoretical and metaphysical framework for theology, he did not advance its imperative status in any relational and therefore existential way.

Thomism and the Reformation

What does biblical theology really owe to Aristotle? The progress of religion in the West has depended not only upon the progress of metaphysics, something that Aristotle masterfully advanced but also upon *transcending* metaphysics. The *Shema Yisrael* "The Lord our God is one Lord" and *YHWH,* "He Who Is" (the LORD or Adonai)—both found in the Torah—are progressive statements in the development of metaphysics.[22] They are significant for asserting divinity as something characterized by *existence* (and by reason, will, and morality) rather than by mere intelligible propositions.

But Gilson and others miss the real significance of the transition from Greek to Christian theology by articulating it as a "continuum of progress" in Western metaphysics. There are key points at which this Western "progress" of theology goes beyond metaphysics. Such is the case of the biblical God, whose direct communication provides an existential dimension transcending Aristotelian essentialism. In the biblical account, God *speaks to Moses* to reveal that he is the "I Am Who I Am" (Exodus 3:14). This is, as Pascal reminds us, the God of Abraham, Isaac, and Jacob.[23] This is a God who deliberately speaks to persons in order to provide moral imperatives, not simply a being existing for inspiration or contemplation. The biblical moral imperatives are not just appeals to absolutes or immaterial forms. God is not presented merely as a co-discoverer of truths above both God and humankind.

God's revealed moral imperatives are intended to communicate directly both man's nature and his destiny. These imperatives are essential to covenants, the blessing and cursing that summarize much of the biblical message. These covenants comprise the existential (moral and political) significance of biblical religion. In asserting that God communicates directly to persons through word and text, revealed theology makes its decisive break with philosophy and with a purely philosophical natural theology. God's speaking to persons in order to communicate ultimate moral imperatives of temporal and eternal consequence is the root of the biblical eschaton in Western theology. The promise of judgment and expectation of covenant faithfulness makes religion ethical and therefore political.

The biblical eschaton is not merely discovered by reason or experience, as might be the case if its discovery was confined to classical metaphysics. Divine revelation is a quantum leap in political thinking. The visions of divine reward and punishment in Plato's *Republic* or *Gorgias* are argued inductively from the nature of justice. They do not claim divine inspiration in the same way the Christian texts do. Plato seems to point us to the gods for the sake of what is true and rational. He is not pointing us to what is true and rational for the sake of the gods.[24] The emphasis is on grasping truth, not establishing a deliberate relationship with the Divine Person who is the source of that truth. This is a substantial difference from biblical religion.

Thomistic metaphysics, though appreciative of Aristotle, expanded the gulf between Christianity and the ancients. Thomistic metaphysics cannot be cast as a mere syncretistic synthesis. Existing things are what they are not only because they possess some apprehensible essence, as argued by Plato or Aristotle, but because they *exist as* the thing that they are in the mind of a willing Creator. They are the product of a deliberate and willed Creation that began in the mind of God. This makes all intelligibility inexorably bound to God's own existence. The fundamental act of Creation becomes the foundation for intelligibility, and there can be no rational intelligibility apart from God's supreme existence and actions.

It is not enough to say that things exist because God exists. That, broadly considered, would simply restate what Aristotle said about the unmoved mover. Rather, things exist because a God who defines himself as "I Am Who I Am" exists and chose willfully to bring about all existing things, particularly other rational and existential beings made in the *Imago Dei.* Behind existence, understood in this way, is a creative will and purposeful mind that has generated these existences and made them as they are. Thus, we can move beyond the "how" a thing is what it is, to answer also the "why" of what it is. It is this "why" that enables a relationship among rational beings. "Why" gives moral purpose. "Why" enables politics and necessitates political theology.

Because their deities are not revelational, Aristotle's "why" can only be "nature" (*phusis*) and Plato's can only be the existence of a cosmos or a transcendent but imprecise realm of forms. The Greeks never get beyond nature or essence. In Thomas Aquinas's metaphysics, by contrast, a thing's essence exists and is communicable because it first existed in the mind of God.[25] It is doubtful that one would understand this point through philosophy only, let alone enter into a relationship with the Creator; the knowledge of real essence and a relationship with its source necessitates the existential act of divine revelation. As Pieper says, "Because his own existential metaphysics has succeeded in forcing its way through that crust of essences which is but the outer coating of reality, Thomas Aquinas can see the pure Act of existing as one sees the presence of the cause in any one of its effects."[26] To apprehend such Self-Existence behind all existing things would push reason to the breaking point.[27] The overwhelming intellectual burden of discovering or comprehending Self-Existence made divine revelation, the source of revealed theology, necessary. To comprehend the source of all things, to comprehend it as willing and acting Self-Existence, requires direct revelation.

Divine revelation does more than reveal something intelligible, however. It also calls one into a relationship with that Self-Existence through covenants. Of note are the biblical virtues: faith, hope and love. These provide not only intellectual support in the face of what would otherwise be intellectually and metaphysically overwhelming; they invite a relationship with the Creator. These biblical virtues are relational virtues. They enhance the existential dimension of biblical religion and give force to its eschaton.

Thomistic metaphysics kept Christianity and its political theology from collapsing into neo-Platonistic dualism and Averroism.[28] Averroism undermines the significance of revealed religion by proposing a dichotomy between the "secular" and the "sacred." Neo-Platonism posits two separate realms, an intelligible realm and a physical realm. In Platonic metaphysics, the senses present an obstacle to knowledge, for they are the gateway to a false world. Aquinas demonstrates neo-Platonic dualism to be incompatible with the biblical text in two significant ways. First, it made the act of Creation of no real consequence for man's rational progress. Second, classical authors had no place for the Incarnation, a doctrine Plato would surely have found abhorrent.[29] According to the biblical text, the Word (*logos* in Greek) became flesh and dwelt among us.[30] By this act, Christ redeems a fallen Creation.[31] Not only this, but Christ ascends with a physical body, a remarkable and exceptional dimension of the Incarnation.[32]

Protestantism further strengthens the existential qualities of Christianity. One need look no further than mottos now associated with the Reformation—*sola scriptura, sola fides, sola gratia.* This heightened emphasis on Scripture (as "God's talk") enhances the existential dimension, underscoring that God communicates directly with those made in the divine image. The emphasis on faith (*sola fides*) and grace (*sola gratia*) underscores one's direct relationship to God through the individual priesthood of the believer, maximizing the responsibility of the acting individual. These are states of being that are sought, won, and felt experientially. They are not merely understood rationally or doctrinally.

A sampling of the existential aspects of Reformation theology is evident even in some of Calvin's presentations. While Calvin's humanist training encouraged him to provide logical justification for doctrinal articulation wherever possible, he also looked to experience as confirmation. For example, Calvin argued against inquiring too much into logical demonstrations of Scripture and the life of faith. He instead referred the reader to the confirmation of experience.[33] In defending his theology of communion, a central Christian sacrament, Calvin asserted in his *Institutes,* "Now, should any one ask me as to the mode, I will not be ashamed to confess that it is too high a mystery either for my mind to comprehend or my words to express; and to speak more plainly, I rather feel than understand it."[34]

This is not to say that Calvin believed that anything from Scripture could be argued from experience alone. Scripture and experience would sometimes be at odds.[35] For example, Calvin wrote, "Faith cannot flow from a naked experience of things, but must have its origin in the Word of God."[36] Experience is brought into Calvin's theology because he knows that faithful exposition of the Scripture does not always produce a truly "rational" synthesis. Of the Christian life, for example, Calvin wrote, "Doctrine is not an affair of the tongue, but of the life; is not apprehended by the intellect and memory merely . . . but is received only when it possesses the whole soul, and finds its seat and habitation in the inmost recesses of the heart" (*Institutes* III.vi.4).

In short, Calvin's theology is often a theology of experience. It is something felt as much as understood. It is in the revival of covenant theology that the existential aspect of Christian theology becomes magnified during the Reformation.

Natural Theology, Modern Atheism, and Gnosticism

It is now appropriate to turn in the direction of natural theology and modern atheism. Ironically, modern atheism has its origins in natural theology. This should not be surprising given that natural theology is sometimes nothing more than an attempt to make God intelligible while ignoring the existential act of divine revelation. Leaving aside the ethical or eschatological implications of divine revelation is understandably attractive to philosophers as it enables them to engage the idea of God while not engaging the person of God. The escape is short-lived; the existential and eschatological reassert themselves with a vengeance in the nineteenth century's climax to philosophical theology. In Hegel and his aftermath, Gnosticism replaces piety and mystery.

The death of revealed religion in modern natural theology began in the seventeenth century in the philosophy of René Descartes. In his *Meditations,* he promises the theology faculty of the University of Paris that he will prove the existence of the soul and God without using what he calls the "circular" argument of faith. Here one sees a deliberate attempt to join philosophy and theology in a way that Thomas Aquinas argued could not be done.[37] The problem here should be self-evident. Unless Descartes was not picky about what kind of god and soul he was going to demonstrate, would he not have to rely on divine revelation (theology) to one degree or another? If Descartes could start with reason and experience, and wind up at the same place as Scripture, then what would be the point of Scripture? Descartes therefore marginalizes the import of God's revealing Himself through divine revelation. The result was logically predictable. What Descartes "proved" by working inductively—and backward from reason alone rather than forward from statements of Scripture—was the existence of something other than the biblical God and soul. This loss of Scripture in the argument is not just the loss of YHWH who is existence itself, Self-Existing and Creating. It is the loss of all the moral imperatives and covenants that accompany such a God.

In asserting that he would demonstrate the existence of God and the soul through philosophy alone, demoting "faith" to a second class form of demonstration, Descartes embraces the dichotomy that Thomas Aquinas rejected. Rather than enabling theology and philosophy to complement one another, Descartes sets up a hierarchy. And insofar as his demonstrations fail, he has done more than fail to fulfill his promise to the Paris academics; he has opened a gulf between revelation and reason and changed Western thought for centuries. Aquinas argued that theology (defined as divine revelation) must inform philosophy, and that philosophy cannot speak comprehensively to many biblical subjects. Descartes replies that divine revelation is not necessary. The resulting antagonistic dichotomy between philosophy and theology continues to this day. There is nothing relevant to the Christian eschaton in Descartes' natural theology. There is no Incarnation, no willing and acting person. There is nothing that can be called supernatural. Furthermore, Descartes' God in the *Discourse* becomes little more than *phusis* under the old pre-Thomistic philosophy. Descartes' argument is not a return to pure Greek essentialism but revives the old challenge the Greek philosophers faced. How can one search for a "why" in the universe without an existential source?

Descartes' legacy continued undiminished so long as natural theologians concurred that one can arrive at God without divine revelation. Natural theologians become theologians only in the general sense that they are studying an idea of god. But they are not studying the existential God, the one who is behind covenant relationships. By the late eighteenth century, exemplified in the work of Hume, it is not surprising that we have returned to the Stoics, to the unknown god. One can say that the philosophers had found a religion that is intelligible but not existential. It was a set of propositions rather than a person.

Atheism was now close at hand. Natural theology went from dichotomizing divine revelation and philosophy to denigrating it. If divine revelation is unnecessary for understanding God, but relational existence remains bound to divine revelation (God speaking to persons), the historical God of the biblical covenants becomes of no real consequence. God, as an existential being, remains stillborn since Descartes. And because humans are themselves living and existential beings, they have no need for a corpse. Nietzsche was therefore right when he asserted that God was "dead." His great insight was to precede the claim by saying that the madman approached those who already did not believe in God and confessed to them what was already the case.[38] The next logical step was to cast off the obvious absurdity of treating an intelligible being now no different from a geometric figure as one would treat an existential being.

Revealed theology was the only thing that could resurrect an existential God, but because of developments in philosophy and elsewhere, it had been given its walking papers from educated circles. Revealed theology was now the purview of an implicitly second-class kind of thinking called "faith." Kant's distinction between *phenomena* and *noumena* helped to emphasize that dichotomy. Kant also took the next step in the revolution when he declared natural theology to be philosophically inept. Seeing the resulting vacuum in practical morality, Kant proposed a rationalist post-Christian morality. But he was only putting the final nails into the coffin of a god who had been dead for more than a century. Friedrich Schleiermacher's attempt to rehabilitate religion not withstanding, God was all but doomed since the determined rise of modern natural theology. When forced to choose between a god with no existential qualities and no god at all, it was only logical to choose no god at all. After all, a god with no existential qualities is no god at all.

In the nineteenth century, the seeds planted by Descartes grew to maturity. Hegel marks the transition from natural philosophy to atheism. This is ironic: Hegel is arguably the most "religious" of the theological philosophers because he makes the most ambitious effort at natural theology. He seeks to provide more information about God than was ever attempted without revelation, even in the face of Kant's coup de grace against natural theology. Hegel transcends anything his predecessors attempted through logical induction. But the result is what Voegelin rightly calls Gnosticism.[39] Unlike previous efforts at natural theology, which realized their eschatological limitations because they never resorted to revealed theology, Hegel provides both eschatology and cosmology. Hegelian philosophy is a kind of Christianity for atheists. Hegel's progeny, Feuerbach and Marx, would follow, promising real liberation for any who would trade the Christian eschaton for their historical dialectic. The West merely traded one eschaton for another. By the time Hegel's eschaton was articulated forcefully by his young disciples such as Marx, the political eschaton rivaled the mansions of heaven. Atheism built on the foundation of Hegel thus became as eschatological as Christianity. Historical progress monopolized moral imperatives and replaced revealed religion with the ersatz religion of ideology.

Many of the atheists who did not embrace this new eschaton left off the existential philosophy of freedom and moral responsibility altogether. This is exemplified in Nietzsche and Freud, who deny an existential nature by essentially denying free will. But not all atheists denied freedom and moral responsibility. Existing requires deciding, as Sartre rightly argued.[40] Postmodern philosophy and critical theory seems to have rediscovered at least the phenomenology of what used to be called "religion."[41] This gives rise to a new kind of political theology as well.

THE FAILURE OF CIVIL RELIGION

Given the existential qualities of Christianity and the existential demands of politics, can revealed imperatives be collapsed into something called a civil religion? What is meant here by the phrase "civil religion" is the pragmatic articulation of religion for political ends. Such a pragmatic articulation may be intended to promote certain virtues, such as loyalty, courage, and charity. It may be intended to provide a transcendent or omnipotent imprimatur for the political regime. Whatever the case, such a scheme does not intend to promote a particular religion in its own right or on its own merits. Rather, civil religion is promoted to advance the goals of the regime.

Robert Bellah is correct when he argues that there is a unique set of advantages and problems for Christianity with respect to civil religion. The tendency of every attempt to resolve the tension between Christianity and politics has been to make religion the servant of the state or else the state the servant of religion.[42] This raises both legal and ontological challenges. The demands of the Bible on members of the church, particularly elements of the political language used in reference to Christ, invite something more complicated than Aristotle's concern that the good citizen also be the good man (for example).[43] Civil religion is an ontological challenge because it challenges one's fundamental identity and forces a choice between the dual citizenships eloquently presented in Augustine's *City of God.*

The political-cum-ontological question is not just determined by whom one is ruled. The Jews told Pontius Pilate, "We have no king but Caesar" (John 19:15). This is an assertion of political loyalty and gets to the heart of both order and identity. It answers the fundamental questions of philosophical anthropology, and therefore politics. It determines the nature of what is overarching in the highest sense—the *arche* in which we "live and move and have our being" (Acts 17:28). This statement was first made by the poet Aratus in his *Phaenomena*, then quoted by Saint Paul, demonstrating the importance of this contested ground of identity.

There is much compatibility between Christianity and some standing political and ethical philosophies. But whereas a political or ethical philosophy, prudently framed, can coexist or even complement religion (and Christianity in particular), the kind of civil religion being indicted here intends either to subvert or to tyrannize the prerogatives of religion.

Finally, one should note the important historical challenge to creating a civil religion that approximates Christianity. To borrow a concept from Heidegger, we are "thrown" into the historical situation of Christianity. Christianity is an experiential and historical reality. A civil religion cannot now be created from whole cloth. We must accommodate the standing Christian tradition. Short of instituting a nationalistic religion (as the Japanese did with Shinto, for example), we cannot think of the civil religion in terms of any radical genesis. For the reasons articulated here, and for many more, a civil religion is not a possibility. And a wholly natural theology is not a solution.

It therefore remains necessary to return to the historical articulation and practice of political theology as we find it in the Western experience. Because of its emphasis on revealed theology, human conscience, and lateral and vertical relationships (person to person and person to God, respectively), covenanting is a political theology par excellence. It is the most intensely ethical and political expression of biblical religion. The chapters that follow explore the legacy of covenant theology as a political theology par excellence.

3 The Biblical Background to Covenanting

The Bible is the main source for Western political theology. It is the most influential text in Anglo-American political thought and probably presents the oldest political constitution in the historical record.[1] But the Bible is significant not because it prescribes a particular type of regime.[2] Regime classification is a Greek and Roman project.[3] It is the relational attributes of biblical religion that make it a political theology par excellence, and central to those relational claims are the biblical covenants.

ORIGIN OF "COVENANT"

In English Bibles, the word "covenant" is translated from the Hebrew word *berith,* which is used more than three hundred times in the Hebrew Bible. The etymology of the word is uncertain, and potential translations include "to cut," "to bind," "to hand," "to fetter," or "to eat." The "cutting" may refer to its use in a ceremony not unlike the one found in the biblical text where an animal is cut in half in a covenant-making ceremony (Genesis 15:9–10). Translating *berith* as "to eat" may refer to a special meal that accompanied a covenanting ceremony (Genesis 31:51–54). Hittite civilization, which preceded the established Israelite society, also used treaties similar to covenants. There is some controversy regarding how closely the biblical covenants parallel treaties used by surrounding civilizations; the latter might safely be considered proto-covenants compared to most of the biblical covenants since they came before, and did not include all the elements of, the biblical covenants.[4] Unlike the covenants of the surrounding cultures, the biblical covenants emphasized a certain level of equality or reciprocity.[5]

The covenants used by surrounding civilizations often established hierarchy or vassal relationships.

Berith becomes *diatheke* in the Greek translation of Hebrew texts, a word that most frequently referred to a last will and testament. This led to the now familiar Christian titles for two parts of the Bible: the Old "Testament" and the New "Testament."[6] *Diatheke* appears more than thirty times in the apostolic Scriptures, with its first usage in Paul's epistles.[7] Some of these usages are quotations of the Old Testament, however. In later Latin usage, the word most used for "covenant" is *foedus*, the root of the English "federal."

There is some controversy in biblical studies concerning the meaning of "the covenant" (*berith*) in the Hebrew Bible. Some argue that *berith* refers to the covenant itself, while others focus on the act of covenanting.[8] Rendtorff focuses on what he calls the "covenant formula," which occurs more than thirty times in the Hebrew Scriptures. The covenant formula includes one or both of two important statements: "I will be a God for you" and "You shall be a people for me." This formula, Rendtorff argues, is used more systematically than the word *berith*.[9] It is the act of election—Rendtorff's "covenant formula"—that defines the covenant and its relational characteristic. God's taking a people for Himself is commonly referred to in theology as "election."[10]

THE HEBREW CHRONOLOGY

Noah

Excluding for now what some Reformed Protestants claim about a prelapsarian (pre-Fall) covenant, the first politically significant biblical covenant is made between God and Noah. God makes a covenant with Noah in the plan for Noah's escape and afterward makes a covenant concerning the whole earth (Genesis 6 and 9).[11] God not only denies Himself the right to repeat the destruction of the Flood, He establishes universal justice. This latter point has great political significance because it may overlap with what has been called "natural law." However much biblical natural law may be similar in ethical content with Greek or Roman philosophy, for example, biblical natural law is not identical to those articulations. The universal and natural law of the Hebrew Scriptures resides first in the will of God. Greek or Roman natural law (as articulated by philosophers) is found in a superintending nature that lacks the qualities of a relational and covenanting God.[12]

The Noahide covenant is an unconditional covenant. This means that there are no stated requirements for human faithfulness and no terms by which the covenant must be kept; God is bound to the covenant regardless of human faithfulness. It is also a unilateral covenant. This means that there is no expectation of performance on the part of humankind. God demands justice in a passage later cited by Locke and Grotius (Genesis 9:6) but it is not clear that this is a condition to ensure God's faithfulness.

Abraham

The covenant with Abraham in Genesis is perhaps the most important biblical covenant. The covenants of God with Abraham promise both people and land, and they require both ceremony and sign (Genesis 15, 17). Genesis 17:5–8 records this promise made by God to Abraham. These Abrahamic covenants are foundational and eventually become the ones of greatest controversy—both theological and political. Particularly controversial is this promise to Abraham in Genesis 22:15–18:

> And the angel of the LORD called to Abraham a second time from heaven and said, "By myself I have sworn, declares the LORD, because you have done this and have not withheld your son, your only son, I will surely bless you, and I will surely multiply your offspring as the stars of heaven and as the sand that is on the seashore. And your offspring shall possess the gate of his enemies, and in your offspring shall all the nations of the earth be blessed, because you have obeyed my voice."[13]

This not only echoes the dominion mandate found earlier in Genesis 1:26, 1:28, and 9:1, in which God tells mankind to be fruitful and multiply and subdue the earth; it also has further political implication. The covenant is made with Abraham and also with his descendants. It is used to establish a "people" and a homeland—two essential ingredients for any human polity. Abraham's descendants are said to possess the "gate of his enemies" that is the seat of political power in the ancient world.

At the heart of differences between Jews and Christians is this promise to Abraham. They disagree in their interpretation of exactly what is promised, and each claims to be the heir of the promise. Each claims to be a "chosen people." As evidenced by Genesis 18:16–25, this is a claim of substantial consequence, blending judicial and legal, social, familial, political, and eschatological matters all together. The judicial and legal point concerns God's justice and Abraham's role in that justice. The social, familial, and political are blended together in the covenantal promise to make Abraham's descendants a powerful nation. The eschatological point concerns the future state of affairs brought by God's justice in its own right ("Judge of all the earth") as well as the covenant with Abraham ("all the nations on earth will be blessed through him").

The biblical narrative of Abraham teaches more about covenants. Abraham is said to have made a covenant of his own with Abimelech, a Philistine king, to establish an alliance (Genesis 21). This demonstrates that covenants do not necessarily require mutual orthodoxy between covenanting parties.[14] Nor do they have to be dictated or approved by God, though they are said to be made in His presence.

Abraham's descendants are also in the covenant and become patriarchs (Genesis 17:19, 21). The case of Jacob (who eventually becomes renamed Israel) provides a provocative insight. He schemes his way into his father's blessing.[15] Jacob also tries to treat the covenant as a contract for his own self-interest. The relevant passages suggest a contractual rather than a covenantal approach on Jacob's part; that is, Jacob approaches the covenant as a bargain to be struck on open terms rather than as something agreed to in a standing moral and legal framework (Genesis 28:12–22). We also learn, in the case of Jacob as presented in Genesis 31:51–54, that a covenant can be used to separate as well as to join.[16]

These subsequent covenants are important because they introduce the idea of a covenant not as something imposed but as something to be negotiated or kept conditionally, based on terms. If the covenant is imposed and also unconditional, then the moral dimension is different. God has bound himself (as in the case of Abraham) regardless. If the covenant appears negotiated, then the human party's status is elevated to more of a partner's role than a vassal's role. If the covenant is conditional, this enhances the moral dimension. Human partners are then cast as moral agents, able to abide by (even if they do not set) the terms of the covenant. If the human partners should fail to keep the terms of the covenant, then God is not bound to the covenant. He is bound conditionally rather than unconditionally. This is the idea of a "bilateral covenant," emphasizing the role and the responsibilities of both parties.

Mount Sinai

The Exodus from Egypt is perhaps the most politically powerful narrative in the Scripture.[17] Included in that narrative are both the aforementioned covenants made with Abraham, Isaac, and Jacob and the covenant made at Mount Sinai (Exodus 2:23–25). God returns to the unconditional covenant He made with Abraham and his descendants, telling Moses that deliverance from Egypt is part of the covenant made with the patriarchs (Exodus 6:2–5). A clear example of the "covenant formula" is evident when Moses is instructed to tell the Israelites: "You yourselves have seen what I did to the Egyptians, and how I bore you on eagles' wings and brought you to myself. Now therefore, if you will indeed obey my voice and keep my covenant, you shall be my treasured possession among all peoples, for all the earth is mine; and you shall be to me a kingdom of priests and a holy nation" (Exodus 19:4–6). This passage not only repeats the usual political details (being a people, kingdom, or nation) but also emphasizes God's role in establishing and maintaining His part of the covenant. As for the Israelites, their terms are imposed; but they are no less bound to keep them.

The covenant at Sinai is a corporate covenant made with Israel and probably the second most important political covenant in the Hebrew Scripture. Moses serves as mediator, not so much in the sense that he negotiates as that he acts as a representative for both God and the people. The Sinai covenant confirms the movement from a familial covenant to a national covenant; it includes not only the Ten Commandments but also the case law and civil law that follow. This becomes the condition of blessing or cursing (Deuteronomy 27, 28; Leviticus 26). The Sinai covenant provides the basis for the new Israelite polity. It also assigns the division of power, separating prophetic, priestly, and civil functions.[18] What was once familial, social, and political becomes more explicitly and institutionally political.

The covenant formula is repeated many times thereafter in the narrative of the chosen people, but there appear to be two variations of covenant. Unconditional election of Israel, first exemplified in the Abrahamic covenant, is what Freeman calls the "gracious covenant"[19] This is the first type of covenant. The second is a kind of "mutual covenant" or conditional covenant, with which comes the promise of blessing or cursing.[20] The Sinaic covenant is a seminal example of the second type. How these two types of covenant work together causes difficulties in the formulation of any Hebraic political theology. If both types of covenant work together, it might mean that Israel may be chastened but never destroyed. But how were the Protestant reformers to take this? They were not the first people to receive the covenant, so what had become of the first covenant people? Had the Jewish people become permanently apostate, as some interpreted St. Paul to say? (Romans 11). Appropriating the Jewish covenants meant that the Christian church became Israel in the biblical narrative. If the Jews could be punished for failing to keep covenants, why could the church not also be punished? As a corporate body, was the church under the Abrahamic or the Mosaic covenant? Or was it under both? This question of covenant faithfulness would vex the inheritors of the biblical covenants.

Joshua

In Joshua 24, we see the first explicit tripartite covenant of human design.[21] Joshua harks back to the patriarchal covenant and reminds the people of God's covenantal faithfulness. They, in turn, pledge their faithfulness. But Joshua himself also makes a covenant with the people, which not only expands on the role of mediator played by Moses but also includes a covenant between the mediator and the people. This has important civil implications because Joshua (like Moses) has a civil role to play. This is a clear example of a mutual and conditional covenant.

The tripartite covenant is rich with civil implications. It further establishes what Kaminsky defines as "corporate responsibility."[22] This means that persons are also judged as nations for their collective faithfulness or unfaithfulness. It appears to grant clergy a right to take the role of prophet, admonishing civil authorities or the people, or both.[23] God appears to give special responsibility to the civil magistrate as evidenced by the record of both Saul and David (I Samuel 16:14; II Samuel 7:16, 22).[24] The leader of Israel was seen to function on God's behalf (Joshua 11:12, 15; Judges 6:25–26). Finally, while God appears to make a covenant with every individual Israelite, these individual covenants serve to complement rather than replace the corporate covenant. The main application of this last covenant, between God and individual persons, is to emphasize that the people owe their primary allegiance to God rather than to the ruler should these obligations come into conflict. God is King.[25] This emphasis on conscience (reappearing in later Protestant manifestations) enabled the right of disobedience and resistance.[26]

The Davidic Monarchy and Its Legacy

The next significant set of covenants surrounds David, a king said to enjoy political power by God's favor (I Samuel 16, II Samuel 3). David, as a ruler, covenants with his people in II Samuel 5:1–3. The Davidic covenant is presented as a continuation of the original patriarchal one, the covenant of election (I Chronicles 16, 17). David also makes a covenant of friendship with Jonathan (I Samuel 18:1–3). The Davidic covenant is perhaps the last major covenant of significance in the Hebrew Scripture; it both parallels the Abrahamic covenant and asserts the covenant to be perpetual (Ezekiel 37:21–28).[27] This may mean that the covenant no longer stands in need of formal renewal. Political rulers (kings) become the successors to the old tribal patriarchs, blending the civil and the religious. The Davidic covenant also revives the promise of a homeland that was first made to Abraham. This promise of land makes covenant theology what Buchanan calls "a theology of conquest."[28] Not only are the covenant people to take possession of a homeland, but also they ultimately cannot be defeated.

The civil implications of the Davidic covenant extend beyond the idea of a perpetual spiritual covenant made with a chosen people. Legal civil authority was also established by covenants, making them an early form of constitution. Although David was anointed by Samuel under God's direction (I Samuel 16), his legal civil authority was recognized through a series of internal covenants (II Samuel 5). These covenants were made not with the people "at large" but with the people via their tribal leadership. This is another example of the tripartite covenant established by Joshua. The ruler covenants with God and also with the people. The covenant of the Israelite monarchy was both vertical and horizontal.

King David's covenant with tribal leaders also demonstrates the principle of federalism wherein a network of covenanted polities and jurisdictions forms a nation rather than one central authority governing a people and forming a nation.

Without the formation of these perpetual covenants between the tribes and the monarch, civil authority was in doubt. Solomon successfully covenanted with the tribes (I Kings 8). But Solomon's son Rehoboam was denied kingship by tribal leaders (I Kings 12, II Chronicles 10). This caused the division of the nation into Judah (the southern kingdom), headed by the Davidic monarchy, and Israel (the northern kingdom), now ruled by the ten northern tribes.

Covenants appear throughout the biblical narrative with every crisis of political leadership. Notable episodes recur in the biblical histories. In restoring the monarchy in Judah from the usurping and murdering Queen Athaliah, Jehoiada the Priest covenants with the royal guard (II Kings 11:4) and later establishes a tripartite covenant between God, himself, and the people that "they should be the LORD's people" (II Chronicles 23:16, II Kings 11:17). King Hezekiah instituted moral reform and the abolition of idolatry established by a covenant (II Chronicles 29). King Josiah, upon discovering "The Book of the Law" (most likely the Book of Deuteronomy), renews the tripartite covenant among himself, God, and the people (II Kings 22–23).

All of these historical episodes tied together the kinds of reform that would determine the attributes and goals of covenantal politics. Covenantal politics therefore includes moral and religious reform, which renewed piety before a holy God. It also includes political reform, which held rulers and people accountable to one another. Successful reform was preconditional to the success of the community before God. Failure was tantamount to rebellion. When the Protestant reformers viewed themselves as a covenanted people effecting reform, they saw themselves bound by these examples.

THE CHRISTIAN INTERPRETATION

Christians not only acknowledge the aforementioned "Old Testament" covenants, they declare themselves inheritors of them through Christ. This move into a new covenant becomes, for Christian theologians, a new Exodus. The author of the letter to the Hebrews, for example, asserts to his readers, "We received the good news just as they did," and draws a direct parallel with the Hebrew covenant (Hebrews 4:2, 10, 12). Reformed theologians were emphatic on the need to return to the Hebrew Scriptures. This is emphasized by Heinrich Bullinger, for example, who wrote, "Let none of us therefore hereafter say, 'What need I to care what is written to the Jews in the old Testament. . . . I am a Christian.'" Bullinger's response is both to cite the use of the Old Testament by Christ and Saint Paul and to address what is kept and lost in the Old Testament ordinances (*Decades* I.2, 58–59).[29] The narrative of Israel is adopted both literally and metaphorically as the narrative of the Christian Church, particularly in light of judgment and redemption promised by the prophet Isaiah.

Christians assert that Christ is the heir of the Davidic kingship. They also use "enthronement psalms" or messianic psalms to adopt the Hebrew covenant narrative.[30] These "enthronement psalms" refer to a king whose reign will not end. Messianic psalms (Psalm 22 or 69, for example) refer to a coming messiah. This is a king who would subdue nations, deliver the saints, usher in the messianic kingdom, and put all enemies under his feet. Particularly important are Psalms 2 and 110. The repeated quotation of Psalm 110 in the New Testament canon (cited more than any other verse from the Hebrew Scriptures) summarizes the essence of Christian covenantalism in appropriating the Davidic covenant.[31] All Christian eschatologies argue that the age of Christ is essentially the messianic age promised in the Hebrew Scriptures. Jesus is given the throne "of his father David" in order to "rule the house of Jacob forever."[32] Thus, Jesus inherits the role of covenantal ruler. The last book of the New Testament canon, John's vision at Patmos, is written in typological format to echo themes of Jewish deliverance.[33] The covenant blessing of Abraham is now to be fulfilled by Christ's Great Commission.

For the Hebrews, life in covenant was life in the fullest sense of the word.[34] Death in the Hebrew Scriptures meant not only the perishing of the Hebrew people but being scattered, having community dissolved, and being made outcasts among foreign nations. In the New Testament, "eternal life" becomes synonymous with covenantal life.[35] Christ also refers to himself as the "bread of life" (John 6:35, 48). The Gospels speak of inheriting eternal life, just as the Israelites had spoken of inheriting the land God had promised to their forefathers.[36] Communion becomes the new Passover, instituted as it was at a Passover meal (Luke 22, Mark 14).

But the translation of the Hebrew Scriptures into the church is not without many questions and complications. How does one reconcile conditional and unconditional covenants? What is the relationship between the individual covenant of salvation in Christ and the corporate covenant? Do Christian modifications embolden or disempower the earthly and political implications of the covenants? After all, many of the covenantal promises become spiritualized. Where is the new Promised Land, the Kingdom of God? Hebrews 11, for example, makes explicit connection between Christ and the patriarchs; but it says that the patriarchs sojourned for a heavenly city, not an earthly promised land. Jesus also tells Pilate that his Kingdom is "not of this world" (John 18:36). Should this diminish the political effect of Christian covenantalism? Or should it make it all the more emphatic? And to complicate matters, Christianity took root outside the Jewish civil and political authority. Was a new *Christian* civil and political authority to take its place? Was this authority to be established by new covenants? This was a challenge faced during the first fifteen hundred years of church history, and the seismic shift of the Protestant Reformation made the challenge all the more difficult. The solutions offered would change the face of Anglo-American politics.

Part II

PART II

4 Founding Covenant Theologies
Bullinger and Calvin

Two theologians whose ideas were most influential for the initial direction of Anglo-American political theology were Jean (John) Calvin (1509–1564) and Heinrich (Henry) Bullinger (1504–1575). Their legacies are the reformations of Geneva and Zurich, respectively, and represent differing but complementary approaches to political theology within the covenant model. There were of course other sixteenth-century theologians of comparable status such as Martin Luther, Martin Bucer, or Peter Martyr (Pietr Martire Vermigli). But none of them exerted the same degree of influence within a civil polity as Calvin or Bullinger. Calvin and Bullinger therefore had unique opportunities to craft political theology.

HEBRAIC CHRISTIANITY: REFORMED THEOLOGY'S RETURN TO THE OLD TESTAMENT

The study of Reformed political theology must begin with its Hebraic roots. While Reformed theologians pursued reforms of Roman Catholicism on points common to all Protestant traditions, the Reformed variant of Protestantism is marked by three important emphases. The first was an emphasis on biblical languages, consistent with the humanist training of the founders of Reformed Protestantism. Reemphasizing Hebrew, sometimes even rabbinic sources, encouraged a new and independently minded study of the Hebrew Scriptures (the "Old Testament").[1] This then led to a second innovation, biblical covenants as a leitmotif of theology and biblical interpretation.[2] The third innovation was the construction of a theological garment that attempted to seamlessly integrate Hebrew Scriptures and the Christian Scriptures—the "Old" and "New" Testaments. This return to the Old Testament together with the articulation of "covenant theology" changed early modern politics.

In order to settle disputes, Christian scholars had always looked back to the Church Fathers.[3] Reformed theologians used the same technique in argument but also went one step further. With the new covenant theology, returning to the "early church" now also meant returning to the patriarchs and the earliest covenants, thousands of years before the Apostolic Church and patristic Christianity. In the Hebrew narratives of the patriarchs, many Reformed theologians argued, one would find the relevant foundations of Christianity. Many reformers considered Hebraic innovations, particularly the revived use of Hebrew Scriptures, to be a return to the primitive and sure foundation of Christianity.

This "Hebraic" revival was not without controversy, and the reformers risked the charge of "judaizing." "Judaizer" was a common insult used by many stripes of polemicist in the sixteenth and seventeenth centuries. The Lutheran author Aegidius Hunnius described John Calvin as a judaizer, for example.[4] Calvin argued that the Lutheran liturgy was judaistic. Roman Catholics asserted that the literalistic hermeneutic of the Lutherans was judaistic. Roman Catholic ceremony and ritual struck many Protestants as judaistic. The controversial Michael Servetus was considered a judaizer; Servetus responded that his persecutors were judaizers.[5] When Bishop John Maxwell, an opponent of Scottish Presbyterian Samuel Rutherford, wanted to heap scorn on the Puritans he referred to them as "our Rabbis."[6]

To understand the seriousness of this charge, recall the controversies of early Christianity. The Apostles debated not only what traditions would be retained from Judaism but also how Jewish Scriptures would be interpreted. The resulting controversies are chronicled throughout the New Testament canon.[7] In their leaving the Roman Catholic Church, reformers saw themselves as leading a break similar to the one between Judaism and Christianity. The first generations of Christians broke with what they considered apostate and corrupt Jewish tradition; the reformers drew a parallel to their own struggle with Roman Catholicism.[8] Like the Early Church, the reformers had canonical texts but no clear hermeneutic. They no longer could implicitly trust the dogma governing biblical interpretation.[9] Furthermore, the Protestant emphasis on faith and grace meant freedom from what they considered to be unnecessary rituals, works, or intermediaries. Anyone who appeared to turn back the clock on this liberation could be charged with "judaizing." Despite the risk of judaizing, however, the reformers proceeded with their controversial Hebraic revival. It was in this fertile and controversial soil of the Hebrew Scriptures that Reformed theology and its political implications took root.

INTERNATIONAL REFORMED PROTESTANTISM AND SWISS LEADERSHIP

By the sixteenth century, the Protestant Reformation had grown into a diverse and international movement. It was hardly something confined to Geneva or what scholars erroneously call "Calvinism." Not only is "Calvinism" not an accurate title for a widespread and diverse theological tradition, but the label of "Calvinism" loses sight of the many important and substantial controversies within Reformed theology. Calvin was but one figure in the simultaneous development of an international movement that had no official leader. Calvin, who desired to be buried in an unmarked grave, did not seek to create "Calvinists" any more than Luther desired to create "Lutherans." Furthermore, Calvin and his followers constituted just one wing of Reformed political theology. Only in hindsight can we speak of the development of covenant or Reformed theology, let alone something called "Calvinism."

In the sixteenth century, early Reformed theology was being founded in Britain, France, Germany, and what is now Switzerland.[10] It was a movement much larger than Calvin's Geneva. The English Reformation was motivated by both the theological innovations of the reformers and the creation of the Church of England by Henry VIII. Reforms progressed under Henry's son, Edward VI. Early English and Scottish reformers were influenced greatly by the Swiss Reformation, either through correspondence with the Swiss or because of time spent among them while in exile from Mary Tudor (whom the Protestants called "Bloody Mary" because of her persecution of Protestants). When England returned to established Protestantism under Elizabeth I, theological division among the returning exiles from the Continent became increasingly problematic.

The French Reformation had early beginnings but was always embattled. It is remembered now largely for its Huguenot movement, named for Besançon Hugues and his religious compatriots who sought an alliance with Geneva. It is also remembered for Strasburg reformers Martin Bucer and Peter Martyr and their leadership from a city that became a sanctuary for other Protestants. Calvin's heart was always with the French Reformation. As for the German Reformation, it was largely Lutheran. But many German Protestants still adhered to Reformed theology, particularly in Heidelberg and Frankfort. Some of the English (and Scottish) exiles from Mary Tudor spent part of their exile in Frankfort.

The Reformations in England, France, and Germany all drew from the Swiss reformers during the sixteenth century. After the death of Huldrych (Ulrich) Zwingli in the Second Cappel War of 1531, the leadership of the "Swiss" Reformation fell largely to leading lights Henry Bullinger and John Calvin. Bullinger began his reforming ministry at an impressively young age (nineteen) and was a contemporary of Zwingli's. At the age of twenty-seven, Bullinger was given Zwingli's position after Zwingli's death and is hence considered his successor. But had Zwingli not died in the Second Cappel War, he and Bullinger would have progressed as contemporaries. John Calvin's international fame started five years after Zwingli's death, but he was as much a "French" reformer as he was a "Swiss" reformer. Not only did both Bullinger and Calvin disagree with Zwingli on important points, but they disagreed with each other as well, and these differences are important for the trajectory of Reformed political theology.

The most common and most substantial error among those who study the Reformation is to ignore or minimize Bullinger and to focus on Calvin instead. Not only did Bullinger gain a position of influence much sooner than Calvin, but his influence was arguably as extensive as Calvin's, if not more so. Archives of known correspondence have three times as many surviving letters from Bullinger as from Calvin, and there are potentially thousands more; his influence penetrated every corner of Europe and Britain.[11] By 1528, when Calvin was still relatively unknown, Bullinger had composed scores of theological works and was an internationally recognized authority.[12] His influence far surpassed Zwingli's.[13] He also outlived Calvin by twelve years, furthering his influence. Bullinger's works circulated widely in England approximately thirty years before Calvin's works. His influence even in France (acknowledged by Franz Hotman in a letter of 1572) can be attributed in part to his early converting influence on Theodore Beza in 1535. During the sixteenth century, there were well over fifty European printers producing hundreds of editions of Bullinger's works in at least five languages. Even Geneva may have been more taken with Bullinger than with Calvin, as Genevan printers worked hard to promote French editions of Bullinger's work. Even the Genevan authorities recognized the importance of Bullinger's scope, depth, and tone and required that Bullinger's doctrinal works be published alongside Calvin's *Institutes.*[14] Within one hundred years, 400 editions of Bullinger's works had been printed in Switzerland and 230 editions in other countries.[15] Bullinger's shadow was at least as long as Calvin's for the next two generations.

COVENANT CONTINUITY IN BULLINGER'S *DE TESTAMENTO*

Just as covenants were central to the Jewish narrative, they would now become central to the Reformed theology. Reformers addressed both individual and corporate covenants in their theology. Because Christians were the new descendants of Abraham, the reformers would have to contend with the meaning of the covenants described in Chapter 3. How the Reformed Protestants crafted their political theologies begins a legacy of complementary but competing disagreement.

Bullinger was the first to appropriate the Abrahamic covenant. In 1523, at the age of nineteen, he was already beginning to employ the traditional *testamentum* (covenant) in his writing. In 1526 he asserted that the New Testament was the fulfillment of the covenant with Israel.[16] By 1534, Bullinger had published his first substantial seminal treatise on the biblical covenants, *De testamento seu foedere dei unico & aeterno.*[17] *De testamento* was the first great contribution of the Reformation's "Hebraic Christianity" and the first great work of covenant or federal theology. Peter Lillback considers this study "of strategic importance" and "the first study of the covenant produced in the history of the church."[18] Most important for Reformed political theology, the work provided a seminal definition and defense of civil government just as the greatest progress of the Reformation was about to be made. Together with his *Decades,* which also addressed covenant continuity, *De testamento* cemented Bullinger's reputation as a political theologian.[19] Calvin's first edition of his *Christianae religionis institutio,* published two years later, did not yet contain any detailed discussion of the covenants.[20]

Bullinger's *De testamento* is evidence of the two-front theological war fought by the reformers. On one front, they sought to articulate the distinguishing marks of a theology reformed from "popery," "superstition," and "works righteousness." On the other hand, they had to counter elements of Anabaptist theology,[21] which undermined the traditional approach to the civil magistrate. Implicit in Anabaptist political theology was a belief that the New Testament covenant was a spiritual covenant while the Old Testament covenant was a carnal (and obsolete) covenant. This belief not only undermined continuity between the Old and New Testaments of Scripture but also challenged any application of Scripture to political practice. The result was a strict separation of Christians from any role in civil politics and no role for the magistrate in religious matters. Bullinger's *De testamento* repeatedly denies this, arguing particularly for continuity between the two testaments and their covenants and thereby rejecting both the Anabaptist theology and its accompanying political theology.[22]

De testamento is entirely dedicated to the defense of covenant continuity between the Hebrew and the Christian Scriptures. Bullinger begins with an introduction providing substantial connection between the Hebrew, Greek, and Latin terms, and he demonstrates their continuity throughout history. He argues that the spiritual quality of Christian faith far excels the ancient Jewish ceremonies and has more in common with the patriarchs because of its spiritual rather than ceremonial qualities.[23]

Bullinger's theology of covenant continuity includes political theology as well. He argues that the promises to the patriarchs of "land . . . wars and victories, Judaic glory and happiness" extend also to Christians. Earthly successes are not to be wholly replaced by "cross and exile" or "persecution."[24] The patriarchs are cast as taking the role of civil magistrates, with a corporate (or civil) covenant implicit in the presentation. Bullinger not only repeats a familiar list of obligations for the civil magistrate but also makes them the motive of the Old Testament's juridical and civil laws. Bullinger argues that Abraham, the first patriarch, was called by God to be a kind of magistrate and pursue civil responsibilities as part of his covenant with God.[25] The prophets played an implicitly political role according to Bullinger, working to hold the people to their covenant with God.[26] Bullinger interprets the parable of the wheat and tares (Matthew 13) as having implications for the civil magistrate's role in regulating religious practice.[27]

On this question of the civil government's role in religion, Bullinger's *De testamento* foreshadows a position taken more clearly in later works. Bullinger believed that the civil magistrate was to take a leading role (rather than a subordinate one) in matters of church discipline and orthodoxy. This is a position opposed by some of his fellow reformers, most notably Calvin and the English Puritans. And it is a position that would later diminish Bullinger's legacy. His charge to the civil magistrate cannot be cast as identical to or motivated by royal supremacy, however; it is a covenantal approach to civil society wherein every party becomes part of an implicit corporate responsibility before God and the magistrate has chief authority for the corporate covenant.[28] Bullinger's approach is best understood as a communal rather than a hierarchical approach.

In addition to explicit political theology, *De testamento* contains implicit political theology concerning the covenant of salvation. Bullinger calls the covenants "the origin of our religion and its primary point," describes the covenant as the "entire sum of piety" and everything handed down to the "saints of all ages, throughout the entire Scripture." By doing this, he is taking the question of soteriology, the theology of redemption and salvation, and making it the centerpiece of Reformed theology.[29] The debate about how this covenant of salvation functions will not only inspire theologies of predestination and divine sovereignty, it will underlie later debates about church polity, church-state relations, and the sacraments.

COVENANT CONTINUITY IN CALVIN'S *INSTITUTES* AND BULLINGER'S *DECADES*

While *De testamento* was really the first great work of covenant theology and political theology, Calvin's *Institutes* and Bullinger's *Decades* became the two great and most enduring works of the Swiss Reformation, the cornerstones of Reformed theology and British Protestantism. Calvin's first great contribution to Reformation controversies, his *Institutes,* grew substantially over five Latin editions through 1559. By then, the length of the *Institutes* was more comparable to the multi-volume edition of Bullinger's *Decades.*

If we focus only on the 1559 edition of the *Institutes*, we can certainly call Calvin's *Institutes* a work of covenant theology. Calvin uses covenantal Latin terms 273 times, and this does not include related terms such as *conjunctionis* or *adoptio* which he uses more than 293 times. Even terms to denote the trinity, election, predestination, or justification are used less frequently.[30] The word count itself does not enable substantive conclusions, of course, but it is clear from Calvin's treatment of covenant continuity in Book II of his *Institutes* that he agrees with Bullinger that it is a theme of central importance for biblical interpretation.

Calvin's specific treatment of covenant continuity has very important political implications. Like Bullinger, he argued that the covenant made with the patriarchs is the same as was made with the church, differing only in administration (*Institutes* II.x.1, 369). Both Calvin and Bullinger considered the promise to the Christian church to be the same as was given to the patriarchs and the Hebrew nations (II.x.1 and 23). By asserting continuity among the patriarchs, the church, and the Hebrew nations, Calvin joins Bullinger in arguing against both Roman Catholic and Anabaptist antagonists. The covenant with the patriarchs is given civil significance and the civil magistrate is not simply an Old Testament device.

But Calvin and Bullinger diverge when interpreting the lives of the patriarchs and appropriating their success or failure. And this is also significant for politics. Calvin takes special note of the Anabaptist contention that the promise given to the Jews was carnal rather than spiritual. His response to this is different than Bullinger's. Whereas Bullinger emphasized and appropriated the earthly successes of the patriarchs, Calvin emphasizes the disappointments of the patriarchs and Hebrew nations. If the patriarchs were promised a kind of final happiness but did not find it in this life, Calvin argues, we can only conclude that these promises to the patriarchs implied the *heavenly* promises now also given to Christians. Contrasted with Bullinger's, Calvin's narrative of the patriarchs is more sorrow than victory. In earthly terms, Noah, Abraham, Isaac, and Jacob all led troubled and unhappy lives (II.x.11 and 12). Calvin concluded, "If these holy Patriarchs expected a happy life from the hand of God (and it is indubitable that they did), they viewed and contemplated a different happiness from that of a terrestrial life" (II.x.13, 378). Their promise therefore was for something later, to future blessedness.

Bullinger argued that the earthly blessings to the patriarchs could be shared by Christians. He wrote, "For no one denies that the promise of the land of Canaan was bound to a specific place; but neither can anyone deny that the same promise or rather a similar promise of earthly things was made equally to all the Gentiles." Bullinger noted the famed riches of Abraham, Isaac, Jacob, and Joseph and concluded, "Now I believe that this was done by the Lord as an example for all the Gentiles, from which they might learn that they also would lack nothing if they feared the Lord after the manner of the patriarchs. And you will find many more promises of this type throughout both Testaments."[31]

For Calvin, the "covenant of [God's] mercy" to the patriarchs did potentially include greater earthly blessing. But this blessing was so that the prophets could direct the people's minds to heaven. Calvin agrees that the prophets used temporal blessings as examples before the people of general covenant blessing. But he also emphasizes that earthly blessing was to lift their minds above the earth (II.x.20, 384). Calvin argues that the same thing is true of modern believers, who should understand "prosperous success" in no other sense than as a manifestation of celestial glory (II.x.16, 380; II.xi.1, 388; II.xi.3, 389). Unlike Bullinger, Calvin is quick to spiritualize or "telescope" the blessing of God into a prophetic or heavenly future. In this seemingly small theological difference, two different political theologies can already be discerned in the works of Bullinger and Calvin. Bullinger sees much greater hope of a unified Christian polity than Calvin does.

THE COVENANT OF SALVATION: PREDESTINATION, ELECTION, AND REPROBATION IN CALVIN AND BULLINGER

Reformed Protestants faced another challenge in their covenant theology in addition to deciding how to interpret the successes or failures of the Hebrew patriarchs. How should they interpret the covenant of salvation, the covenant God made with his elect and redeemed people? The covenant of salvation, argued to extend all the way back to Abraham, was by far the most important of all the biblical covenants. It addressed questions of eternal life and fellowship with God. While life after death may appear a question too esoteric for political application, quite the opposite was true. Deciding how the covenant of salvation operated addressed a number of important political concerns. First, how the reformers interpreted the covenant of salvation would determine whether wheat and tares were to be separated in worship and administration of the sacraments (Matthew 13:24–30). Was separation to be done at all? If so, was it to be done by the magistrate or by the church? Or was it to be done by both church and state? Or were wheat and tares to be kept together in the church until Christ's second coming? If wheat and tares were to be kept together, did this mean that God would still judge entire nations for their faithfulness or unfaithfulness? Or did he judge only those in the church? Questions of God's election to salvation also raised questions about reprobation to damnation. If some were saved by God's sovereign and deliberate election, did this mean that the rest were damned by God's sovereign and deliberate election? (This was referred to as "double predestination"—predestination to salvation working together with predestination to damnation to decide the fate of all persons.) If damnation was the will of God, and damnation came as a result of evil and Adam's Fall, then what exactly was God's role in evil? This raised questions about the source of evil, especially political evil (tyranny), and the Christian's proper reaction to it. It was therefore in these seemingly abstract questions of soteriology (a branch of theology concerned with salvation) that more groundwork was laid for political matters.

"Predestination," the idea that God unilaterally selects persons for salvation, is not a debate exclusive to the Reformation.[32] The centuries-old debate between Augustine and Pelagius became a touchstone for the reformers and was continually cited by them. Nor was the study of predestination derived only from New Testament Scriptures. Part of Reformed Hebraism meant reviving the question of divine election (being "chosen") under the biblical covenants. The Hebrew Scriptures do not teach that the covenant is necessarily imposed. There is a call for human cooperation that is simultaneous with divine sovereignty. There are multiple passages calling God's people to "hearken" to the terms of the covenants given.[33] Persons are summoned to terms of agreement, individually and corporately, and the consequences for disobedience are stated.[34]

There was fundamental agreement in placing the grace of God and the sinfulness of human nature at the forefront of any argument. All Reformed theologians would agree that the terms of the covenant of salvation are set by God in His eternal decree, and communicated in the Scriptures. No Reformed theologian, regardless of their other disagreements, would confuse a covenant with a contract giving or receiving something in exchange for something else, as in the sense of a quid pro quo.[35] In theological principle, Calvin and Bullinger would also agree that God is the guarantor of human participation. This means that persons could not ultimately attribute covenant faithfulness to their own merit or will. Neither would any of the Reformed Protestants say that the Christian truly aids God in his or her own redemption. But this was all mainly agreement in principle. Exhortation, admonishment, or warning would still come from pen or pulpit, and the Christian was not to be passive and presume upon divine grace. How these two ideas—divine sovereignty and human responsibility—were reconciled has come to define the boundaries of scholarly debates over Reformed soteriology and political theology.

Scholars have debated whether there is a substantial difference between the theologies of Calvin in Geneva and the Rhineland theologians Zwingli, Bullinger, and Johannes Oecolampadius (an earlier German reformer).[36] The assertion of a difference emphasizes Calvin's belief in double predestination and suggests that he taught a "unilateral covenant" scheme wherein human participation became irrelevant when considered in the light of divine sovereignty. By contrast, Bullinger's theology is cast as more sincerely allowing for human cooperation in the covenant. In this latter view, God's promise is therefore conditional on man's response. Because man is able to fulfill or not fulfill the terms of the covenant, this latter view is called a "bilateral covenant."

This thesis of two distinct Reformed traditions has been carried forward into the study of political theology by J. Wayne Baker, who argued Bullinger to represent a Reformed tradition distinct from Calvin's.[37] The difference between the two types of covenant is sometimes expressed as the difference between "testament" and "covenant" respectively.[38] A testament, which is something bequeathed or disposed, is the more unilateral; a covenant, implying something close but not quite equal to a contract, is the more bilateral. The thesis concerning the "two Reformed traditions" has profound implications for politics. Any alleged similarities and differences between Bullinger and Calvin on this question of soteriology are of fundamental importance and must therefore be investigated.

The basic philological question is, How did Calvin use the words related to the covenant? Did Calvin see "testament" and "covenant" as essentially similar terms, as Bullinger did? Or did he see them with conceptual differences between them? (as Baker implies). On the surface, Calvin and Bullinger appear to be in agreement. In his Latin translation of the Bible, Calvin uses *pactum, foedus,* and *testamentum* (seen in 143 instances) without distinctly different meanings. He appears to use them in a manner consistent with the introduction of Bullinger's *De testamento,* as if they were essentially terms for the same thing.[39] This is further demonstrated in Calvin's commentaries on the Bible, which indicate no substantial differences between his thought and that of Bullinger.

We then proceed to some examination of Calvin's discussion of covenants in his *Institutes* and his commentaries on the Bible. If the bilateral covenant thesis is read to claim that Calvin never urged his audience to piety, or that he taught a kind of sterile fatalism, this cannot be reconciled with Calvin's writing. If it is arguing that the other Reformed theologians believed fallen persons could respond to demands of the covenant without God's assistance, this cannot be found in their writing. If the two traditions thesis is arguing that Calvin thought human cooperation to be essentially enabled by divine grace, it is simply echoing what was taught by any other Reformed theologian—especially Bullinger.

Like Bullinger, Calvin acknowledges human responsibility and urges his audience to appeal for divine assistance and to fulfill their duties before God. He joins human striving and divine sovereignty, using theological concepts such as adoption, calling, and works:

> Hence, if we would not deprive ourselves of the privilege of adoption, we must always strive in the direction of our calling. On the other hand, however, let us remember, that the completion of the divine mercy depends not on the works of believers, but that God himself fulfills the promise of salvation to those who by right conduct correspond to their calling, because he recognizes the true badges of sons in those only who are directed to good by his Spirit. *(Institutes* III.xvii.6, 109)

In his commentary on Genesis 17, a touchstone of Reformed theology, Calvin states, "We now consider how the covenant is rightly kept . . . for as God binds himself to keep the promise given to us; so the consent of faith and of obedience is demanded from us."[40] Clearly, Calvin argues, the Christian cannot simply claim the covenant of salvation and then do nothing. He speaks of Abraham's "twofold class of sons" in the church, distinguishing those who are gathered (but not redeemed) from those who are reckoned the sons of God by faith "in the innermost sanctuary of God." What distinguishes the true sons of God is "gratuitous election" (known only to the hidden counsel of God). We are able to distinguish these two classes of children by the "respective marks of faith and unbelief."[41] Hence, Calvin is quite capable of speaking of the covenant of Abraham as a covenant that involves actions on both God's part and man's part. Not all of Abraham's descendants persevered in saving faith. The remnant of believers is preserved in the first covenant, which is sustained by God. The rest (who are not saved) are in the second. Those who are excised from the covenant (outside the remnant) did indeed break the covenant. But it is also true that they were never part of the everlasting and saving covenant at all. Calvin says that this was true of Ishmael and Esau, for example (III.xxi.6, 209). And it is true of some Christians, whom he compares to Ishmael and Esau when he writes, "Such persons never adhered to Christ with that heartfelt confidence by which I say that the certainty of our election is established" (III.xxiv.7, 246). Later English Puritans such as William Perkins investigated these notions of salvific confidence more robustly, but it certainly can be said of Calvin that he hardly urged anything that could be characterized as "unilateral" redemption (wherein God did everything and man was called to do nothing).

But while Calvin would readily exhort his hearers or readers to covenant faithfulness, he also reminded them that they could only persevere by the grace of God. He argues throughout that it is the will of God that keeps His people faithful and capable of doing good works. He wrote, "This passage, therefore, tends in no degree to establish the freedom of the human will. . . . [I]t is one thing to withdraw from man, and look to what he will do when thus abandoned and left to himself, and another thing to assist his powers (whatever they may be), in proportion to their weakness" (II.v.12 and 13, 285–86). God has first place in the Christian's good works. Calvin asks whether Christians can take any credit for assisting Him. "If the only thing here insisted on were, that good works are termed *ours,* I, in my turn, would reply, that the bread which we ask God to give us is also termed *ours*" (II.v.14, 286). Christians must ask for their bread because all bread comes from the hand of God. In the same way, all good works must be sought but ascribed to God alone according to the phrase, "Give us this day our daily bread." These statements by Calvin demonstrate a complicated relationship between divine responsibility and human responsibility.

All persons are invited to hear what Calvin calls the "universal call" that is found in preaching. Those who do not heed this call are ordained to a more severe condemnation. Those who persevere and are not "abandoned" by God are those who received a "special call" (III.xxiv.8, 247). Explaining the difference in responses to the universal call, Calvin refers to those persons who will not persevere as merely "enlightened" but "without repentance" unless they take heed to Saint Paul's warning in Romans 11:22. Those who are "members of Christ in name only" are bound to God, but God is not bound to them. They are enlightened for a time but then fall into ingratitude and a "greater blindness" (III.xxiv.8, 247). Excision "cannot happen to the elect." The prescription here, in other words, is not fatalism or inaction. Calvin warns his audience that they "have yet need of such warning, in order to subdue the pride of the flesh which, as it is in fact opposed to their salvation, ought justly to be terror-stricken through fear of damnation"[42] Calvin preached reprobation in order to elicit pious conduct and considered it a doctrine of great comfort for God's people, arguing that the great and unmerited mercy of election could be known to God's remnant only by asserting the equal decree of reprobation (III.xxi.5, 206; 6, 209; 7, 210). This demonstrated the "gratuitous" love of a free covenant (III.xxi.5, 207; 6, 209). Calvin believed the equal assertion of election to salvation and reprobation "bore godly fruit," gave glory to God, and enabled humility (III.xxi.1, 203).

According to Calvin, it was certainly possible, at least in the existential reality of the individual professing Christian, to fall away from the saving covenant. In the "innermost sanctuary of God" (the inaccessible will of God), those who fell away were never in the covenant to begin with. But the solution to this problem, Calvin argues, is not to press into the counsel of God and try to discern God's electing decision. Calvin repeatedly warns against inquiring into the eternal counsels of the divine will on this matter (III.xxi.1, 202–3; III.xxiii.2, 227; III.xxiii.7, 231, for example). One can only pursue faithfulness by attending to the Word and sacraments as means of grace. In speaking of the Deuteronomic covenant, for example, Calvin distinguishes the everlasting "covenant of mercy," which would transform the heart, from the covenant that obliged keeping the law (II.v.12, 285). In other words, Calvin is speaking of two different covenants. Both call persons to faithfulness. One will succeed because God will enable faithfulness, but the other cannot succeed, because fallen and unregenerate persons are unable to be faithful.

Calvin, like Bullinger, argues that God is bound by all His covenants. But the terms by which He is bound depend upon the particular covenant. The former covenant with the Hebrew nations was made with an absolute condition that, if broken, would make them "covenant-breakers and traitors." This covenant was broken, in order for God to make way for the covenant He would make with the Christian church. Bullinger agreed concerning the spiritual legacy of Abraham's descendants, demonstrating substantial concord with Calvin in their interpretation of Genesis 17.[43]

Despite their fundamental agreement on covenant conditionality and the need for both faithfulness and divine enabling, however, there is important disagreement too. On the subject of reprobation, for example, Calvin is quite forceful where Bullinger is reticent.[44] It is on the question of reprobation and Adam's fall that they are divided. Calvin emphasized reprobation as the willing action of God. This is evident in his *Institutes* and commentaries and is stated in his 1538 catechism for Geneva.[45] It is also the subject of a 1552 treatise, *De aeterna Praedestinatione Dei* (Concerning the Eternal Predestination of God).[46] Albertus Pighius and Georgius Siculus had earlier attacked Calvin in the 1540s concerning his position on sin and free will. In his 1559 edition of the *Institutes,* Calvin pursues the question of reprobation and Adam's fall methodically and systematically. All things happen by the will of God, he argues. There are neither two divine wills nor a manifold divine will (I.xviii.3, 202–3). No distinction is made between will and permission (III.xxiii.8, 232). To those who hope to untangle the difference between them, Calvin replies, "If anyone object that this is beyond his comprehension, I confess it. But what wonder if the immense and incomprehensible majesty of God exceed the limits of our intellect?"[47]

Calvin denies categorically any hope of equating prescience with predestination, or prescience with determination (III.xxiii.6, 231; xxi.5, 206). And he is clear that no human works are taken into account in either reprobation or salvation (III.xxii.3, 214). In denying any reference to merit or works, Calvin repeatedly repairs to Romans 9. But even in his appeal to the penultimate chapter on predestination, he again gives a warning to his reader against searching into the hidden counsels of God.[48] In his *Institutes,* Calvin applies this "mysterious majesty" of the hidden counsels of God to the whole narrative of the Fall. Sin and evil are somehow part of God's plan, but this in no way makes God the cause nor does it diminish human responsibility. "Man therefore falls, divine providence so ordaining, but he falls by his own fault" (III.xxiii.8, 233). Calvin argues that God created Adam (whom he calls "the noblest of creatures") solely with the purpose of bringing glory to Himself. To argue that God created Adam with no particular purpose strikes Calvin as a "frigid fiction" (III.xxiii.7, 231). He says quite emphatically, "God not only foresaw the fall of the first man, and in him the ruin of his posterity; but also at his own pleasure arranged it" (III.xxiii.7, 232). At another place, Calvin blends the two wills together, just as he did in his discussion of the covenant of Abraham. He states that Adam fell by his "own will . . . though not without God's knowledge and ordination."[49] Calvin also argues that Adam had free will to decide for himself: "Adam, therefore, might have stood if he chose, since it was only by his own will that he fell . . . he had a free choice of good and evil" (I.xv.8, 169).

As for Adam's descendants, Calvin argues that they are all at fault and that God's judgment is a perfect justice (III.xxiv.14, 254). Man ruined his own nature (a nature that God proclaimed to be good at Creation) and thereby earned reprobation (III.xxiii.9, 233; 3 and 4, 228). The root of human disobedience, and even the cause of the hardening of hearts, is the inscrutable judgment of God's glory (III.xxiv.14, 253; III.xxiii.1, 227; 4, 228). But that judgment is hidden and unknowable. The evident sinfulness of persons, including Adam, is cause enough for their condemnation. If there is a "necessary" quality inherent in human sinning, it is not the same as compulsion (II.iii.5, 253–54). Calvin argues that the "blame of our ruin rests with our own carnality, not with God" (II.ii.10, 219). To assert the will of God does not remove man's guilt.[50] And neither does it make God a tyrant. In a phrase also full of political implication, Calvin wrote, "We give no countenance to the fiction of absolute power. . . . the will of God is not only free from all vice, but is the supreme standard of perfection, the law of all laws" (III.xxiii.2, 227–28).

When Bullinger explicitly takes up predestination in his *Decades,* it is in the context of God's providence rather than soteriology (IV.iv, 181–83). Though Bullinger will call election a "fore-appointment" (*praefinito*), he is more reluctant than Calvin to discern or even place the will of God in the operation of election. He urges his audience to pursue salvation with all effort and haste, praying incessantly for an increase of faith (IV.iv, 185, 192). Bullinger took this approach throughout his ministry, up to and including his writing of the Second Helvetic Confession.[51]

Unlike Calvin, who rooted covenants of salvation in the unknowable will of God, Bullinger made those covenants more accessible by putting them in the context of human covenants and agreements. Bullinger casts the biblical covenants as something which God condescended to make with persons, mimicking the covenants persons already made with one another (III.vi, 169). In writing on the Lord's Supper and the binding of persons to God and to one another, for example, Bullinger compares the sacrament to historical human confederacies (V.vi, 238–39). The point here was not to argue that Bullinger thought covenants were an agreement between equals or to make the biblical covenants akin to human contracts, but rather to stress the accommodation of God. The unknowable mystery in Calvin is why God chose to save one person rather than another; the unknowable mystery in Bullinger is the role of God's will in predestination (IV.iv, 185–88).

Bullinger always emphasizes an existential approach to predestination, discouraging his reader from turning what should be a relational question into an academic one. Doubt about one's election, Bullinger argues, is the work of the Devil (IV.iv, 192). If a person experiences fellowship with Christ, then he is predestinated to life. If not, then he is predestinated to death. Bullinger concludes,

"Higher and deeper I will not creep into the seat of God's counsel" (IV.iv, 187). Emidio Campi puts it this way: "For Bullinger the decisive matter in eternal election or damnation from the human perspective is not God's eternal decree, but rather communion with Christ as realized by faith."[52]

This does not mean that persons can hope to fulfill (on their own) the promises made in the covenant of salvation or that the covenant is conditional to the point that those truly in the covenant of salvation can break it. As in Calvin, God's grace is essential and must be sought. While Bullinger will indeed speak of the duties of the covenant more readily than Calvin (III.vi, 170), he also credits sanctification entirely to God *(Decades* IV.i, 32; IV.ii, 99–102).[53] Man's duty is to walk upright before God, in faith, hope, and charity (III.vi, 171). This makes the covenant of salvation neither conditional nor "bilateral." It does not mean that persons can do good works by free will without regeneration (IV.ii, 102–3). As in Calvin, the covenant remains eternal. Perseverance is the work of God. Resembling Calvin's comparison of good works to daily bread, Bullinger wrote that, although works are imputed to men, "There is none other well-spring, from whence good works do flow, than God himself, which is the author of all good things" (III.ix, 322, 324). He criticizes Pelagius, who claimed (in disagreement with Augustine) that he could keep the commandments of God by free will (IV.i, 11).

As for sin, Bullinger only partially agrees with Calvin's argument. As God made it, the created nature of man was good and hence cannot be blamed for sin (III.x, 362, 368–69, 373, 377). But whereas Calvin discourages the conclusion that God *abused* his absolute power in *causing* the fall into sin, Bullinger discourages the conclusion that God *should have used* his absolute power to *prevent* the fall into sin (III.x, 365). And whereas they agree that God cannot be made the author of sin, what Calvin will allow and what Bullinger will allow in their discussions of Adam are quite different. Bullinger argues that God chose to work with Adam by law rather than by divine interference (III.x, 365–70, 375). In short, Adam was given terms of an agreement which he broke. Calvin and Bullinger seem to agree that Adam's sin was the cause of the agreement's being broken. But Calvin will assert God's role in that chain of events, whereas Bullinger will not.

Disagreement over these matters led to one of the few "public" disagreements between Calvin and Bullinger. In October 1551, Jerome Bolsec charged that Calvin's ideas of reprobation and double predestination could not be reconciled with Scripture.[54] The events that followed revealed some of the weakness of Calvin's reputation among some Swiss Reformed brethren and also his disagreements with Bullinger.[55] Bolsec, a refugee from France, was a former Carmelite monk who also held a doctorate in theology from the University of Paris. During a formal Bible study meeting (a *congregation,* the regular Friday meeting instituted by William Farel and Calvin since 1536), Bolsec argued that Calvin's predestination made God into a tyrant, removed predestination from its proper context in Christ, and suggested an unbiblical view of God's will. After he was arrested, Bolsec was brought before the civil authorities.[56] Bolsec's defense was that it was he and not Calvin who held to orthodoxy. Geneva's clergy asked the Council to withhold judgment until they could consult with Bullinger. Calvin also appealed to Bullinger, claiming that Bolsec was a liar.

The debate hinged on the source of salvation and the cause of reprobation. In his reply to Calvin, Bullinger stated three things clearly: (1) God wills that all men be saved and come to knowledge of the truth; (2) No man is saved by his own works but by the grace of God alone; and (3) Damnation and reprobation is the result of unbelief and sin alone.[57] Bullinger made it clear to Calvin that he disagreed with him not only theologically but also pastorally.[58] The reply from Bullinger and the Zurich clergy included an appeal to Article XVI of the *Consensus Tigurinus* of 1549 and corresponding Scripture. Although the *Consensus Tigurinus* was a document of recent vintage that was agreed upon by both Zurich and Geneva, appealing to its sparse explication of the matter was a curious gesture of support. In a statement of November 27, 1551, the Zurich ministers argued that every man's sin was his own and without excuse. This was a more indirect explanation for reprobation and not the one Calvin had offered.

This disagreement revealed substantial differences between Calvin and Bullinger, particularly concerning the intersection of foreknowledge and foreordination. Bullinger takes up this intersection in the context of Adam rather than in the context of general predestination. He argues that God's foreknowledge does not necessitate anything. Those who blame God for not intervening in Adam's fall are guilty of "railing against the majesty of God almighty" (III.x, 377). It was the choice of mankind's first parents to abandon the Word of God and thereby fall into sin. By this, they broke the law. Adam's fall had nothing to do with God's ordination. The source of the first sin is threefold: the devil, human free choice, and the sinner's hope for a false good (III.x, 370). Bullinger is quite clear that Adam had the power to sin or not to sin, and he defends the decision of God to give Adam that freedom. Whereas Calvin repeatedly rehearsed the election and reprobation of Jacob and Esau in Romans 9 to defend the sovereign decision of God to bring some persons to redemption and others to destruction, Bullinger uses the same narrative in Romans 9 to defend God's making Adam and Eve fallible rather than impervious to sin (III.x, 375). Bullinger's response to the penultimate passage of election (Romans 9:18), "So then he has mercy on whomever he wills, and he hardens whomever he wills," is to say, "We must not so wrest it to say, that God doth of necessity drive any man to sin, and that therefore he is the cause of sin" (III.x, 384). This is consistent with what he says elsewhere: "We do not make man subject to fatal necessity, nor turn upon God the blame of iniquity" (IV.ii, 102). This distinction of

Bullinger's will become very important for explaining differences between himself and Calvin on the subject of tyranny. Calvin will readily ascribe its cause to God. Bullinger will not.

Unlike Calvin, Bullinger denies that God either hardens or spiritually blinds men. Nor does Bullinger believe that God's desire for divine glory is the first cause of anything that happens to man. God needs neither election nor reprobation of persons to bring glory to Himself (III.x, 378–79). Bullinger urges his hearers to prevail upon the means of salvation, even in the face of the eternal decree (IV.iv, 183–94). When God is said to "harden" persons, as in the case of Pharaoh, it is by their own sinful presuming on His goodness and long suffering. If God tells Moses that He will harden Pharaoh, it is in order to warn Moses of a long struggle against him (III.x, 381–82) and not to make Himself the cause. Bullinger agrees with Calvin that the gospel is to be preached to all. But he does not think the limited response that inevitably follows enables us to draw either theoretical or practical conclusions. In a passage directed against any fatalistic conclusion or resignation, Bullinger wrote:

> For we must not imagine that in heaven there are laid two books, in the one whereof the names of them are written that are to be saved, and so to be saved, as it were of necessity, that, do what they will against the word of Christ and commit they never so heinous offences, they cannot possibly choose but be saved; and that in the other are contained the names of them which, do what they can and live they never so holily, yet cannot avoid everlasting damnation. Let us rather hold, that the holy gospel of Christ doth generally preach to the whole world the grace of God, the remission of sins, and life everlasting. (IV.i, 32–33)

Bullinger follows this with a host of passages indicating God's desire that all should be saved, including I Timothy 2:3–4: "This is good, and it is pleasing in the sight of God our Savior, who desires all people to be saved and to come to the knowledge of the truth." Concerning any supposed universality implied in that passage, Calvin simply interprets Timothy only to say "the way of salvation was not shut against any order of men" *(Institutes* III.xxiv.16, 254–55). Bullinger says only that many are called but few are chosen, as evidenced by Christ's parables (Luke 14; *Decades* IV.i, 32–34).

Insight into Bullinger's view of the covenant of salvation can also be discerned from his discussion of circumcision, the covenantal ceremony that maintained a "people" in the Old Testament. Circumcision was understood by Reformed theologians as being the Old Testament equivalent of baptism, and theologians debated how baptized children by way of a covenantal sacrament became members of a chosen people (V.ii, 73; V.vii, 299, 316, 322, 323). Bullinger wrote that the circumcised were bound by a lifelong duty to become confederates of God, and to dedicate their lives to the will of God rather than to their own "lust and pleasure." Circumcision is the token of what Bullinger calls "the bargain and agreement between God and men, which hath certain conditions and articles" (V.vi, 280). This "bargain and agreement" is not just applied to the Old Testament, or what Bullinger's contemporaries would have identified as the "works of the law." Consistent with themes of both covenant continuity and faithfulness on the part of Christians, he compares physical circumcision to a spiritual circumcision or circumcision of the heart (III.vi, 176–77).[59] In light of both covenant continuity and the way in which circumcision (now baptism) creates an entire nation, it is not unexpected that Bullinger draws from this a covenantal conclusion, creating corporate responsibility for the polity before God. This corporate responsibility includes multiple warnings against persons who either treat the covenant with disrespect or ignore it altogether (III.vi, 178; V.vii, 295–96; V.viii, 366).

DRAWING CONCLUSIONS FOR POLITICS

Asserting covenant continuity with Abraham began as an exercise by Reformed Protestants intent on recovering the foundations of a defensible soteriology. But in returning to the Old Testament, Calvin and Bullinger raised important questions about the nature of covenants and their implications for individuals and for society. Though Calvin and Bullinger did not fundamentally disagree about covenant continuity, the particulars of their respective soteriologies are pregnant with implications for politics. As we will see in the next chapter, how one understands the particulars of covenant salvation informs political questions central to the sixteenth century and the centuries that follow. This includes the role of church discipline, church-state relations, resistance against tyranny, political legitimacy, popular approval of magistrates, and the importance of the individual conscience.

5 Regime, Discipline, and Resistance
The Covenant and the Civil Magistrate

The political implications of Bullinger's and Calvin's theologies now deserve a more intentional analysis. Their legacies remain in a state of both competition and cooperation throughout the Anglo-American experience. Only by continuing to view them side-by-side can one fully appreciate the development of the Reformed Protestant inheritance for politics.

Looking at the circumstances of the mid–sixteenth century, one would not expect that Calvin and Bullinger should loom large in the political heritage of Britain and America. Neither held any official civil office in their own city-states. Calvin was hardly the powerful theocrat that some have cast him to be. It would have been hard to wield any legal authority when he was not even offered Genevan citizenship in 1559, five years before his death. For most of his time in Geneva, Calvin was the victim of anti-French sentiment and often found his plans thwarted by the city authorities of Bern (with whom Geneva held an important political alliance).[1] Bullinger was more popular than Calvin, and the pastors in Zurich enjoyed more independence than did those in Geneva in setting "official" church doctrine.[2] But like Calvin, Bullinger did not hold any civil authority. And in neither city did the church hold the independent excommunication power that the Roman Catholic Church hierarchy had used to influence civil authorities in Catholic realms. Nevertheless, both Bullinger and Calvin arguably shaped political thinking across the Protestant realms more than did philosophers, statesmen, diplomats, or armies. Ironically, their legacies of influence were guaranteed by the persecuting policies of a Catholic monarch, Mary Tudor, who drove her Protestants into the waiting arms of the reformers on the continent. While on the Continent in exile, these English and Scottish reformers would be deeply influenced by their time in Protestant strongholds such as Zurich and Geneva. They would later return to Scotland and England to continue the work of reformation.

THE CHURCH'S RELATIONSHIP TO THE CIVIL MAGISTRATE

The vital church-state questions at the time of Bullinger and Calvin consisted of church polity and church discipline (excommunication), worship (ritual and vestments), and sacraments. Presupposing there was a Christian magistrate, Bullinger recognized that magistrate's right to determine certain religious questions. This minimized but did not eliminate any right of excommunication by church leaders. In the English controversies, Bullinger did not flinch at the royal supremacy asserted by Henry VIII, Edward VI, and Elizabeth I. Rejecting any adversarial approach taken by dissenting clergy, Bullinger in his political theology emphasized community and reconciliation. Zurich was cast as a traditional *corpus christianum* (Christian body) wherein the church and state were partners. Through their role as prophets and evangelists, the clergy served only to influence the magistrate but never themselves to rule.[3] Bullinger did not insist upon an ecclesiastical discipline in opposition to the authority of the civil magistrate. This mercifully saved Zurich from a host of embroilments and saved the clergy from being viewed as competitors by the civil magistrates. This might seem to have diminished the clergy's power in Zurich. From Bullinger's position, however, it maintained their integrity as prophetic voices within the civil realm. It also stood in contrast to the papacy's previous interference in civil polities.

Calvin asserted the need for a more independent church, though the church was hardly without civil support. And though Calvin did not seek a "purified" church on the Anabaptist model, he did want to cleanse the church and its communion of those living in unrepentant sin. Calvin's *ideal* church-state relationship is unclear. He certainly did not confuse their respective authorities or assert that the punishment and justice of one should stand in for the other (*Institutes* IV.xi.3, 441–42). But the line between civil piety and pious orthodoxy was not always clear. On the one hand, Calvin expected the civil magistrate to be a partner of the church (IV.xx.9, 657–58).[4] The civil magistrate in Geneva both exiled and executed heretics, though not necessarily for heresy itself so much as for heresy's presumed relationship to civil discord. On the other hand, Calvin argued that civil laws do not touch the conscience, and particularly not when they concern "necessary" religious matters.

Bullinger's ideal is not precisely clear either, apart from vague prohibitions against "any new religions" or altering established modes of worship. In his *Decades*, Bullinger charges the magistrate with the "maintaining of religion, honesty, justice, and public peace" (*Decades* II.vii, 323). This includes judging among various doctrines and also executing "those that do stubbornly teach against the scriptures, and draw the people from the true God" (II.vii, 324–25). This is necessary in order to keep the commonwealth both safe and prosperous since church and commonwealth required the Word of God (II.vii, 324). Bullinger's model includes not only the Hebrew patriarchs and monarchs, but also Melchizadech, the priest-king who met with Abraham and is later compared to Christ (II.vii, 324–27, 333–36; Genesis 14, Hebrews 7, Psalm 110).

From the perspective of the sixteenth century, the civil and ecclesiastical were then not so easily separated. Public piety was seen as essential to good civil order. Religious dissent and variation were seen as posing a threat to civil peace. The Hebraic nature of Reformed theology also added a covenantal dimension of corporate responsibility. Ancient Israel was never far from the Reformed mind, and boy kings such as Edward VI had the potential to restore the covenant like King Josiah.[5] Even Calvin, who asserted the church's right to administer discipline and to bar even princes from the sacraments, used the civil authorities to challenge and punish his theological opponents. What divided Calvin and Bullinger was their respective understandings of "papist" practice. Bullinger associated clerical supremacy and ecclesiastical autonomy with Romanism.[6] Papal tyranny over the magistrate and papal theological errors was a violation of the public covenant with God.[7] This included not only the papal bulls issued against political opponents in England but also the use of church councils (Protestant or Catholic) to resolve theological matters. There was an important difference between *plenitud potestatis* and *cura religionis.*

To further understand the differences between the political theology of Bullinger and Calvin, contrast their first encounters with the civil magistrate. Calvin, in the tradition of the French-speaking Reformation, viewed baptism and the Lord's Supper as ordinances that could be used for church discipline. When Calvin and William Farel first partnered in Geneva in 1537, they submitted to the Genevan people three things they considered necessary for a true church: a series of articles for organization, a confession of faith, and a catechism. Their proposed catechism of 1538 for the citizens of Geneva became the standard for church discipline. The Articles and Confession were accepted by the Magistracy of Geneva but later rejected by the Genevan city council. The Genevan church insisted on the right of discipline,[8] including the public reading of the names of outcasts.[9] Under pressure at home and from Bern, the Genevan Council had banned both Calvin and Farel from Geneva by Easter 1538. After a brief and somewhat unfruitful trip to Zurich (where he and Bullinger were able to communicate only in Latin and through interpreters), Calvin sought asylum with Martin Bucer at Strasburg. Despite their differences, Bullinger appealed to get Calvin back to Geneva.[10] While Calvin made some compromises in his *Ecclesiastical Ordinances* of 1541 and was not allowed to sit on any of the Genevan councils,[11] he did reassert (largely unsuccessfully) the right to excommunicate. His Consistory of pastors and elders continued its regulation of morality consistent with that power (including an infamous decision to refuse baptism to children deemed to have superstitious names). Calvin's arrangement was never tantamount to ecclesiastical autonomy, however. Until 1555, the Genevan Senate claimed that the Consistory could only admonish and *recommend* excommunication.[12] It could not actually excommunicate on its own authority.

By contrast, Bullinger took a cooperative rather than a competitive approach to the civil authorities. When he first appeared before the Zurich Council as successor to Zwingli to swear allegiance to the civil magistrate, Bullinger neither asserted specific autonomous powers for the church nor presumed to subject civil magistrates to church discipline. He asserted that the church could not run the state and the state could not run the church. The civil magistrates would be expected to live up to their reputations as Christians and to abide by a Christian conscience. The church would do likewise. Both would be governed by conscience. The ministers would agree to abide by twice-yearly general synods and not to meddle in doubtful teaching or doctrine. They would also agree to admonish civil authorities as was within their power. The civil council of Zurich agreed to commit authority to the church "free, unhindered, and without restrictions."[13] Bullinger was thus free to proceed with the reformation of Zurich without the kind of contentious relationship that Calvin endured for decades in Geneva.

Calvin insisted on church discipline apart from partnership with the civil magistrate (*Institutes* IV.xii.1–7, 453–58). In this he was consistent with both Bucer and Oecolampadius, though Oecolampadius later changed his own position.[14] Church discipline included excommunication and barring a person from the sacraments. Not even princes were exempt from excommunication, Calvin argued (IV.xii.7, 457–58; IV.xi.3, 442).[15] Civil magistrates should have no desire to exempt themselves from "the common subjection of the children of God" (IV.xi.4, 442). The Genevan clergy thus acted as gatekeepers to the Lord's Supper (IV.iii.6, 320). By making some attempt to separate the wheat and the tares *now,* Calvin's emphasis on church discipline had the effect of discouraging the *corpus christianum* of Bullinger and the reformers' medieval predecessors. It also created a dilemma for Reformed Protestants after Calvin.

Bullinger's position on church discipline is more difficult to discern. Ella asserts that Bullinger and Zwingli, in the German-speaking tradition, never sought to use threats of exclusion against those who sat under the gospel. Bruce Gordon asserts the same thing. Baker argues that Bullinger believed excommunication was unheard of in the Apostolic church and was begun by popes and emperors in the third century.[16] Zurich's position could rightly be cast as an implicitly covenantal approach emphasizing inclusive community and the primacy of the gospel.[17] However, Bullinger does assert the right of the church to discipline ministers, and he extends "the same admonition and correction to the whole church" (V.x, 505–7). He does not deny powers of discipline to church leaders entirely but warns against the consequences of such discipline if it should be used against anyone other than "wicked orders, and pernicious men." The church must not threaten discipline against those characterized by "weakness of the flesh," "those judged heretical only by bishops," or "poor persons." Bullinger warns against causing division in the church and also cites the much-used parable of the wheat and tares. In contrast to Calvin's devoting many pages to church discipline in his *Institutes* (IV.xi and xii), Bullinger's discussion is relatively short and concludes by citing the power of the civil magistrate, which he summarized earlier in his *Decades* (V.x, 508–9). That power includes the power to punish substantial heterodoxy and impiety (II.viii, 357–69). Bullinger is quite careful, however. He never endorsed the idea that civil laws can create faith. His interest is in the preservation of orthodoxy and civil peace and not in confusing the church militant with the church triumphant or the visible church with the invisible church.

Calvin had evangelical motives for asserting the clerical right to excommunication, believing that the threat of it would encourage piety. He also believed that for its own sake the visible church required a certain degree of purity before God and the world. Calvin thus emphasized a corporate responsibility of the church before God. Calvin repeats this theme in his *Institutes,* calling the gospel the life of the church, and the church's discipline the "sinews" to defend itself against those who would threaten its life (IV.xii.1, 453). In his 1538 catechism, Calvin wrote that discipline was "necessary among believers for the reason that the church, since it is Christ's body, ought not to be polluted and befouled by unclean members who bring shame upon the head."[18] Furthermore, chastisement of sin might bring shame where indulgence would bring stubbornness.[19] This all goes back to the wheat and tares dilemma and emphasized individual covenant faithfulness. When Calvin complained to Bullinger concerning the "wretched people" in his church, Bullinger's reply was to say that the pure church would be gathered in heaven and that the New Testament church was composed of a "mixed" body.[20]

Bullinger remained suspicious of Calvin's Geneva model of competition between church and civil magistrate. In particular, he believed that Calvin's approach to church discipline would introduce auricular confession similar to that used by the Catholics. Bullinger called such confession a "corrupt evil in the church."[21] He wrote to a fellow pastor in 1543, "One introduces confession again and builds a fence around the Lord's Supper so that only a few Table guests may partake of it and the meal of thanksgiving becomes a torturing of conscience."[22] What concerned Bullinger further was the possibility that externals (small theological matters) would be put before theological essentials and that the church would be torn apart. Unlike Calvin, Bullinger was content not to try to purge the tares from among his wheat. These questions of church discipline did not substantially divide Calvin and Bullinger at the time, but they would later divide the English and American churches and tear apart the covenantal social fabric.

THE CIVIL MAGISTRATE, TYRANNY, RESISTANCE, AND CONSCIENCE

In addition to questions of church discipline and the church-state relationship, the *Institutes* and the *Decades* have much to say on the role of the civil magistrate. In keeping with the Augustinian tradition, Calvin (IV.xx.1, 651–52; xi.3, 441–42) and Bullinger (II.vii, 329) both speak to the twofold nature of government—the temporal and the civil, or the spiritual and the ecclesiastical. Neither government may subsume the other or presume to do its work. To frame the discussion in this way enabled them to respond to the excesses of both Anabaptist and Roman Catholic opponents *(Institutes* IV.xx.5, 654–55). Both Calvin (IV.xx.1–3, 651–53) and Bullinger (II.v, 276–77) also deny that any separation of jurisdictions releases Christians from their duties to their country, the laws, or the magistrate. Both assert that government is essential and honorable, and not a necessary evil *(Institutes* IV.xx.3, 652–53; xx.22, 668; *Decades* II.v, 279–80). Both cite Saint Peter's admonition to "Fear God, honor the king" (I Peter 2:17), and both extol the virtues of those who serve their country *(Institutes* IV.xx.5, 654; IV.xx.22, 668; *Decades* II.v, 279, 280). Calvin praised the civil magistrate's office as the highest station in mortal life (IV.xx.4, 653–54). Bullinger discourages not only seditions and conspiracies against the magistrate but also cursing and speaking evil of him (II.v, 280; II.vi, 311). Both agree that the magistrate's function is to punish evil and to defend the country by going to war if necessary *(Decades* II.vi, 307–8, 313; *Institutes* IV.xx.9, 659; xx.11, 661). Bullinger casts civil magistry as a service to God Himself (II.vi, 308). Calvin urges magistrates to take both consolation and encouragement from the knowledge that their duty is prescribed and governed by God (IV.xx.6, 655). Bullinger, consistent with his hope for civil-ecclesiastical cooperation, argues that magistrates should be selected for their belief that God will reward or punish their faithfulness to the civil vocation (II.vi, 319). Much of this is implicitly covenantal insofar as it depends on a scheme of promises and faithfulness by both magistrate and citizens.

Both Bullinger and Calvin are reticent to prescribe clearly any particular regime type based on the classical regime taxonomy (monarchy-aristocracy-democracy). Both argue, implicitly or explicitly, that circumstances are the primary consideration in selecting the best regime. Bullinger wrote, "It maketh not greatly to my purpose to dispute which ought to be preferred before [the] other" (II.vi, 311). Calvin argues that it is a "very idle occupation" for private persons to debate the question of the best regime. He concludes only that the best regime is "where liberty is framed with becoming moderation" (IV.xx.8, 656–57). If one reads between the lines, it becomes clear that they prefer aristocratic republicanism. Bullinger sees great perils and "infinite discommodities" in democracy when compared to aristocracy. Citing I Samuel 8, he argues that a "good and upright prince" is hard to find (II.vi, 309–11). Calvin also believed that each regime type had its vices but argues that aristocracy avoids the particularly destructive vices of democracy and monarchy. In commenting on the Davidic monarchy, Calvin strikes a preemptive blow against the yet-to-be-asserted divine right of kings by arguing that God's approval of monarchy was merely "an image of the Messiah in David."[23] Furthermore, God Himself established an "aristocracy bordering on popular government among the Israelites" (IV.xx.8, 657).

These hints of republicanism cannot be conclusively tied to the covenant theologies of these thinkers, however. Scorn for democracy went back to the ancients and both Bullinger and Calvin were familiar with those critiques. Covenanting did imply a cooperation of equals, but it neither necessitated republicanism nor forbade monarchy. The republicanism of Calvin and Bullinger could also just as easily be ascribed to their Swiss context.

On the question of tyranny and resistance, their respective diagnoses and prescriptions reveal important differences and hearken back to differences between them over soteriology. If not read carefully, Calvin and Bullinger may seem to prescribe obedience in almost any case. Bullinger, for example, declares that where rulers falter because of their "infirmities," they should nevertheless be supported "so long as justice is maintained and good laws and public peace defended" (II.v, 280–81). Likewise, Calvin says that God's command to obey the magistrate is not limited to those who honestly and faithfully perform their duty; allegiance is to all princes, "by whatever means they have so become, although there is nothing they less perform than the duty of princes" (IV.xx.25, 670). Both Calvin and Bullinger also suggest that the first remedy against tyranny is repentance and prayer *(Decades* II.vi, 316–17; *Institutes* IV.xx.29, 673–74). Both caution against resistance by citing the refusal of David to slay Saul *(Decades* II.vi, 316; *Institutes* IV.xx.28, 673). But both also open the door for resistance, suggesting from Scripture that God has previously used avengers from among his people to return liberty and displace tyrants *(Decades* II.vi, 318; *Institutes* IV.xx.30–31, 674).

The more interesting differences in political theories hinge on theologies of divine providence and covenant faithfulness. Bullinger provides an important theological condemnation of political tyranny. Calvin also changes the trajectory of resistance theory by advocating interposition by the "lesser magistrate," and he offers a provocative doctrine of individual conscience. These must be investigated if the contributions of covenant theology are to be fully understood.

While Calvin and Bullinger agree that the office of the magistrate is good, they disagree on why that office is sometimes held by tyrants and what role is played by divine providence *(Decades* II.vi, 314; *Institutes* IV.xx.22, 669). Both argue that tyranny is a type of divine punishment for disobeying God *(Decades* II.vi, 314–15; *Institutes* IV.xx.25, 670–71). But in ascribing a cause, as with their respective theodicies, they differ. Consistent with his discussion of reprobation and the sin of Adam, Bullinger will not argue that God is the source of a bad magistrate. Unlike Calvin, who had said that God "arranged" the fall of Adam, Bullinger uses every opportunity to disassociate sin and evil from the divine will. Bullinger's approach to political evil is the same as his approach to moral evil. He wrote, "Whether an evil, that is, a tyrannical, magistrate, be of God or no? To this I answer, that God is the author of good, and not of evil" (II.vi, 314). Just as Adam neglected the ordinance of God and brought about evil, so the prince or the people neglected the ordinance of God when enabling the evil of tyranny. Tyranny, like Adam's fall, is caused by the cooperation of the devil's temptation with human sinfulness. The divine will is not the cause of the evil, but only the cause of the just punishment that follows. Tyranny is therefore condemned, with Christ's own sanction, as a work of the devil. Tyrants are called servants of the devil. Bullinger puts the condemnation of the tyrant directly into Christ's mouth (II.vi, 315; also Luke 22:52, 53). This is far more than Calvin was willing to do.

Consistent with his discussion of divine providence, Calvin will readily repair to God's sovereign pleasure in occasions of both political good and evil. He not only makes no effort to mitigate God's role in tyranny but devotes a lengthy discussion to establishing God's role in ordaining tyrants *(Institutes* IV.xx.25–28, 670–73; xx.30, 674). Calvin wrote, "We need not labor to prove that an impious king is a mark of the Lord's anger" (IV.xx.25, 670). God delegates authority to earthly magistrates and this includes the execution of divine justice. Calvin will ascribe tyranny to the will and arrangement of God much in the same way that he related the Fall to the will and arrangement of God's sovereignty. The argument is derived by Calvin largely from the Nebuchadnezzar narrative in the biblical book of Daniel. All of the changes in Nebuchadnezzar's condition, Calvin argues, were the result of "Divine Providence" (IV.xx.26, 671). By contrast, Bullinger draws on God's sovereignty only to encourage faith that God is able and willing to *cure or cast down* tyrants *(Decades,* II.vi, 318). Included in Bullinger's argument that God is willing to cast down tyrants is the same Nebuchadnezzar narrative Calvin used to argue that God established tyrants! (II.vi, 317). Just as in the case of Pharaoh's "hardening," one sees how the two reformers interpret the same narrative to different ends and apply divine sovereignty to different practical conclusions. Where Calvin used the example of Nebuchadnezzar to cite God's sovereignty in establishing tyrants, Bullinger used it as an example of God's sovereignty in delivering His people from them.

Bullinger had two conflicting views of the magistrate. On the one hand, there was his fond desire to see the polity as a Christian community headed by a godly magistrate. On the other hand, how could Bullinger sidestep the fact that Roman Catholic magistrates (in France, Spain, or England, for example) threatened the Reformation? Bullinger never seems to quite resolve this problem. When consulted by John Knox in 1555 on the question of tyrannicide, Bullinger gave a mixed reply. Concerning Bloody Mary's succession to the throne, Bullinger would only tell Knox that these questions were particular to the laws of the realm and not abrogated by Scripture. Concerning Mary's proposed marriage to Phillip II of Spain (a Catholic monarch) and the potential transfer of power, Bullinger deferred to the laws and customs of the realm. But he does add, "If the reigning sovereign be not a Deborah, but an ungodly and tyrannous ruler of the kingdom, godly persons have an example and consolation in the case of Athaliah. The Lord will in his own time destroy unjust governments by his own people, to whom he will supply proper qualifications for this purpose, as he formerly did to Jerubbaal, and the Maccabees, and Jehoiada."[24] This all seems like pretty strong stuff, but the explicit conclusion was actually quite conservative. Bullinger would conclude that only "mandated idolatry" should be disobeyed whatever the case, citing biblical examples of armed resistance and tyrannicide only in that context. When pressed by Knox as to which side the faithful should take if "religious nobles" took action, Bullinger only repeated his warning and deferred the decision to those fully apprised of all relevant facts.

One should not conclude from this that Bullinger opposed resistance. He cautions against it but never forbids it. To those pondering tyrannicide, he cautions that they clearly discern their calling and not make things worse. His *Decades* makes reference to "noble captains and valiant men to displace tyrants" and makes no clear distinction between private persons and lesser magistrates (II. vi, 318). Another discussion in the *Decades* of those who love their country references those "valiantly fighting for [their country], if need be, to save it from violent robbers" (II.v, 276–77; II.vi, 318). Included in that list is Judas Maccabeus, whom the more radical Christopher Goodman later portrayed as a "worthy captain" against tyranny.[25] In his earlier writings *Ermanung* and *Lucretia and Brutus,* for example, Bullinger emphasized that those in authority were under the eternal justice of God. Bullinger praises the actions of the Swiss people that led to independence and sees God's providential hand in popular rebellion. Bullinger believed it would sometimes require a clear urging of the people to make civil magistrates act in accordance with God's justice. This may even extend to tyrannicide. In his *Anklag und ernstliches ermanen Gottes,* Bullinger cites Solomon's beheading of Joab as an example of what to do with unrepentant tyrants.[26] But if Bullinger supports resistance from lesser magistrates, why not say this more clearly to Knox? To modern ears, Bullinger's defense of resistance may sound hollow.[27] Resistance (or at least disobedience) is tied only to idolatry, and the relationship to conscience is not explicitly pursued beyond the usual passages of Scripture (Acts 5:29, for example).

Ironically, Calvin's response to Knox was even more tepid than Bullinger's.[28] But it is Calvin and not Bullinger who will assert the right of interposition by other magistrates as well as the exercise of conscience in disobeying civil authorities. In Calvin's early work, he was clearly more reticent on the subject. In his

1538 *Catechism,* for example, Calvin prescribes that the Christian "endure those who insolently abuse their power, until freed from their yoke by a lawful order."[29] But as his co-religionists faced increasing persecution in France, Calvin is less half-hearted.[30] In his final edition (1559) of his *Institutes,* Calvin strikes a balance between presumption and prudence. He warns against private action and defers to "popular magistrates . . . appointed to curb the tyranny of kings," calling popular magistrates the appointed guardians of liberty (IV.xx.31–32, 674–75).[31] So while Bullinger was bold enough to explicitly condemn tyranny as evil in any case, it is really Calvin who articulates the mechanism and justification for resistance against it. Thus, their political theologies became complementary on this important point. Bullinger provided the moral justification and Calvin provided the means.

Calvin's famous prescription to use magistrates rather than private persons is implicitly more covenantal because it works within the standing framework of authority and includes the consent of the people. By the early 1560s, Calvin is explicitly referencing the covenant as the basis of resistance. Preaching on I Samuel 8, Calvin argues, "Since kings and princes are bound by covenant to the people, to administer the law in truest equality, sincerity, and integrity; if they break faith and usurp tyrannical power . . . is it not possible for the people to consider together taking measures in order to remedy the evil?"[32]

A covenantal theory of resistance can also be discerned in Calvin's discussion of conscience. It is notable that these discussions are not in the chapter of Calvin's *Institutes* devoted to the civil magistrates (IV.xx). Calvin's first discussion of conscience is in the context of offending a brother in Christ (III.xix.15–16, 140–42). The second discussion is found in the middle of a critique of papal authority and councils (IV.x.3–6, 415–18). Calvin lays out a relationship between law and conscience arguably more seminal for politics than anything found elsewhere in his *Institutes.* In these two sections, hundreds of pages away from his chapter dedicated to civil government, Calvin concludes many things about the authority of the Roman Catholic hierarchy, the importance of a chaste mind, and not offending one's Christian brother. But what he also says about conscience goes beyond bishops and brethren.

Most important is Calvin's reference to a passage from Saint Paul's famous chapter on civil government, wherein Saint Paul requires obedience to the magistrate, "not only to avoid God's wrath, *but also for the sake of conscience*" (Romans 13:5, emphasis added). This verse, following on the heels of Saint Paul's admonition "Let every person be subject to the governing authorities," provides Calvin with a backdoor approach to reexamine whether resistance is allowed by Romans 13:1. Calvin begins each discussion of conscience with a dualistic anthropology, dividing the "spiritual" and the "civil" (III.xix.15, 140, 141) or the "external forum and the forum of conscience" (IV.x.3, 415). The dichotomous approach to human affairs here is striking. "When the one is considered, we should call off our minds, and not allow them to think of the other. For there exists in man a kind of two worlds, over which *different kings and different laws can preside*" (III.xix.15, 140–41, emphasis added). From this Calvin reaches a conclusion already drawn in his chapter on civil government: spiritual liberty does not lead to civil license. But this is only a qualified conclusion.

Citing other passages from Scripture, Calvin defines the conscience as that by which men know something of divine justice and have their sins revealed before God (III.xix.15, 141; IV.x.4, 416). The function of law therefore is to bind us to God alone. "Hence a law is said to bind the conscience, because it simply binds the individual, without looking at men, or taking any account of them" (III.xix.16, 142; an almost identical passage is found at IV.x.4, 416). Calvin twice entertains the possibility that Saint Paul is asserting (Romans 13:5) that all civil law should bind the conscience, but he rejects that conclusion because of what has already been said about "spiritual government" (III.xix.15, 140–41; IV.x.3, 415). It may be that Calvin here has posited a simple distinction between obligations to God and obligations to Caesar. He would then be repeating Saint Peter's oft-cited claim, "We must obey God rather than men" (Acts 5:29) or Christ's statement, "Render to Caesar the things that are Caesar's, and to God the things that are God's" (Matthew 22:21). But Calvin already includes Peter's admonition in his chapter devoted to civil government. In fact, Peter's claim is repeated as the second-to-last verse cited in the *Institutes* as part of Calvin's discussion of the civil magistrate. While the verse is no small detail, it is one already well-known. Calvin would not feel obliged to construct twice an explicit theory of the conscience in order to make a fairly straightforward point.

In revisiting Saint Paul's famous statement in Romans 13:1, Calvin wrote that we are bound by "the general command of God" as the *genus* of our obligation. Our obligation to the civil magistrate is but a *species* of this obligation. Therefore, it is not the civil laws that reach to our conscience but the command of God to obey the civil laws. Hence, civil obedience is *conditional on* divine obedience. (The species could not subvert the genus.) It will not suffice merely to rephrase this as obedience to God necessitating obedience to the civil magistrate. In fact, Calvin is quite explicit about this interpretation and rejects it. "[Saint Paul] does not at all teach that the laws enacted by them reach to the internal government of the soul, since he everywhere proclaims that the worship of God, and the spiritual rule of living righteously, are superior to all the decrees of men" (IV.x.5, 417).

Why should we not just presume that here Calvin is denying ecclesiastical authority to the magistrate? If Calvin were to leave things at "the worship of God," then we would return to the first conclusion: that Calvin is putting boundaries on the civil vis-à-vis the ecclesiastical. But we know that Calvin himself used civil authorities for ecclesiastical purposes, and he adds to "the worship of

God" the phrase "living righteously." In light of everything he has said about the conscience binding us to God alone in all conduct pertaining to law, the phrase "living righteously" opens up a reading of civil law beyond church-state relations. It brings back to mind the idea of covenant faithfulness. Calvin has opened the door for regulating obedience to the magistrate by one's obedience to God. He has enabled John Bradshaw to say at the trial and execution of Charles I, almost one hundred years later, "Resistance to Tyrants is Obedience to God." But even earlier than that, Calvin has provided justification for contemporaries John Knox or John Ponet to place final authority in the individual conscience.[33]

FORMULATIONS OF THE COVENANTED SOCIETY

Bullinger and Calvin were each constructing a political theology with the Hebrew polities in mind, and each theology included both vertical and horizontal responsibilities. Individuals had "horizontal" responsibilities to the community and vice versa. The magistrate had a "vertical" responsibility to God and to the community. Polities had corporate responsibility which was more than the aggregate of the individual responsibilities of their members. In all this, Calvin and Bullinger were generally agreed. Bullinger's consistent model is an implicitly covenantal one, asserting the binding of the community by baptism. Calvin began with an explicitly covenantal model in his attempt to bind Genevans to his 1538 Catechism.[34] When that failed, he withdrew to an approach that was more implicitly covenantal. What was not reconciled in their two models was the precise role of civil government and the status of the wheat and the tares. These were New Testament modifications on the Hebraic model and would be taken up more explicitly by the English Reformed Protestants in the late sixteenth and seventeenth centuries.

The explicit covenanting of Calvin is on display in his 1538 Geneva catechism. If Calvin had succeeded in gaining full subscription, he hoped that it would serve as a means toward ecclesiastical and civil unity. There was associated with the catechism a confession "published with solemn oath-taking by the whole people to be adjoined."[35] With the compliance of the Geneva Senate, Calvin literally wanted citizens of Geneva (on threat of losing their citizenship) to subscribe to the confession. This was not his invention, Calvin insisted, but something that was only part of their clerical offices as mediators of the covenant. Calvin cast full subscription as an act of testimony in the Lord for the sake of harmony and love. It was not enough that Genevans had been confirmed into the covenant once by right of baptism. Calvin compared those he considered apostate to be equivalent to deserters from military service. If the first oath (baptism) was violated, then that covenant was obviously not sufficient.[36]

When full subscription failed and Calvin returned from exile, he retreated to a more implicit covenantal approach, including a providential view of history. This covenantal approach is evident in his sermons on Deuteronomy 27 and 28, which he preached in 1555 and 1556.[37] Here Calvin took a more moderate view of applying the Old Testament covenant of national blessing and cursing, but it was still a literal view nevertheless. While God continues to reward both individuals and communities according to the biblical covenant model, New Testament believers are under a more "mature" system of rewards and punishments. Since Christians have the Word, two things follow. God's corporate judgment may be slower or less severe, and Christians are to rely on the revelation of the Bible more than providential blessings and curses.[38]

Bullinger's covenantal view of the civil polity is more consistently implicit and based on faithfulness to various oaths. Bullinger wrote to the Zurich magistrates, "Dear Confederates, remember now that in baptism you have bound yourselves to me with an oath stronger than the one with which you have bound one state to another among yourselves."[39] There is no record of any attempt by Bullinger to have explicit civil covenanting as was done previously by Calvin or later by the Presbyterian Scots. But Bullinger presumed persons to be part of God's covenant by baptism unless the individual later rejected the covenant by not keeping its conditions.[40] As Baker characterizes this, "Election was a matter of inclusion within the covenant, not of exclusion."[41] Bullinger's political theology is predicated on the magistrate's being a Christian. The pastor's role was to interpret the covenant and preach, rebuke, and exhort accordingly.[42] It was the magistrate's duty to restrain, punish, or establish religion. The magistrate was to aid in the condition of piety, not to force belief *(Decades* II.viii, 363–69). Faith was a gift of God alone. But this did not confine preaching to just Christians. All could benefit from hearing the Word.[43] Pastors were also to encourage the magistrate in his duties, though clergy held no power or sanction against a magistrate any more than against any other Christian. It was the magistrate's duty to assist the people in carrying out the basic functions of political life: public peace, property, business transactions, justice and equity.[44] One might argue that this kind of medieval corporatism resembles the later "City on a Hill" idea. And it is Bullinger's implicit covenantalism that may have found its way to Britain through his broad influence from Zurich.[45]

THE LEGACY OF THE COVENANTED REFORMATION: THE COVENANT AS POLITICS

Calvin and Bullinger's embrace of explicit or implicit covenanting served as a catalyst to a new movement within political theory. What was prescribed by

Reformed Protestants in the sixteenth century should not be cast as entirely original, of course, for they were steeped in humanist and legal training, and the influence of medieval and classical political theory can never be discounted.[46] But although the reformers were indeed steeped in the humanist legal tradition, they also looked to Scripture for political advice—to texts that predated Solon, Gaius, or Justinian I. Even when the reformers are not entirely original, they make an important contribution by articulating political theory in the language of the new theology. Hostility toward medieval scholarship (or at least recognizably Catholic authors and persons) made it necessary for political theories to be reformulated and made palpable to new audiences. This required the voice, rhetoric, and argumentation of Protestants. In the stream of the Western (and Anglo-American) legal conversation, "old" ideas became "new" when associated with Protestants and Reformation.[47] This enabled the passing of political theory to a Protestant posterity.

In its most passive and subtle form, covenantal political theory largely echoes the traditional "commonwealth" approach of Roman law. This means that the biblical covenant becomes a "new" symbol to justify standing ideas and institutions. And this is not surprising, given the humanistic training of the reformers. In this more passive form of covenantalism, the nation is also viewed as a common pursuit of *salus populi.* In the seventeenth century, for example, Samuel Rutherford explicitly centered civil government on the great principle of Cicero: *salus populi, suprema lex.*[48] This common good was pursued with two important biblical caveats. First, all government is derived from God's supreme authority. Magistrates are accountable to the limits of authority interpreted from Scripture. Second, the will of the people, though not necessarily represented by direct elections, is a means by which the authority of God is legitimately transferred to civil magistrates. Again, although neither of these ideas is new within political thought, the argument from Scripture is part of the Protestant re-formation of politics. These two ideas also demonstrate the two dimensions of the covenant relationship: vertical and horizontal. Commonwealth thinking by Reformed Protestants was largely a passive adoption of the covenant as a political model.

At the other end of the spectrum from commonwealth thinking and passive covenantalism is active or aggressive covenantalism, which displays a more explicit scriptural argumentation. Aggressive covenantalism does not reject the essential goals of passive covenantalism: *salus populi.* It agrees with the need for appropriate civil order, but it makes resistance and limits on civil authority a religious duty rather than a right. For example, Quentin Skinner characterizes Christopher Goodman, John Ponet, and John Knox as arguing that those who fail to resist tyrants would be damned.[49] And while all covenantal political theologians argued, for example, that the magistrate has some responsibility for the maintenance of true religion, the more aggressive form of covenantalism emphasizes this as a means of obtaining divine corporate blessing or avoiding covenantal sanction.

With the additional force and warrant of the covenant, tyranny is cast not simply as the abuse of reason or freedom, it becomes the violation of both divine delegation and popular trust. This opens the door for an aggressive doctrine of resistance or revolution. Inheritors of this tradition over two centuries could assert, "Resistance to tyrants is obedience to God."[50] This included John Bradshaw, prosecutor of Charles I, and Benjamin Franklin and Thomas Jefferson, who wanted the phrase as the motto of the United States. This assertion is a far more powerful claim than "Resistance to tyrants is the assertion of our natural rights" or "Resistance to tyrants is the restoration of *nomos*," where nature or *nomos* simply means some superintending impersonal mechanism. The notion of an argument only from nature does not create the same kind of moral imperative as one that is tied to personal revelation and divine judgment. This existential approach makes the covenanted commonwealth approach much more wary of the abuse of power and of conscience and more prepared to act in the face of tyranny. It makes covenantal political theory a political theology par excellence.

Bullinger and Calvin were both prepared to apply the covenant to politics, to assert the idea of corporate responsibility, but it was their contemporaries elsewhere who put it into radical practice. John Knox first explicitly and radically applied the covenant to politics, though reluctantly at first.[51] Knox was selective in his application of the civil covenant, predicated largely on religious circumstances. His first assertion that a covenant had been violated was during the accession of Mary Tudor. In 1554 he argued that to participate in the Mass was to violate "the league and covenant of God" that forbade idolatry.[52] This was consistent with both the Protestant critique of Roman Catholic ritual and its condemnation of the doctrine of transubstantiation. The covenant Knox was referring to was technically not a civil covenant. Knox was referring to the covenant between God and His elect, but an important precedent was set by casting civil disobedience as necessary to avoid damnation. By 1558, in *The Appellation to the Nobility and Estates,* Knox is prepared to articulate a doctrine of resistance that hinges on a more robust theory of covenanting. Knox seems most clearly to have used the *Appellation* as a call to the inferior or lesser magistrates of England to rebel against the monarchy. At no point did Knox call on the Scottish nobility to rebel. Whereas England was a covenanted nation, having officially subscribed to Protestantism, Scotland was not.[53] After Scotland subscribed to Protestantism, however, Knox issued the same covenantal warning and admonition. In a sermon to the General Assembly in 1564, Knox applied the same arguments to the Scottish nobility.[54]

The most famous and robust development of a civil covenant was developed by Philippe Du Plessis Mornay in the *Vindiciae, Contra Tyrannos* (1579), which was published in the wake of three other French covenantal political theologies: Theodore Beza's *De jure magistratuum* (1575), an anonymously published *Le Reveille-matin des François* (1573-1574), and Francis Hotman's *Franco Gallia* (1575).[55] According to Mornay, there are two covenants of political significance. These covenants established the root of the monarch's power as coming from both God and the people. The first covenant is between God, the king, and the people; the second is between the king and the people. The first enables the people to act should the king turn away from God. The second obliges the king to act in the interests of the common good.[56]

Covenantal political theory, though hardly democratic in any modern sense, was certainly more egalitarian than previous political theory in spirit and its distrust of monarchy. It was also more desirous of consent.[57] In his *Lex, Rex,* Scottish Presbyterian Samuel Rutherford wrote, "The power of creating a man a king is from the people."[58] He urges the "election" of the king by the people.[59] Goodman, tying election to the obligations of covenant, states, "If we will be the people of God, let us then search and diligently follow the Laws of God, especially in so weighty matters, as the election of princes and kings."[60]

What most of the reformers meant by "consent" was not the same as we would view it today. Consent was obtained through narrow suffrage and largely by local magistrates and nobility.[61] Extremely limited suffrage and indirect representation was a reflection of the time. But for the reformers, working through the estates or other lower civil offices was not merely a device to limit suffrage or "mob rule." The creation of these offices mirrored the federalism of covenant theology. Smaller units could enjoy both community and independence and play a prominent role in checking tyranny (a concept understood by the reformers in terms more modern than classical). Smaller and dispersed units of sovereignty also reflected the Protestant imperative for dialogue and self-examination.[62] Such institutional and rhetorical bulwarks were an important contribution of covenant theology.

The notion of a civil covenant enabled the more radical reformers to put civil magistrates on notice regarding their abuse of power or lack of rightful protection. The author of *Vindiciae, Contra Tyrannos* states, "To what purpose should the magistrates bear the sword, if it be not to serve God, who has committed it to them, to defend the good and punish the bad? Can they do better service than to preserve the church from the violence of the wicked, and to deliver the flock of Christ from the swords of murderers?"[63] Marian exile Christopher Goodman, a colleague of both Calvin and Knox, commended the rule of Edward VI and noted the comfortable enjoyment of both religion and property under Edward's reign.[64] Knox likewise urged a "two table" duty on the civil magistrate.[65] In regard to the first table, the nobility had a duty to safeguard the people from corrupt bishops. Knox wrote to the nobility, "For if your bishops be proved to be no bishops but deceivable thieves and ravening wolves . . . then shall your permission and defense of them be reputed before God a participation with their theft and murder."[66] Two-table prescriptions were all rooted in various manifestations of covenantal theorizing. In the case of heresy, there were concerns about collective responsibility before God, a seminal covenant idea. Consistent with federal theology (developed later in the sixteenth century), it also was thought that unbelievers could benefit from hearing the Bible and thereby learn more of their responsibilities under the covenant of works.

Though Calvin and Bullinger were reluctant to prescribe resistance against tyrants in the case of Mary Tudor, Bullinger's condemnation of tyranny and Calvin's doctrine of interposition were not lost on their colleagues. Marian exile John Ponet advocated resistance against Mary Tudor. The Scot George Buchanan justified the deposition of Mary Queen of Scots. Hotman, like his Huguenot co-religionist Mornay, believed that the crown was rooted in the consent of the estates and could be deprived of its power by the estates. Knox believed an ungodly ruler to be a judgment from God, but he also urged resistance.[67] Repentance was not the last remedy. Knox scolds the realms and estates for their election of Mary and urges them to refuse submission to her commands. He adds, "She is a traitress and rebel against God. . . . They must study to repress her inordinate pride and tyranny to the uttermost of their power."[68] Should the nobility or lesser magistrates fail in their duty, they would suffer under the wrath of God.[69]

Christopher Goodman clearly advocated tyrannicide under a covenantal model. Like his co-religionists, Goodman did believe that citizens under tyranny should look first to their own sin. But if tyranny was a corporate sanction, the only way out of it might be to depose an idolatrous ruler. In a textbook case of active covenantalism and popular revolution, Goodman wrote to the people:

> And therefore your study in this case, ought to be, to seek how you may dispose and punish according to the Laws, such rebels against God, and oppressors of yourself and your country: and not how to please them, obey them, and flatter them as you do in their impiety. Which is not the way to obtain peace, and quietness, but to fall into the hand of the Almighty God, and to be subject to His fearful plagues and punishments.[70]

Using an argument not unique to Reformed Protestantism but revisited by its political theology, Goodman asserts that any magistrate who abandons his God-given duties forsakes legitimacy altogether. Such magistrates cease to be "public persons" with authority.[71] God alone was the primary chief and master of all human authority, and he set the limits of masters under his charge.[72] Goodman's essay ties calls for revolution against false religion to true piety.[73] Covenant faithfulness is the cornerstone of his resistance theory, indicting Mary as an idolatrous ruler. To profess a false religion was equal to being a tyrant. Both were forms of rebellion against God. Disobedience to such rulers was not only permissible, it was commanded. Goodman repeated throughout his work that Christians were in rebellion to God if they obeyed a wicked ruler. Referring to the stoning of false prophets by the people of Israel, Goodman emphasizes that the people were not led by a civil magistrate.[74] But it is the laxness of the "common and simple people" that often leads to their own destruction.[75] To make his point, Goodman promotes the example of Mattathias, a character from the Apocrypha.[76] Mattathias not only refused to sacrifice to the Greek gods but took up his sword against those who did—including a government official. He thereby initiated the War of the Maccabees and Jewish independence.

For the French reformers dear to Calvin's heart, the question of legitimacy was explicitly tied to the covenant. The king who breaks his trust with the people and the law, the heart of the second covenant, becomes a tyrant. Mornay also added a whole litany of acts that defined a tyrant.[77] This list included ignoring counsel, abusing taxation to fund extravagance, and the lawless persecution of subjects. Mornay not only gave permission for resistance but considered it a duty. Resisting a tyrant was to be done by those who were officers or lower magistrates, however. The three-party covenant in the *Vindiciae* not only described the legal structure of accountability but also created obligations punishable by covenantal sanction. If a tyrant was allowed to rule, the wrath of God would be poured out not only upon the evil ruler but also upon his surety, the people. If the lower magistrates failed in their duty, the common people had no choice but to leave.[78]

Though Reformed Protestants were not advocating the kind of freedom that is familiar to modern democratic liberalism, it would be hard to find a more emphatic defense of liberty in the sixteenth century. Though all the offending Marys who inspired the Anglo-Scottish polemics eventually lost power, the idea of dissent lingered in Britain. The ideas of conscience and disobedience under covenantal political theology would soon split the English church and change the face of politics in England and Scotland. Contemporary with the split of the English church and the British political implosion, American Reformed Protestants would attempt to establish an even purer covenant on the shores of the New World. The Anglo-American and Scottish experiments with covenantal political theology in the seventeenth century would eventually prove that the complications of political covenanting were perhaps impossible to resolve.

6 The Legacies of Geneva and Zurich in England and Scotland

The Anglo-American trajectory of Reformed political theology begins in Zurich and Geneva in the sixteenth century. These legacies then combined with new elements of English and Reformed Protestantism in the late sixteenth and early seventeenth centuries. Reformed political theology developed further during both the crucible of war in Britain during the mid–sixteenth century and the Reformed Protestant migration to the New World at roughly the same time. The threads that run from Geneva and Zurich to America concern the same theological questions that were raised by the first generation of reformers. Who is in the covenant? What is the jurisdiction of the church vis-á-vis the state? What is necessary to keep covenant faithfulness in either, if not both together? What should be done with a civil authority who violates the terms of the covenant?

THE INFLUENCE OF CALVIN AND BULLINGER ON EARLY REFORMATIONS IN ENGLAND AND SCOTLAND

Although the English Reformation was accelerated by Henry VIII's break with Rome, many English churchmen were already sincerely interested in the new theology and motivated beyond Henry's political expediency. Thomas Cranmer, Henry's archbishop, was an early English reader of Luther, though Henry himself was not. Both Cranmer and Henry were also admirers of Phillip Melanchthon. But the influence of Luther and Melanchthon did not hold. Archbishop Cranmer was corresponding with Bullinger and others in the Reformed tradition as early as 1536. He had the highest regard for Bullinger's work and approved its publication in England. Henry VIII, after his break with Rome, also approved of Bullinger's work.[1] Cranmer invited Jan Laski, Martin Bucer, and Peter Martyr

Vermigli to take prestigious posts in England. All three had done impressive work in helping to establish the particulars of Reformed theology. Bucer and Peter Martyr would have a special legacy in Cranmer's view of communion and liturgy, respectively.

Archbishop Cranmer is representative of the complexity of the English Reformation. He was author of the Forty-Two Articles in 1552, predecessor to the Thirty-Nine Articles (1563). Both are in agreement with the reformers on major points of theology. Cranmer tried unsuccessfully in 1552 to organize an ecumenical council with Calvin, Bullinger, and Melanchthon. His great legacy, the *Book of Common Prayer,* official liturgy of the English church, reflects his work with key Reformed theologians, primarily Peter Martyr and Martin Bucer.[2] But Cranmer is not necessarily remembered as someone in the tradition of the reformers, let alone Reformed theology. Later in the sixteenth century, the *Book of Common Prayer* was deemed by Puritans to be a tool of Rome. Its reputation among English Protestants and Scottish Presbyterians was further poisoned by Laudian excesses in the seventeenth century. It is ironic that Cranmer's legacy is not better known among Reformed Protestants, given the fact that he died under Bloody Mary as an opponent of the Mass.

Both Calvin and Bullinger were widely read by English clergy. The first English edition of Calvin's *Institutes* was translated by Cranmer's son-in-law, Thomas Norton, in 1561. The sermons in Bullinger's *Decades* began to appear in the 1540s, with the final work published between 1549 and 1551, eight years before Calvin's magnum opus. English clergy were using the *Decades* in its Latin edition by 1552, in its German edition by 1566, and in English translation by 1577.[3] Bishop Cooper was ordering clergy to read the *Decades* in 1573, before the complete English-language edition was published.[4] In 1577 Bishop Cooper required clergy to buy it in English or Latin and read one sermon each week and be able to give an accounting of it.[5] In 1586, Archbishop Whitgift and the Convocation required ministers in training to read the *Decades* along with their Bibles.[6]

The English reformers had extensive contact with prominent continental reformers at home, in correspondence, and especially during the Marian exile. Laski, Vermigli, and Bucer took up residence in England and worked with members of the English church during the reign of Edward and Elizabeth Tudor. The Swiss reformers had regular correspondence with many prominent persons in the English church throughout the sixteenth century. Of the thousand or so Marian exiles, about one-quarter made their way to Geneva and established an English church.[7] Other exiles went to other Reformation centers, including Zurich and Frankfort. Mary Tudor's intention was to end the Protestant advance in Britain, but her persecution ended up in fact advancing its most radical elements. The most disruptive controversies of the British Reformation took shape during the Marian exile.

The English exodus to the continent raised Geneva's international prominence and the influence of its political theology. The more catholic elements of the English Reformation would have been much less troublesome if Bullinger (or Martin Bucer or Peter Martyr) had been the leading influence in Britain after Mary's death. Calvin was, after all, an unlikely "English" reformer. His intended legacy was the French Reformation. He corresponded sparingly with Edward VI and his tone indicates a more distant relationship.[8] Elizabeth had no fondness for either Calvin or Geneva.[9] She was suspicious of the Marian exiles who returned from Geneva, particularly Goodman and Knox. Calvin made some effort to repair the damage, even dedicating his commentary on Isaiah to her, but Elizabeth refused the dedication, and neither Calvin nor Beza was able to mend the relationship.[10]

By contrast, Bullinger was long held in high esteem by the English ecclesiastical establishment and intentionally took the role of prophet in the English Reformation.[11] Bullinger was actively working to influence the English Reformation from the beginning, dedicating earlier works to Henry VIII and dedicating portions of his *Decades* to Edward VI. Bullinger's influence could be found among both advocates of conformity (such as Whitgift) and dissenters (such as Hooper and Grindal). Bishop John Hooper was reading Bullinger's commentaries in England in the 1530s and was won over to Reformed theology through them. Bishop Hooper and Bishop John Ponet, author of the influential *A Shorte Treatise of Politike Power* (a defense of rebellion against Mary Tudor), were both correspondents and guests of Bullinger.[12] Hooper was particularly close to him and made him godfather of his daughter.[13] Edmund Grindal (later an archbishop under Elizabeth) credited Bullinger's *De Origine Erroris* with his conversion to the Reformed view of the eucharist.[14] Bullinger's influence continued under Elizabeth I. When Elizabeth came to power, she thanked Bullinger and the Zurich church for their friendship and sent a silver cup as token.[15] When Elizabeth was formally excommunicated by Pius V in 1570, Bullinger rushed to her defense by condemning papal overreach in his *Refutatio Bullae papisticae contra Angliae Reginam Elizabetham.*[16]

Prior to the Marian exile, it was most likely that Bullinger would be the English Reformation's leading light, but Marian exiles who fled to Geneva would later raise Calvin's profile while Bullinger's outspoken defense of conformity cast doubt on Bullinger's legacy in England. One can imagine an alternate history in which Calvin was little more than just another theologian for English clergy to draw from and Bullinger's allies were the vanguard. Instead, English exiles from Geneva helped become de facto leadership for dissenting positions that would eventually tear England apart. Was this what Calvin intended? Geneva's divisive legacy in England cannot be attributed directly to any intent on Calvin's part. Bishop John Hooper, who first protested over prescribed vestments under

Edward VI, was Bullinger's close friend and not Calvin's. (Bullinger urged him to conform, however.)[17] Calvin's discussion of worship in the *Institutes* (IV.x) was cited by both sides in polemics written during Elizabethan Settlement controversies.[18] Calvin also became the face of the English church's soteriology.[19] Furthermore, Calvin discouraged the early protestations of the Elizabethan Settlement.

But Calvin's successor, Beza, certainly became a patron of the Presbyterian controversies that would begin in 1572, led by Thomas Cartwright, and it was tools and ideas gained in the previous exile in Geneva under Mary that solidified Calvin's legacy as the prime mover of English dissenters. Not content with the previous English translation commissioned by Henry VIII (the Great Bible), British exiles in Geneva crafted the Geneva Bible (also called the Breeches Bible) from 1557 to 1560. Its notes were crafted by many English reformers and reflected covenantal resistance theory. Its seditious content prompted Elizabeth I to commission the Bishop's Bible, and James I to commission the "King James Bible" as replacements for the Geneva Bible.[20] The British refugees in Geneva learned to question the episcopal system and to embrace the equality of clergy. Whereas Calvin taught that there were four offices of relative equality and each with separate duties (doctor, pastor, elder, deacon), the English church prescribed a hierarchy of bishops, priests, and deacons. Another legacy of Geneva was the Psalter and exclusive psalm singing, which were both iconoclastic and egalitarian, and defied English practice in the sixteenth century.[21]

Genevan exiles drew from Calvin's theology on two additional points. They agreed with Calvin on the prerogatives of elders (rather than magistrates) for prescription and discipline. They also adopted Geneva's version of covenantal soteriology, advanced by Beza beyond what Calvin defended. This soteriology made the English dissenters from Geneva more offensive to moderate predestinarians and also to the rising anti-Calvinist faction of the English church. These arguments on church discipline and soteriology, when combined, clashed with the default English theology of coterminous membership in church and the Commonwealth.

Finally, there was the matter of ritual. Though Calvin scolded the Frankfort rabble-rousing of Knox and Goodman against Bishop Cox during the Marian exile, both Knox and Goodman enjoyed sanctuary in Geneva after losing control of the church to Cox. While in Geneva together, Goodman and Knox authored an alternative to the *Book of Common Prayer,* which they called the *Book of Common Order,* and they pastored an English church. Goodman worked on the Geneva Bible, though Knox's involvement was probably minimal.[22] All this took place in Geneva on Calvin's watch. One can see how it would be the legacy of Geneva rather than Zurich that would define the dissenting movements (Puritanism and Presbyterianism) in the English church.

AFTER ELIZABETH: THE DIVIDED LEGACIES OF GENEVA AND ZURICH AFTER 1559

English Protestants welcomed the passing of Mary and the new reign of Elizabeth I. They were not only revived by their time spent abroad but also inspired by Marian martyrs such as Hooper and Cranmer. Many hoped to proceed beyond even the aggressive reformation begun by Edward VI and ended by Bloody Mary. Using covenantal language, Peter Martyr identified England as an "elect nation" under the "anointed kingship" of Elizabeth.[23] Elizabeth was certainly not Roman Catholic, but she was hardly prepared to embrace *semper reformandum.* John Knox described Elizabeth as "neither good Protestant nor yet resolute Papist."[24] Elizabeth, for her part, already knew more than she cared to about Knox's opinions from his *First Blast of the Trumpet against the Monstrous Regiment of Women* (1558), written against Elizabeth's second cousin (Mary I of Scotland) and half sister (Mary I of England). Knox's polemic was no doubt read by Elizabeth as both misogynistic and rebellious to the point of advocating tyrannicide. Elizabeth was certainly aware of the radical ideas returning with some of the exiles from Geneva (notably Thomas Sampson, Anthony Gilby, Thomas Lever, Lawrence Humphrey, and Willliam Whittingham) and worked to marginalize their influence in the English church.[25] She was also sensitive to the diverse constituencies within the English church (including conservatives such as Cox). Beza knew that Geneva's stature was diminished in Elizabeth's eyes because of the reputation of exiles such as Knox. In a letter to Bullinger in 1566, Beza lamented the rhetorical excesses of Knox and Goodman and appealed for Zurich's assistance in reconciliation with Elizabeth and the bishops.[26]

Elizabeth's plan for avoiding controversy was prudent. Her bishops would prescribe in things mainly affecting ritual and ceremony and she would exclude Genevan exiles from high office in the new church. This, she hoped, allowed the substantive matters of the Reformation to move forward while retaining some of the status quo on *adiaphora* (things indifferent, such as vestments or minor elements of ritual and ceremony). But for many English reformers, ritual and ceremony were in fact among the substantive matters and *not* things indifferent. Repeatedly the English proved themselves worthy of a remark Bullinger made to Beza in a letter dated March 1567: "England has many characters of this sort, who cannot be at rest, who can never be satisfied, and who have always something or other to complain about."[27] In 1566, even Beza admitted to Bullinger, "Some of them [the English exiles], I admit, are rather hard to please, but in so much affliction it is difficult to keep within bounds."[28] Much of the English rhetoric had to do with covenantal political theology, arguing that reformation of the church was their responsibility before God. The continental reformers counseled prudence to the English, but to little avail. The Pandora's Box of the covenantal ethos had been opened. The English dissenters were compelled by that ethos to reform the English church in all matters pertaining to worship and governance.

The first English controversy under Elizabeth Tudor was a replay of earlier disagreements regarding ritual, vestments, and worship. This was a protest that began under Edward VI and heated up even during the Marian exile. Bishop John Hooper, Bullinger's close friend, was first persecuted under Edward VI for his refusal to wear vestments. Among the British exiles in Frankfort in 1554 there was subsequent controversy regarding vestments. Other controversies arose among Marian exiles in Basle, Emden, and Wesel.[29] Problems *did not* break out among exiles in Strassburg and Zurich, where the exiles adhered to Cranmer's 1552 prayer book, a fact that further emphasizes the different legacies of Geneva and Zurich.[30] Now back in England and under Elizabeth's reign, certain ministers and bishops were chafing at the garments and rituals prescribed by Archbishop Parker's *Advertisements* and the Settlement of 1559—Elizabeth's attempts to satisfy her diverse church constituencies.[31] Bishops Grindal and Horne described the situation in a letter to Bullinger and Gualter in 1567: the dissenters refused to adopt the "distinction of habits now prescribed by public authority," as "impious, papistical, and idolatrous." Grindal and Horne disagreed with the dissenters, arguing that these vestments were simply a question of "things indifferent."[32] The other bishops were divided on this question, though most were not given over to the more radical and separating factions. The answer of the Swiss divines was the same now as it had been to Bishop Hooper during the Edwardian reformation: conform outwardly but preach as conscience requires.

Bullinger himself wore no robe or vestments; but he never quarreled over the matter, and he urged the English dissenters to conform. Calvin, who wore the plain black "Geneva robe" (later the choice of Presbyterians) also encouraged conformity.[33] A book was published by order of Elizabeth's commissioners containing the earlier judgment of Vermigli and Bucer that wearing the habits was not sinful. Dissenting books protesting the Settlement were prohibited and their printers arrested. A handful of ministers was briefly imprisoned and threatened with further punishment by the queen and the privy council.[34] More ministers were suspended or deprived of their current offices. Opponents of the prescribed vestments threatened to leave the ministry rather than "serve the church with these rags of popery."[35] Open and sometimes violent protests began in 1566.

Bullinger's public and systematic response to inquiries on the matter from England, his *Epistle ad Episcopos et fraters in Anglia,* was included in some English editions of his *Decades.*[36] Many of the central political theologies of the Reformation are on display in Bullinger's letter. He argues that Christian liberty is not violated by the vestments.[37] Not only was the idea of a clerical habit not necessarily "papist," it was introduced for "civil regulation and good order."[38] On the matter of conscience, Bullinger argued that the greater offense to conscience was abandoning the pulpit and leaving the church flock to the care of "wolves, or at least teachers who are far from competent."[39] Perhaps most important, Bullinger takes sides on the long-running question of civil authority in ecclesiastical matters. In responding to the question as to whether the clergy must consent to the wearing of vestments in this case, Bullinger answers:

> I answer, if the consent of the clergy is always to be waited for by the sovereign, it is probable that those most wise and pious kings, Asa, Hezekiah, Jehoshaphat, and Josiah, and other godly princes, would never have brought into proper order the Levites and ministers of the churches. Though I would not altogether have the bishops excluded from the consultations of churchmen. But on the other hand, I would not have them assume to themselves that power, which they heretofore usurped over kings and magistrates in the time of popery. Nor again, would I have the bishops sanction by their silence the unjust ordinances of princes.[40]

Bullinger's irenic and prudent style is on display, as is the importance of the Reformation's Hebraic and covenantal Christianity. The Vestiarian controversy was a classic episode of political theology, wherein theological struggles would test the "secular" constitutional framework, raise questions about liberty and order, and redefine the church-state relationship.

This episode of protest was not the event that gave serious impetus to the Puritan movement. It was relatively small and confined mostly to radicals with little future in English Puritanism. Many of those who would later become Puritans (such as Grindal) could not at this time join with the dissenters or "Precisians" in their zeal to condemn the vestments or leave their churches. But the controversy was important as the first salvo in a longer debate over royal supremacy. The fact that Bullinger came out so clearly against the dissenters marked him and his English confederates as conformists or royal supremacists at a time when the intentionally reforming element within the English church was moving in the opposite direction.

Though only a relatively small number of clergy were substantially affected by the Vestiarian controversy led by the Prescians or early Puritans, it revealed real division within the Church of England. In a move that would foreshadow the English Civil War, growing opposition forces took their case to Parliament.[41] This led to the *Admonition* controversy and the budding of the Puritan movement. Written by John Wilcox and John Field in 1572, the *Admonition* was an appeal to Parliament for relief from what the growing dissenting movement considered lingering elements of Roman Catholicism in the Elizabethan church. Appealing to Parliament was in keeping with the Calvinist prescription of interposition. It also was consistent with the standing belief that the civil magistrate should be a partner of the church in the greater covenant of civil society. The English Presbyterians, a movement against the English church's current episcopacy and also inspired by Geneva, especially Beza, continued to draw on Old Testament law in their attempt to purify the New Testament church.[42] Walter Travers, a colleague of Presbyterian Thomas Cartwright, asserted along with Calvin that Christ was the new Moses who would prescribe precise worship for the church (*Institutes* IV.x.17, 426). Dissenters tied ecclesiological orthodoxy to faithfulness in the covenant of salvation.[43]

The respective English legacies of Geneva and Zurich continued to grow apart. Regarding the English Presbyterians, Bullinger's son-in-law and colleague Rudolph Gualter wrote to Bishop Cox in March 1574, "I wish they would think about reviving that simplicity of faith and purity of morals, which formerly flourished, and not attack the commonwealth. . . . Saul did not do his duty; but Samuel did not therefore appoint a new senate, nay, nor even David . . . would not make any alteration in the commonwealth."[44] Bullinger hated the division and longed for unity. He strongly criticized both the denial of ecclesiastical authority to the civil magistrate and the demand by some English Puritans for the exclusive institution of presbyteries.[45] Bullinger wrote to Bishop Edwin Sandys, "I wish there were no lust of dominion in the originators of this [English] presbytery."[46] Sandys revealed the weight of the conformity in his reply of August 1574. He accepted Bullinger's counsel but then added, "I hope that this new fabric of new discipline [under the Elizabethan settlement] will shortly fall in pieces by its own weight, since it appears that many of our countrymen who formerly admired it, are now grown weary of it."[47]

On one side of the *Admonition* controversy were defenders of royal supremacy. Most notable among these was John Whitgift, later Archbishop of Caterbury, who defended conformity from the political writings of Vermigli, Bullinger, and Gualter.[48] On the other side was Cartwright and other members of the burgeoning Puritan and Presbyterian movement. Cartwright defended clerical parity as early as 1570 and was subsequently welcomed in Geneva by Beza, who was himself increasingly critical of the English church polity.[49] In a letter to Bullinger in 1566, Beza lamented that the English were "hard to please." He also wrote, "You will learn that the papacy was never abolished in that country, but rather transferred to the sovereign; . . . I once thought the matter was only about caps and I know not what other externals, but I afterwards understood that the controversy was of a far different character."[50] Embryonic English presbyteries began to form in the 1570s and 1580s in opposition to episcopacy. Even those such as Bishop Grindal who were on the conforming side found themselves increasingly put upon by Whitgift and others stressing conformity in the 1570s. Grindal's defense of Puritan "prophesying" eventually cost him his position in 1577.

DEFINING AND REJECTING *CORPUS CHRISTIANUM*

Throughout these controversies, Bullinger's influence continued but was confined increasingly to the conformist side.[51] A substantial blow was dealt to Bullinger's legacy among the Puritan dissenters when a 1573 letter from him to Bishop Horn, which was interpreted to compare dissenters to Anabaptists, was published in both Latin and English by Archbishop Whitgift in the hope of advancing conformism.[52] Meanwhile, Geneva's influence rose as dissenters in their defense took to printing Beza's attacks on the English church. But while Bullinger was less important in the growing English Puritan movement, his use by English conformists shows the continued influence Reformed theology had in the Church of England even as the Puritan faction was withdrawing. For conformists in the English church, Bullinger remained the leading continental influence. Bishop John Jewel, who saw nothing amiss in the Elizabethan reforms, called Bullinger "the only light of our age," the "oracle of the churches," and said that Bullinger's influence put religion "on the same footing on which it stood in King Edward's time."[53] That was high praise, given that King Edward's aggressive reforms made him a "Josiah" in the minds of many Reformed Protestants.

Ironically, both conformists and dissenters in the 1570s were still more or less arguing for variations of church-state cooperation and the idea of *corpus christianum.* None were arguing for a clear church-state separation. Cartwright largely wanted state Presbyterianism with no tolerance for nonconformity.[54] He asserted a God-given partnership between the civil magistrate (for temporal well-being) and the church (for spiritual well-being). He argued that neither institution could exist without the other.[55] Both realms were to see to the souls of the people. The civil magistrate did this by securing wealth and quietness on earth; the church concerned itself with eternal life and maintained piety through church discipline.[56] Whitgift wanted something closer to Erastianism with royal supremacy and full state control of church discipline, arguing that the existence of a godly prince was a great blessing to the church and necessitated agreement between the church and state regimes.[57] Partisans in the *Admonition* controversy were therefore repeating the debate over excommunication and the right of church discipline along lines drawn earlier in other corners of the Protestant Reformation, notably Switzerland.[58] The debate would even be carried into the Westminster Assembly in 1644.[59] In short, the controversy was still not settled seventy years later.

The English debate between conformists such as Whitgift and dissenters (mostly Presbyterians) such as Cartwright in the 1570s was also a repeat of the wheat and tares debate that had already begun in continental circles in prior decades. It was not, as one might suspect, a debate between "Anglicans" and "Calvinists" as if an Anglican tradition had fully taken shape by this point. It was an internecine debate between predestinarians in the covenant tradition. Whitgift, a conformist in the Episcopal (bishop-led) tradition, cited double predestination as readily as his dissenting and Presbyterian opponents (who were opposed to bishop leadership). Like his Reformed predecessors, Whitgift used the common Reformed Protestant insult against his Presbyterian opponents, comparing them to Anabaptists. Conformists and dissenters in the late sixteenth century disagreed not on soteriology but on ecclesiology and the church-state relationship. Whereas Cartwright wanted an active and independent use of excommunication power by clergy as a means of upholding faithfulness in the corporate entities of church and state, Whitgift opposed that power, fearing that independent and active excommunication would split church and state.[60] Cartwright also wanted Presbyterian church government and equality among the clergy for the same reason that Whitgift wanted hierarchy and bishops. Both believed that their form of church polity was best for maintaining the Gospel piety necessary for covenant faithfulness among both individuals and the nation as a whole. Where they differed was in how they interpreted vertical (man to God) and horizontal (man to man) covenantal relationships. A covenant question was therefore central to both sides of the debate.[61] Which model would best preserve the idea of corporate responsibility before God?

But while Cartwright and Whitgift were both still willing to have quite a few tares among the wheat, their respective visions of the covenanted body would be rejected by Robert Browne and the Separatist movement in 1582.[62] Whitgift had agreed with Bullinger that one purged the church only of the most undesirable elements and maintained a close church-state partnership. Cartwright agreed with Calvin that one should probably purge more undesirable elements and should have the independent authority to do that (*Institutes,* IV.i.15, 293–94). The church purged itself of faithless undesirables. One did not purge oneself of the church as if it was faithless and undesirable. But purging oneself of the unfaithful and undesirable national church was precisely the goal of Browne's Separatists. The Separatist congregations purged themselves of the English church itself by setting up autonomous, independent churches that would be locally and democratically governed. These congregations took the dissenting logic of covenantal faithfulness one step further. Under the banner of the Protestant ethos "always reforming," Puritan Separatists insisted that a truly covenanted church had to be "gathered" and covenanted away from the national church and the civil magistrate. They insisted on the parity of ministers beyond what Presbyterians asserted under Geneva's influence.[63] This movement was so threatening to the covenantal status quo in England that some Separatists were banished, exiled, or hanged. But the movement continued in spite of persecution, and gave rise to Independency, Congregationalism, and a new interpretation of covenant faithfulness.[64] This new vision of church polity was yet another step in the progression of the covenantal ethos.

RECOVERING THE CIVIL COVENANT WITH TWO INNOVATIONS: FEDERAL THEOLOGY AND THE RECOVERY OF CONSCIENCE

The rise of English Congregational/Independent church polity in the last two decades of the sixteenth century was the greatest threat yet to the idea of a national church as one support of the corporate or national covenant. Even if one presumes the Church of England could discard both episcopacy and presbyteries and be constituted by self-governing churches, who would then constitute those self-governing churches? Would citizenship and church membership or baptism remain more or less coterminous? Though the Presbyterian vision would certainly have meant a stricter church discipline, more autonomous from civil authority, both Cartwright and Whitgift were contesting the control of something that would remain largely a collection of wheat and tares. Both visions were compatible with a national church and the standing vision of a corporate covenant. But insofar as Congregationalists or Independents wanted to constitute the church "correctly" in the first place and covenant amongst themselves congregation by congregation, they threatened not only the national church but also the national covenant first sought by Calvin and Bullinger and hearkening back to the national covenants of the Israelites.

There were two innovations in Reformed theology that saved the civil-ecclesiastical partnership from impending ruin in the late sixteenth century. The first innovation articulated a covenant of works that extended to all persons. The second explored the idea of partial spiritual illumination suggested by Scripture (Matthew 13) and integral to predestinarian theology. Both innovations took root among the Puritans and cannot be said to have descended from Geneva or Zurich. By 1590 these two new aspects of covenant theology were becoming commonplace in Reformed theology. They did not first appear within American Puritanism, as Perry Miller's work seems to imply; nor were they psychological reactions to implicit fatalism within early predestinarian theology.[65]

The first innovation that preserved the covenantal corporate framework was called federal theology. It asserted the existence of a "covenant of works."[66] Whereas Calvin and Bullinger had emphasized the continuity of the covenant of grace and redemption, later Reformed theologians argued that there was also a continuous covenant of works which began in the Garden of Eden. This covenant of works was binding on all persons unless superseded by the covenant of grace and redemption in persons elected to salvation (a covenant of works and a covenant of grace). This dual covenant scheme was first proposed in 1562 by German reformer, Zacharias Ursinus.[67] It was most likely another German reformer Caspar Olevianus (also with expertise in Hebrew), who proposed the existence of a "covenant of works" (*foedus operum*) and also joined it to the Sinaic covenant (*foedus legale*).[68] In 1585, English theologist Dudley Fenner, part of the

Presbyterian faction and a colleague of Cartwright, expounded the idea of two covenants in his *Sacra Theologia.* The idea of a binding "covenant of works" is also discerned in the work of a host of other English and Scottish theologians: Thomas Cartwright, Franciscus Junius, John Howie, Edward Fisher, William Ames, John Ball, and Robert Rollock.[69] The idea expanded and can be clearly discerned in mid–seventeenth century Reformed theology such as the Westminster standards or Samuel Rutherford's *The Covenant of Life Opened.*[70]

The idea of a binding moral covenant on all persons, with salutary relevance even for the spiritually unregenerate, gave the covenant of works tremendous impetus for political theology.[71] Even though the Fall into sin guaranteed that no one would perfectly keep the covenant of works, persons did not become released from its obligations nevertheless. A prelapsarian covenant of works motivated the imprinting of the natural law upon the human heart at Eden and supported the covenantal implications of the Decalogue. It was a means by which, according to the Reformed reading of the Genesis account, God enabled moral (and therefore political) order. Natural law could therefore govern the conscience of all men.[72]

The covenant of works was indeed a redemptive failure because no one could successfully fulfill its terms. But that redemptive failure created an additional benefit of showing persons the superiority of the covenant of grace. Just as these two covenants worked together in the economy of salvation, so the civil and ecclesiastical could work together in the polity. On this question of the covenant of works and the law, for example, David Weir cites the example of Sabbath laws applied to all persons in civil law.[73] The reason for having the magistrate preserve religious orthodoxy or require pious acts such as Sabbath-keeping was to enable even unregenerate persons to live good lives under the provisions of the covenant of works. The civil magistrate did not mandate church attendance or moral conduct because reformers believed that they could force true belief. Nor did enforcing religious rules and religious orthodoxy presume that all were under the covenant of grace. Rather, such civil action demonstrated that all were under the covenant of works until graciously transitioned to the covenant of grace. The covenant of works became a justification for civil action, and the covenant of grace became justification for ecclesiastical action, working together in a theological and civil (corporate) framework.

The second innovation that preserved the covenantal corporate framework was a deepening theological inquiry into preparation and conscience as the means of explaining the work of the Holy Spirit in redemption and man's part in that redemption.[74] Puritan William Perkins, whose works were outselling Calvin's by the time of Perkins's death in 1602, pursued both the idea of conditional covenants and the question of temporary spiritual enlightenment. So did Perkins's student William Ames.[75] This innovation included a theology of "preparation." Having a robust theology of preparation meant that there was now room for experimental piety, which could prepare the human heart for the activity of the Holy Spirit. Though conversion could not be forced or resisted, the appropriate place for any person was certainly within the church, rather than outside it. This theology of preparation also justified a civil-ecclesiastical partnership.

Just as the English covenantal system was beginning to collapse because of internal dissent and disagreement about church-state cooperation or separation, these theological developments in the late sixteenth and early seventeenth centuries gave it new life. Both innovations not only energized the joining of church and state and the national corporate covenant but also opened another door for a gracious accommodation of natural law into Reformed political theology.[76] Prelapsarian theology (the covenant of works) relies on the possibility of rational persons.[77] Likewise, the idea of natural law presumed human reason. Preparation theology, which explored the role of partial spiritual enlightenment and preconditions for salvation, expanded the integration of theology and psychology, introducing a new era of philosophical anthropology to explore human attributes of will and conscience. Reformed Protestants began moving away from what they condemned as inane questions and moving toward "practical theology," which was intended to build a practical bridge between the covenants and both moral duty and experiential salvation. And although federal theologians such as Perkins or Ames had little explicit to offer in terms of politics, their presentations of the covenant of works and theological psychologies gave new life to Reformed political theology.

7 Covenant, Revolution, War, and Eschatology

Continuing the historical narrative of covenant theology's legacy in Britain, we come now to the "Wars of the Three Kingdoms."[1] Reformed theology and covenants played a prominent political role in the late sixteenth and early seventeenth centuries in England and Scotland. The most obvious contribution of Reformed political theology was to provide justification for revolution against King Charles I and the subsequent rise of Cromwell's Commonwealth. The justification for revolution was in many ways a replay of arguments previously used by Reformed Protestants against Catholic regents in the sixteenth century.

Covenant theology also became the basis for a proto-constitutionalist view of government, inspiring two national covenants in Scotland during the sixteenth century (National Covenant in 1638 and Solemn League and Covenant in 1643). These literal expressions of a national corporate covenant, protests against the ecclesiastical dictates of Charles I and his bishops, were prominent and explicit expressions of Reformed political theology. The conflict over these national covenants and their interpretation, together with eschatological differences between Scottish and English reformers, further divided Separatists (who would be called "Independents" or "Congregationalists" in the early seventeenth century) and Presbyterians.

Before providing a detailed exploration of the national covenants and the bloody division of Reformed churches in England and Scotland, however, we must first review the important role of Reformed Protestants in the bloody events of seventeenth-century Britain. Included in this overview is the evolution of Reformed political theology in late sixteenth-century England and Scotland as it grew increasingly independent of mentors in Zurich and Geneva.

OVERVIEW OF THE BRITISH WARS AND THE ROLE OF REFORMED PROTESTANTISM

As Reformed theology advanced in England in the late sixteenth century, the legacies of Zurich and Geneva began to move further apart because of the growing dissent within the English church. The legacy of Geneva was largely one of resistance, while the legacy of Zurich was largely one of accommodation. But both legacies could still lay claim to the soteriology and covenantal logic that was dividing the English church.

Protests against the Elizabethan Settlement of 1559 began with matters of worship and ritual. Because these elements were of central importance to corporate life in England, and because the magistrate was supposed to play a key role in their prescription, the resistance of the English dissenters had great political importance. When controversies turned to questions of church discipline (as they had on the continent a few decades earlier) and church government, this prefigured the coming of a great conflagration that would consume not only the church but also the state.

To complicate matters further, the Reformations of England and Scotland were progressing at different rates. "Puritan" was originally used as a term of derision against those who wanted to reform or separate from the Church of England. It was later used by Scottish bishops against their opponents in the 1590s.[2] But can it accurately be said that there were Scottish "Puritans"?[3] By the end of the sixteenth century, Scottish reformers had secured many reforms in worship, church polity, and behavior that English reformers were unsuccessful in winning by that same time. Hence, it is difficult to determine what was left for Scottish "Puritans" to purify in their Reformation, except perhaps the total abolition of episcopacy.[4] There were other important differences between the English and Scottish Reformations. While both were influenced by the continental reformers, the Scottish reformation was also rooted in its own humanist traditions, including the work of John Mair.[5] Added to this was also the work of John Knox and the other Marian exiles, and the result was something of a "miniature Reformation" of its own in Scotland—particularly in matters of political theory.[6]

The Swiss reformers had mixed feelings toward the civil consequences of Presbyterianism in England and Scotland. Bullinger's son-in-law and successor Rudolph Gualter did not join Calvin's successor Beza in supporting Presbyterianism in England. Gualter and Bullinger believed this to be a divisive movement and destructive of piety. In a letter to Bishop Cox in 1574, Gualter wrote that he suspected the English Presbyterians of "affectation of oligarchy, which may at length degenerate into monarchy, or even open tyranny."[7] Gualter's support for unity and peace in England's religious affairs did not dampen his desire for constitutional republicanism advocated by Scotland's Presbyterians, however. He commended George Buchanan and endorsed his work of Reformed political theology, *De jure regni apud Scotos.*[8] Published in 1579, Buchanan's *De jure* was a work of political theory arguing that kings were accountable to the people. Dedicated to James VI (whom Buchanan had tutored as a youth), it was a landmark prescription of constitutional limits and popular accountability for rulers. The reason for Gualter's reticence concerning English Presbyterians, in contrast to his support of Scottish Presbyterians, is not hard to deduce. In Scotland, Presbyterianism had achieved increasing legal recognition since 1572. In England, Presbyterianism was an unaccommodated threat to both the ecclesiastical and political order.

Scottish Presbyterians had made surprising progress in their reformation, so they could not claim the same grievances as the English Puritans were claiming under Elizabeth's reign. Whereas beginning in the 1560s dissenting English bishops had been largely unsuccessful in appealing to Parliament for Geneva-style reforms, the Scottish Parliament created the Kirk in 1560 and gave sanction to the Geneva-style reforms sought by Scottish reformers. The tidal wave of reforms in Scotland far outpaced what Elizabeth would allow in England. Reformed Protestants in Scotland executed the first successful interposition by "lesser magistrates" against Mary of Guise (serving as Scottish regent) in 1560. This was the first use of Reformed Protestant resistance theory. They adopted the *Book of Common Order* (replacing the English *Book of Common Prayer)* and the Geneva Bible. Both had been created by the English exile congregation in Geneva in the 1550s. (In Zurich, the English congregations had used the *Book of Common Prayer.)* The *Book of Common Order* and the Geneva Bible, the Reformed Scots believed, were superior to the English *Book of Common Prayer* and previous English editions of the Bible. Just as Calvin fought Bern over the remembrance of days other than Sunday, the Scottish reformers convinced the Scottish Parliament in 1561 to deny the recognition of Christmas. (Bullinger in Zurich recognized Christmas, emphasizing the importance of any occasion to celebrate the Incarnation.) Reformed theology seeped into Gaelic culture by way of translations of both Calvin's catechism and the *Book of Common Order.*[9] Though James VI did not consent to all that the Scottish Puritans wanted, he did allow the growth of presbyteries as a concession for increasing the power of the bishops and the Crown. The Presbyterian General Assembly was also given a role alongside the Scottish Parliament.

But Presbyterians are never an easy lot to satisfy, and it was increasingly clear that contentions over church polity were not far removed from civil polity. When judged against the episcopal system, Presbyterianism is very egalitarian.[10] Given the close partnership of church and state in the sixteenth and seventeenth centuries, and the way in which polemics about church spilled over into polemics about state, the civil consequences of Presbyterianism were clear. This was certainly evident to Archbishop Whitgift, who asserted during the *Admonition* controversy that incongruity between church and civil polity could not be tolerated.[11] As reformers in England and Scotland chafed under monarchs and their bishops, doctrines of conscience and resistance became more pronounced and articulate.[12] The Presbyterian threat was not lost on Elizabeth I. On July 6, 1590, she wrote to James VI in Scotland: "There is risen both in your realm and mine a sect of perilous consequence, such as would have no kings but a presbytery, and take our place while they enjoy our privilege, with a shade of God's word, which none is judged to follow right without by their censure they be so deemed. Yea, look we well unto them."[13] James agreed that kingship was tied to the bishops and the episcopal system. This he tersely stated as "No Bishop, no King." And while Buchanan's republicanism in *De jure regni apud Scotos* may have warmed Gualter's heart in Zurich, it did not warm the hearts of the civil authorities in England. Only five years after its publication, the work was condemned by an act of Parliament in 1584 and twice thereafter in the seventeenth century.[14]

The 1603 ascendance of James VI of Scotland to become James I of England was a crucible for both political theory and church-state relations. As James I, he hoped to consolidate Scotland, England and Ireland under one civil and church polity. But this plan was continually met with resistance—particularly in matters of religion. Upon taking the throne, James was confronted by English Puritans with the Millenary Petition, demanding further reform of the Church of England. James made some concessions, but he was unwilling to tamper with the episcopal hierarchy in the church system. Episcopal church government was already weakened in Scotland and under a decades-long attack in England. In 1617 his Five Articles of Perth insisted on a series of reforms within the Kirk that would bring the Scottish church into greater conformity with the English church. The Scottish General Assembly reluctantly agreed in 1618, and in 1621 the Scottish Parliament ratified them. But despite small successes such as this, James was never able to accomplish much of his consolidation agenda before his death in 1625.

It was the excesses of James's son and heir, Charles I, that provoked the beginning of literal national covenanting—first in Scotland and later in England. The creation of civil covenants, literal expressions of the collective theological communities sought by Calvin and Bullinger in the sixteenth century, was motivated by attacks from both Charles and Archbishop Laud on Presbyterianism and Puritan worship beginning in the 1630s. Most notable in Charles's counter-reformation was the imposition of a new *Book of Common Prayer* (replacing the *Book of Common Order*) in 1637. In that same year, Laud began making martyrs of English Puritan dissenters. No matter whether these controversies provoked by Charles and Laud were akin to the Vestiarian controversy of the mid–sixteenth century, were motivated by the rise of English sacramentalism, or constituted a growing Arminian resistance against Reformed soteriology, one thing became clear.[15] The naked authoritarianism of Laud and Charles finally moved popular sovereignty from Reformed ecclesiology into mainstream political theory.[16] The fight against ecclesiastical tyranny and the fight against political tyranny were again becoming synonomous—a textbook case of political theology in practice.

Charles Stuart's days were numbered in both Scotland and England. Scottish popular rejection of bishops and the English prayer book led first to the making of the National Covenant (1638) and then to the Bishops' Wars of 1639–1640.[17] Charles's war against the Scots was averted through the Treaty of Berwick, but this only bought him a little time. Constitutionalists and parliamentarians in Scotland and England grew more fearful that Charles's personal rule in church and state institutionalized unaccountable monarchy. Abuses of power included Charles's repeated (but unsuccessful) demands for taxes, his perpetual warmongering, and his years of rule with a dissolved Parliament. Such power was inconsistent with everything Reformed Protestants had taught about the danger of monarchy, the need for interposition by lesser magistrates, and the importance of popular consent. Reformed Protestantism did not invent either constitutional limits on power or popular sovereignty. But thanks to the innovative political theology of the sixteenth century, abuses of power could now be condemned from Scripture as violations of the covenants among God, the ruler, and the people. Knox had already prescribed the "election" of the monarch and relentlessly attacked any claim to "divine right" in the sixteenth century. He wrote in *The Second Blast,* "It is not birth only nor propinquity of blood that maketh a king lawfully to reign above a people . . . but in his election must the ordinance which God hath established in the election of inferior judges be observed."[18] Scottish Presbyterian Rutherford echoed Knox a generation later in 1644: "If his first-born shall be born an idiot and a fool, they are not obliged to make him king."[19]

Religious controversies under Charles harked back to earlier protests of the sixteenth-century covenant theologians. The Three Resolutions not only called on merchants to refuse the King's collection of tonnage and poundage but also protested against the perceived rise of doctrinal Arminianism (a prominent alternative to Reformed soteriology). Clergy chose sides. When Roger Manwaring's sermons supporting absolute monarchy were printed in 1628, Parliamentarians protested and had Manwaring arrested, imprisoned and fined.[20] Perceived movement toward Arminianism in the Church of England was read as the eventual establishment of Roman Catholicism. Any move by Charles or his bishops against the Scottish Kirk was perceived as tantamount to promotion of the Mass. This was a point the Scottish Jenny Geddes made quite bluntly by throwing her folding wooden stool at the priest during the first reading of the new *Book of Common Prayer* in 1637. John Kenyon, contra S. R. Gardiner and almost two generations of British historians, argues that it was not the state of the monarchy but rather the religious protests that were the "rolling stone" of the wars which followed.[21]

The English Civil War began in 1642 shortly after Charles unsuccessfully attempted the arrest of five members of the House of Commons on a charge of treason. The Scots, who had originally made peace with Charles in 1641, were troubled to hear that Irish Catholics threatened to join the Royalists. Most important in the Scots' alliance with the English was the role of the political covenant, however. The Scottish Presbyterians allied with English Puritans only after the English agreed to the Solemn League and Covenant in 1643. The Scottish Presbyterians hoped that this common allegiance to the Solemn League and Covenant would lead to Presbyterian reform of church polity in England. Beset by numerous setbacks and the New Model Army's efficiency, Charles I surrendered to the Scottish Presbyterians in 1646 and shortly thereafter was ransomed to the English. The legacy of Geneva's theology of resistance was in the pocket of every soldier under Cromwell's command: a pocket edition of quotations from the Geneva Bible.[22]

Samuel Rutherford cast the conflict in covenantal terms. In his 1644 *Lex, Rex or The Law and the Prince,* Rutherford used Old Testament examples to argue the existence of a covenant between the king and the people.[23] God works through the people in this covenant.[24] There are three parties to this covenant, though the interests of God and the people are the same. There also exists a covenant between the king and God.[25] This obligates the king to maintain religion and civil piety. Rutherford wrote, "The covenant is so mutual, that if the people break the covenant, God is loosed from his part of the covenant, Zech. xi.10. The covenant giveth to the believer a sort of action of law, and *jus quoddam,* to plead with God in respect of his fidelity to stand to that covenant that bindeth him by reason of his fidelity."[26] Rutherford's argument drew on multiple sources, appealing to Scripture, natural law, and acts of Parliament.[27]

Lex, Rex further develops the political theology of the sixteenth century that resistance to tyrants is obedience to God. Like Bullinger, Rutherford argues that tyranny was the work of Satan.[28] God worked through the people to remove the ruler.[29] Resisting was the duty of the common people as well as of the lower magistrates.[30] The people and the lower magistrates were not to engage in passive resistance only, but were to actively resist the king by removing him from power.[31] Drawing on the theology of resistance of the past hundred years, Rutherford wrote, "We teach that any private man may kill a tyrant, void of all title. And if he have not the consent of the people, he is an usurper, for we know no external lawful calling that kings have now, or their family, to the crown, but only the call of the people."[32]

Though the Solemn League and Covenant was originally intended to give Presbyterian Scots a greater voice in English affairs and a united Presbyterian church in England and Scotland, the Scottish role was increasingly marginalized and never came to its intended fulfillment.[33] During the Commonwealth, religious and political factions in Scotland contested over piety and politics, while Scottish Covenanters debated how best to protect the king from execution by the English. Tensions between English and Scottish Protestants came to a head in the trial and execution of Charles I in 1649. Though the Covenanters had supported the civil war, they viewed the trial and execution as a violation of the agreement to preserve the king's person stated in the Solemn League and Covenant.[34] Routed militarily by Oliver Cromwell at Dunbar and purged from Parliament, Presbyterians faded from influence in Scotland. Presbyterians also faded from influence in England as English Reformed Protestants turned to Independency as their preferred church polity. The Reformed Protestant experiment in ruling England thus became an affair dominated by English Independents and led politically by Oliver Cromwell. When the Commonwealth collapsed and the Stuart monarchy was restored by Charles II, Reformed Protestantism again found itself under suspicion and even persecution in both England and Scotland. By order of the Restoration Settlement under Charles II in 1661, the Solemn League and Covenant was burned by the public hangman.

Having provided an overview of the competing reformations in Scotland and England, and the role of Reformed Protestants in the wars of the mid–seventeenth century, it is now appropriate to turn to a detailed consideration of the Reformed Protestant political theology that developed during the mid–seventeenth century. In particular, it is important to see how the Scots created literal and legal expressions of collective responsibility and theological unity before God. In addition to using the covenant as a form of civil constitution, Reformed clergy played the role of prophet that Calvin and Bullinger sought in Geneva and Zurich. It is also important to examine more carefully the disagreement that grew between Scottish and English Reformed Protestants during this period. This disagreement included important differences in eschatology, a theological subject with great political importance.

THE NATIONAL COVENANT, SOLEMN LEAGUE AND COVENANT, AND THE WESTMINSTER ASSEMBLY

The introduction of the 1637 revision of the *Book of Common Prayer* by Charles and Archbishop Laud recalled to the minds of Reformed Scots the abuses of Catholic regents in the sixteenth century. Ironically, the 1637 edition was crafted by Scottish bishops in an effort to indulge Scottish sensibilities already offended by the 1559 *Book of Common Prayer* and rejected and revised by Marian exiles (such as Knox) in Geneva. But Charles and Laud were spectacularly unsuccessful in their efforts at liturgical union between Scotland and England. The 1637 revision was crafted in secret, not sanctioned or directed by Reformed leadership in Scotland, and was summarily rejected by both Scottish church leadership and laypersons. Plus, Reformed Scots were still resentful of what they considered setbacks in the 1621 Articles of Perth. The Scottish response was to follow the example of the Swiss reformers. They took a page out of Old Testament history and asserted a political-social covenant of unity before God. But whereas Calvin and Bullinger gave only tepid support to Knox's attack on Mary Tudor, the Scots would go much further. In their national covenants they demanded civil and ecclesiastical accountability from Charles, who was now head of both the English and Scottish churches. They also prepared for war.

Scots Alexander Henderson and Archibald Johnston drew up the National Covenant in 1638. It was based on the Confession of Faith of 1581 (signed by James VI) and reflected both the Reformed theology of covenant and the tradition of religious "banding" that had been popular in Scotland since the late sixteenth century.[35] The National Covenant and the succeeding document, the Solemn League and Covenant (1643), became literal and legal expressions of Reformed political theology coupled with historical and cultural circumstance. The National Covenant cited numerous Acts of Parliament to show that the Reformed faith had been duly established in Scotland. It bound its signatories to maintain freedom of church and to defend Presbyterianism. It provided legal warrant for deposing and excommunicating bishops, and it condemned the Book of Canons (a 1635 set of clerical rules issued by Charles), the new Liturgy, and the Perth Articles. Giving rise to the Covenanter movement, the National Covenant was first signed by noblemen, gentry, clergy, and burgesses. It was later distributed for a formal canvass and loyalty oath. The National Covenant not only asserted Presbyterianism as true church polity, it also asserted Scottish nationalism, civic loyalty to the Crown, and the supremacy of parliamentary statute.

Most significant, the National Covenant was characteristic of earlier covenantal thought because it emphasized the conditional nature of authority and of allegiance before God, and stressed corporate accountability before God.[36] Its subscribers argued that the king had driven them to articulate their revolutionary principles.[37] Researching terms of resistance led Johnston to look for inspiration in writings of prominent federal theologians, including the covenant theology of William Ames. Johnston also used the *Politica Methodice Digesta* (1603) of Johannes Althusius, a substantial work of Reformed theology and a pioneering work of political federalism.[38]

While the Scots remained committed to the preservation of monarchy and to accountability only to duly appointed representatives, there was an important populist leap taken in the National Covenant.[39] First, "Tables" (elected by nobility, gentry, burgesses, and clergy) rather than nobles themselves were to exercise the right of resistance.[40] Second, persons outside the "Tables" were now called upon to testify personally to their loyalty and to affirm their support.[41] During their joint struggle against Charles I, the parliaments of England and Scotland eventually required that all persons above the age of eighteen in both countries swear allegiance to the Solemn League and Covenant. By this requirement the National Covenant contributed to the significance of the individual conscience in resisting unjust authority. Steele notes, "With all of society bound by a covenant in subordination to God, conventional social and political allegiance thus took a back seat to faith and the 'Politick Christian' was created."[42]

For many reasons, the alliance enabled by the Solemn League and Covenant was not a perfect one. The Scots were more concerned with religious matters while the English were more concerned with constitutional matters such as taxation.[43] Dissent over theology (and thus political theology) soon became apparent in the Westminster Assembly approved by Parliamentary Ordinance on June 12, 1643. Most prominent in the Assembly debates were Scottish Presbyterians Alexander Henderson, Samuel Rutherford, and George Gillespie. Other groups were also represented, including Independents and Erastians. Originally charged with reforming the Thirty-Nine Articles of the Church of England, the Westminster Assembly abandoned this work for a new charge from Parliament on October 12, 1643. The outcome was a public directory for worship, catechisms for adults and children, and *The Westminster Confession of Faith.* Independents represented in the Assembly resisted efforts toward the imposition of Presbyterianism.[44] Presbyterians even disagreed with one another. Scottish Presbyterian George Gillespie insisted on a kind of divine-right Presbyterianism while other Westminster divines were willing to endorse the Presbyterian system only on prudential grounds.[45] Against Erastians and in the tradition of Geneva and the Scottish Presbyterians, Gillespie argued that there were distinct civil and ecclesiastical jurisdictions.[46]

A COVENANTED NATION: THE PARLIAMENTARY SERMONS

Besides the obvious case of the national covenanting, another prominent application of covenant theology is apparent in sermons preached during the Long Parliament (1640–1648). Beginning in November 1640, the Long Parliament instituted the practice of regular sermons from Reformed clergy. These sermons were preached to the English Parliament until 1652 and serve as a window into the covenantalism common to both Independents and Presbyterians. The language of the sermons was nationalist, often taking ancient Israel as a model.[47] Britain's history and contemporary situation were reconstructed in light of a narrative wherein people could enjoy security and purity through a close relationship between church and state.[48] It is evident from the sermons that clergy did not see themselves having any constitutional authority over Parliament. Rather, clergy mimicked the Hebrew prophets. They had prophetic authority to remind magistrates of both the individual covenant of salvation and the corporate covenant of collective responsibility. This was consistent with the precedent of Zurich and Geneva.

The Solemn League and Covenant was initially intended by both Scot Presbyterians (such as Alexander Henderson) and English Independents (such as Philip Nye) as the realization of hopes for a united national church. The Solemn League and Covenant also advanced conceptions of corporate and national piety. Joseph Caryl, despite being an Independent, praised the Solemn League and Covenant in his work *The Nature, Solemnity, Grounds, Property, and Benefits, of a Sacred Covenant.* He defined the end of a political covenant as "the glory of God and their common good," which would enable a "holy and a happy people."[49] Other clergy also looked to the Solemn League and Covenant as a means of unifying the nation and gaining favor with God.[50]

As a covenanted nation, rulers were "appointed" by God though not with any sense of autonomous divine right. Appointment justified accountability, and the vehicle for accountability was found in constitutional politics and godly preaching. The people and the commonwealth were committed to serving their governors, but all were charged with reform of the church. Cornelius Burges told the Parliament in 1640, "My business is, merely to persuade you into a *Religious Covenant with God,* as himself hath prescribed and commanded; and his people, in the best times of Reformation, have readily admitted: namely, every man to stir up himself and to lift up his Soul to take hold of God, to be glued and united to him, in all faithfulness, sincerity, care, and diligence, to be only his for ever."[51] Covenantal political theology argued that righteous and religious leaders are a blessing. Government was a divine office, but one that still required the tutoring of the preachers.

By 1645 the clergy were becoming increasingly explicit in attributing troubled times to the failure of the people and nation to uphold covenant obligations. Stephen Marshall and Edmund Calamy, for example, blamed the troubled times on divisions and faction. Others blamed heresy. With transgressions came both covenantal chastisement and deliverance. Though a covenanted nation could provoke God, He would not reject them if they repented.[52] National repentance included nationwide prayer and resembled individual repentance.[53] But it was not just repentance that concerned the clergy during the Commonwealth era. An eschatological framework also pervades these sermons. Consistent with a covenantal cosmology, piety was given historical meaning in this eschatological framework.[54] And with eschatological thinking came a new set of challenges for Reformed Protestants and their political theology.

THE CHALLENGE OF MILLENARIANISM

Millenarianism, the belief in an impending divine transformation of society caused by eschatological developments, has clear and important political consequence. While it detaches some people from politics, it turns others into zealots. William Lamont rightly argues that millenarianism, especially in the case of seventeenth-century England, is more about involvement with the world than alienation from it.[55] Millenarianism's reputation for radicalism stands in sharp contrast to the more moderate influence of traditional Augustinian eschatology. J. G. A. Pocock attributes this millenarian radicalism to "imminent transcendence," a concept akin to Voegelin's description of Gnosticism or metastatic faith.[56]

There are varieties of eschatology. Some are more spiritual and others more literal and political.[57] Calvin, so often considered the prototype of Reformed theology, was not especially interested in eschatology and condemned millenarianism. In this respect he was like Augustine. But Calvin was not the inspiration for political eschatology among the Puritans. Protestant historiography began with Philip Melanchthon's revision of Johannes Carion's history of the world from Adam (*Carion's Chronicles,* 1532), Luther's exposition of the Apocalypse, and Matthias Flacius Illyricus's *Magdeburg Centuries* (1559).[58] English variants on historiography appeared soon thereafter, beginning with Henrican and Marian exiles William Tyndale, John Bale, and John Foxe.[59] The Puritan eschatology owes something to to John Wycliffe and Bullinger as well.[60] Bullinger's and Wycliffe's attention to the Book of Revelation and their reading of it to foretell the destruction of the papacy, coupled with the martyrology of the exiles, gave rise to a new dimension of theological politics.

Many influential eschatological works asserted a special role for the place of the English church in history. This was first argued by John Bale in his *King John* (1530s) and *Image of Both Churches* (1541–1547). Bale offered no particularly dramatic vision of the end nor a precise timetable, but he cast the English church as locked in a long-standing struggle against papacy and superstition. Bale's work is notable for its explicit rejection of Augustine, casting the saint as a tool of papacy and superstition. This not only gave the English church a sense of divine destiny but also discredited the more moderate Augustinian approach to eschatology.[61]

The more radical English eschatology has been traced to the work of John Foxe, a friend of Bale's and a fellow Marian exile.[62] Foxe's *Acts and Monuments,* placed throughout English churches for popular reading, provided both an ambitious interpretation of contemporary events and a fuller church history than Bale's work. Foxe urged clergy to attend to ecclesiastical history. He was politically conservative in many respects and supported the status quo, including the hierarchy of bishops and monarchy. Foxe is best understood as supporting the standing thesis that England (and the English church) held an important place in the sacred history.[63] Like Bullinger, he put considerable faith in the role of the godly monarch. Such a presumption had become an implausible thesis by 1641, however. Many had lost faith in a godly prince because of Charles, but could not agree on the alternative.[64] In the early part of the seventeenth century it fell to Thomas Brightman and Joseph Mede to orient eschatology toward the future. This meant not simply interpreting the future but also transforming it.[65] Under the influence of Brightman and Mede, expectations for the millennium began.[66] This had a profound effect on British politics, particularly in terms of revolutionary rhetoric. Many clergy, particularly Independents, began to look at current events with an eye to an apocalyptic future. The message from Brightman was clear to them. God's saints must aid in bringing about the conditions for the millennial age.

To determine whether millenarianism was essential or accidental within Reformed political theology, one must determine if theologies of like mind can be found to disagree in their application of millenarianism. If disagreement is found, it is important to ask how and why they disagreed. Ideally, a case is found wherein one group of covenant theologians rejects the millennial radicalism of their colleagues outright, especially on covenantal grounds. That appears to be the case in what transpired between Independents and Presbyterians over the trial and execution of Charles I. While the disagreements between the Regicides and their opponents have been attributed to a variety of factors, their opposing theologies substantially explain their differences.

Eschatology, the study of last things, is part of any systematic theology. Prophetic history is part of the Bible, and it was certainly part of the notes within the Geneva Bible.[67] But not all eschatology is "millenarian." John F. Wilson describes the division over eschatology as *prophetic eschatology* versus *apocalyptic eschatology,* with the latter appearing as early as 1642.[68] On the one hand, *Apocalyptic* eschatology does not have an open future. According to the apocalyptic interpretation of the future, God ruled the course of human events and would bring things to pass in the context of a certain future. The vision of this future was withheld from the worldly-wise but delivered to faithful elite.[69] *Prophetic* eschatology, on the other hand, emphasized the covenant relationship and the delivery of a "word" from God. It embodied both judgment and mercy. Its vision of the future presented eventualities in context of an open future. This was a scriptural admonition to a covenanted people, not a prediction of events coming on a short horizon. Asserting a special place in Providence or echoing the Old Testament cosmology of deliverance and judgment characteristic of prophetic eschatology is not the same as the utopianism and immanent earthly reign that found its way into the thinking of the more radical clergy and sects and their apocalyptic theology. Whereas prophetic preachers counseled reformation, apocalyptic preachers exalted radical and destructive acts, both violence and revolution. This latter variant of eschatology encouraged the trial and execution of Charles I.[70]

DISSENT OVER REGICIDE: MILLENARIANISM AND THE COVENANT

Scottish Presbyterians had provided some of the most articulate arguments for resistance and revolution and supported the war against Charles I, but they did not support his public trial and execution. Underlying disagreements about jurisprudence between Scots and English were significant differences in theology. These differences included disagreements about the role of the church in the civil polity and the right use of reason and Scripture in constructing legal and political theory—including the use of natural law. These disagreements resulted in two different views of the covenant. Presbyterians, who were cobelligerents with Independents against Charles in the revolution and coreligionists because of their Reformed theology, disagreed with the hyper-millenarianism of the Independents. The Scottish Presbyterians and the English Independents also had fundamental disagreements about covenant theology and the relevance of the Fall. This last point inclined the Presbyterians to differ from Independents in their approach to church-state relations.[71]

Both Presbyterians and Independents, inheritors of the eschatology developed in the sixteenth century, saw history in providential and prophetic terms.[72] Even James I himself was a student of biblical prophecy. But whereas Presbyterians took a prophetic approach to eschatology, Independents had an apocalyptic eschatology underlying both their political theology and their ecclesiastical polity.[73] G. P. Gooch goes so far as to say, "At the basis of the creed of every religious body of the time, except the Presbyterians, lay the Millenarian idea."[74] The apocalyptic eschatology was championed early in the sermons of Independent clergy Richard Sibbes and Thomas Goodwin.[75] It is found in the sermons of John Owen, Cromwell's chaplain.[76] It is found in the writings of John Milton, who was a prominent critic of the Presbyterians. Millenarianism was not confined to England, either.[77] Across the ocean in New England, American Puritan John Cotton was a millenarian, an influential correspondent of Cromwell, and a supporter of the execution.[78] Thomas Hooker argued that clear fulfillment of prophecy trumped any other interpretive method of Scripture.[79] In 1645, Hugh Peters preached before Parliament that the New Model Army was the instrument for the downfall of the Antichrist and the millennial kingdom of Christ.[80] John Cooke, solicitor general and chief prosecutor of Charles I, was not alone in anticipating the arrival of the millennium (Christ's earthly reign) in the wake of the king's execution.[81] (Cooke continued to look for it even as he was condemned to die after the Restoration.)[82] Thomas Goodwin, who would be appointed to a state chaplaincy under Cromwell, predicted that the millennium would begin by 1695.[83] When such radical eschatology trickled down from the educated clergy to the army, Fifth Monarchists, and Levellers, the radical effect on the English political climate multiplied.[84]

Why did Independents assert this radical political theology, and why did Presbyterians dissent? The Independents' eschatology was tied to both their view of the church and their view of sin and grace.[85] When the English failed to secure the ecclesiastical reforms pursued by the Scots, the English turned their attention toward eschatology.[86] Independency was bound to eschatology and invited a disdain for the more humane and earthy politics of their opponents. Independents also rejected monarchy either as inherently evil or as simply an Old Testament "type" that represented Christ but had no contemporary application to politics.[87] As Independents increasingly asserted themselves as a separate party within the Protestant movement, they condemned the "spiritual prostitution" that would result from either Presbyterian supremacy or Erastianism.[88] This was not a controversy that began or ended with the British civil wars. It revealed a longer-standing fissure in Reformed covenant theology. Both Independents and Presbyterians believed that the church had to be protected against heresy, but the Independents believed this protection did not need any head other than Christ Himself, particularly if Britain was on the eve of the millennium. For some Independents, this was also an argument about the efficacy of the religious establishment and the dangers of persecuting the righteous. Demonstrating his concern for the accidental persecutions of the righteous while enforcing civil orthodoxy, Goodwin declared, "rather [let] some beastly men be, than that their suffering should occasion the . . . suffering of his [true] saints."[89]

Presbyterians leveled criticism against what they deemed chiliastic and antinomian eschatology and ecclesiology among the Independents. Apocalyptic millenarianism was condemned by Richard Baxter, who also opposed the execution of Charles I and refused the oath of allegiance under Cromwell.[90] Presbyterian Robert Baillie, representative of other Westminster divines, rejected the biblical literalism of Cotton and other Independents—calling the Independents "Chiliasts."[91] Rutherford, though very much a providentialist in his outlook on history, likewise took a position against what he saw as a kind of utopian eschatology on the part of the Independents.[92] Alexander Henderson, the iconic Scottish Presbyterian, provided direct criticism of millenarianism in a sermon preached to the House of Lords.[93] John Lightfoot, a rabbinical scholar, Hebraist, and influential member of the Westminster Assembly, devoted a complete sermon to members of the House of Commons in August 1645 to errors of the "millenary" opinion. He asserted that England was not as special to God as Israel had been and argued that England resembled Egypt and the Pharaohs more than Israel.[94] Other clergy criticized eschatological excesses as corrupted Judaism or mysticism.[95]

Presbyterian conflicts with Independents not only turned on eschatological interpretations, they also reflected disagreement about the political application of differences between the regenerate and the unregenerate—the two covenants of federal theology (grace and works). Disagreement about soteriology once again had profound implications for political theology and the relationship between church and state. Independents, including prominent leaders such as John Owen, advocated some degree of denominational toleration. The motivation for this was not so much freedom as such but the goal of a purer church. Many Independents in England continued to work within the English parish model, but they did not expect every member of the parish to be fit for membership. While Independents remained evangelical in outlook, they did not believe that the visible church should be corrupted or confused by the presence of the unregenerate. As we have seen, this was a running controversy among Reformed Protestants.[96]

Independents rejected the more inclusive civil theology of the Presbyterians, including the role played by federal theology and the covenant of works. As far as the Independents saw things, natural law and conscience (more prominent in certain strains of federal theology) could not justify the broader and more inclusive ecclesiology sought by the Presbyterians.[97] The Independents wanted a "purer" church than the Presbyterians, taking pains to discern the spiritually regenerate from unregenerate.[98] The quasi-parish model used by the Church of England, including Presbyterians, did not intend the same degree of purity sought by the Independents.

Presbyterian resistance to separating church from state rested ironically on their greater appreciation of natural law and the ability of all persons to reason. Gathering only examined Christians into the churches denied the covenant of works, standing universal moral duties, and the chance for preparatory steps toward conversion. By emphasizing the adequacy of natural law in enabling the covenant of works, Presbyterian theology held all people accountable for living a moral life. This goal could be supported by ecclesiastical methods. For the Presbyterians there was more continuity between law and grace than the Independents would acknowledge, and this continuity continued to justify a national church.[99] Presbyterians accommodated the Mosaic covenant and law (now equated with the covenant of works) to the covenant of grace. By contrast, Independents equated such a theology with legalism, and confusion of the spiritual order with natural reason.[100] Presbyterians criticized Independents as encouraging practical antinomianism by neglecting the Mosaic Law in the covenant of grace.[101]

Differences over ecclesiastical and civil polity grew wider after 1647. To Independents such as Owen and Milton, this Presbyterian regime of church and polity cooperation looked like spiritual tyranny. Worse still, it resembled papacy and the ancient league between popes and princes.[102] This is summarized in Milton's last line of *On the New Forcers of Conscience under the Long Parliament:* "New Presbyter is but old Priest writ large." Fierce literary combat exploded as Presbyterians and Independents traded polemics. Presbyterians accused Independents of both millennial enthusiasm and undermining social order.[103] Independents responded with attacks on monarchy and a defense of their eschatology and church government—often tying eschatology and church government together.[104] Independents insisted on a clear distinction between the regenerate and the unregenerate, thus rejecting any assertion of a "visible church" and a "national church." Samuel Rutherford, William Prynne, and Robert Baillie viewed the Independent approach to the Mosaic Law as detrimental to the social order.

Some prominent Presbyterians were common lawyers. Presbyterians such as Prynne, for example, were willing to make use of the new common law method. Cooke, Owen, Milton, and other Independents rejected it.[105] Independents behind the king's trial were cast by Presbyterians as having abandoned the Bible, the written Word, and the law of nature. Prynne declared the whole trial and execution of Charles Stuart to be illegal according to the standing civil law.[106] By contrast, Independents took a dim view of both reason and the common law emphasis on precedent. In contrast to the openness to regime type that characterized Calvin, Bullinger, or even many seventeenth-century Reformed Protestants, the Independents increasingly associated monarchy with the biblical Antichrist. Many Independents such as Milton argued that monarchy was only a "type" preceding the monarchy of Jesus Christ over the invisible church.[107] Owen denounced what he perceived to be scholastic jurisprudence in the Presbyterians, taking care to admonish both Francisco Suarez's philosophy of law and Rutherford's use of it.[108] Not only did the Independent view mean rejecting the scholastic doctrine connecting law with reason, it also meant a rejection of any "artificial reason" (as taught by Sir Edward Coke) used to interpret law. Milton, for example, placed what he considered to be justice above that staple of common law—precedent. He argued there to be no contradiction since both came from the same God.[109] And whereas the Old Order (by which he meant the English traditional civil law) venerated mixed monarchy (monarchy mixed with elements of aristocracy), precedent, and statute law, the New Age of the Spirit would see the frailties of human law and overturn their imperfection.[110] Both William Dell and John Cooke, for example, employed current legal terminology: fundamental law, natural law, reason, and *salus populi.* But these terms essentially had been appropriated by them to advance a revolutionary confusion of civil law and theology. Independents rejected the standing (or progressive) jurisprudence as "empty forms" created and corrupted by the natural reason of men who were not members of the invisible church.[111] In other words, it was unfit for use by Christians.

For Independents, religious orthodoxy was the basis of legal orthodoxy. Religious orthodoxy was rooted in a firm emphasis on regeneration. The government ought to be controlled only by regenerate men because only they could discern the will of God against mere human precedent.[112] Cooke opposed contemporary legal theory as "spiritually obtuse and pedantic," particularly as the theory was applied by parliamentarians and Presbyterians. Previous cases and opinions in law, for the Independents, had to be reviewed in light of the biblical imperative to destroy the kingdom of the Antichrist. Furthermore, it was years of anti-Christian influence that had distorted and corrupted the law; all this would soon be overthrown by Christ's kingdom.[113] Peter Sterry, state chaplain for Cromwell, defended the regicide in spiritual terms.[114] Just as the ceremonial law had been overthrown by Christ, the laws of the Old Covenant (and the civil magistrate) must give way to a New Covenant after the regicide.[115]

Millenarianism is not necessarily inherent in or essential to covenantal politics, as is demonstrated in the Presbyterian opposition to eschatological excesses. Nevertheless, such excesses proved tempting to Reformed Protestants, revealing fissures in their political theology. But likewise were some of the covenant's virtues more pronounced during this episode as well. The covenant had proved itself a voice for liberty against the excesses of Charles I. The question remained as to whether this could be a balanced and reasonable voice, and that question would be tested again in the case of America.

8 Reaching Limits
The Covenant in America

New England was settled by Protestants in the Reformed tradition. Most of them were Puritans holding largely to the Congregational style of church polity. Like the English Independents, Congregationalists believed in local self-rule by churches independent of a larger church hierarchy, presbytery, or bishops. Presbyterians began arriving as early as 1634. Cotton Mather reported at least four thousand Presbyterians (among the twenty-one thousand American Puritans) between 1620 and 1640. But the Presbyterian label is difficult one to apply, even in hindsight.[1]

With the emigrating English Puritans came their covenant symbol and device. A series of covenants joined church, town, and commonwealth in New England. Many of the settlers who followed, particularly Presbyterians and Baptists in the Middle Colonies, were already familiar with covenanting.[2] No person or segment of society was left out of the series of covenants. Even immigrants without families were required to submit to the authority of a household covenant. Children were trained to assume covenantal responsibilities.[3] Believing that God had called them to continue the work of reforming religion, these early Americans gave the covenant its fullest and most extensive application. But in doing so, they also had to contend with Reformed theology's political challenges.

America was cast in the Puritan mind as the land where God's people could finally live in covenanted faithfulness. All the elements of seventeenth-century English Reformed theology migrated with the colonists. They brought the Reformed soteriology, now including its federal modifications to some degree. They brought the budding apocalyptic theology that had flowered during the English Civil War.[4] They brought with them a providential view of history that was bound up with covenantal expectation of blessing and chastisement.[5] They brought the jeremiad tradition.[6] They brought the long-standing but imprecise theology of corporate faithfulness, including the relationship between unconditional (gracious) covenants and conditional (legal) covenants.[7]

Instead of a political Eden, America became a place where the covenant was pushed to its limits, faded, and eventually blended with other approaches to politics. Many explanations have been offered, then and now, for its demise. Clergy in the eighteenth century blamed general worldliness and sin. Modern scholars credit philosophical or sociological factors such as secularism, class struggle, financial prosperity, or immigration. But it is just as reasonable to assert that the covenant, when fully applied to political realities, collapsed under the weight of its transcendent demands.

NEW ENGLAND COVENANTS, COMPACTS, AND CHARTERS

At the civil and ecclesiastical level, New Englanders were bound to one another by covenants. Ecclesiastical covenants were used for the founding of churches. Charters were the bedrock of civil authority in the colonies, and provided foundations for the civil covenants.[8] Some charters established new colonies; others consolidated existing ones or revised the terms of authority.[9] Civil covenants, founded on the charters, transferred or awarded the power of governance and law enforcement to a local town, plantation, or colony. Given the distance from England, the colonists were often left to establish their own local governments by combination, compact, charter, patent, or legislative action. The Fundamental Orders of Connecticut provide an example of a civil covenant. Though much is made of the Mayflower Compact, it was never presumed by its authors to grant political authority. This had already been established by the 1606 Charter of Virginia. Instead, the Mayflower Compact was a civil covenant conceived for survival of the local government.[10]

Civil covenants differ one from another in their religious content or provision for a state-supported church.[11] Extremes of religious prescription soon faded; the New Haven Plantation and Colony, the most religious, was joined to the more secular Connecticut Colony after only one generation. Providence Plantation, founded by Roger Williams and the most secular, became less secular when joined to the Rhode Island colony.[12] What is perhaps most interesting about a comprehensive examination of New England covenants is not what the patents and charters actually say about religion, but rather what they do not say about religion.[13] Though New England colonists used the covenant as a legal device, its ethos would not and could not be sustained by official religious language or religious institution in the covenants themselves. This was true from the beginning but became more difficult after the Restoration in 1660.[14] Covenantal political theology had to survive on its own merits; it could not rely on the law.

UNDERMINING THE STANDING ORDER: ROGER WILLIAMS

Roger Williams dealt the first substantial blow to the covenant in New England. Though he was warmly greeted by John Winthrop upon his arrival in 1631, Williams soon proved to be too radical in his understanding of the public covenant. Though some in early twentieth-century scholarship cast Williams as a democrat or proto-liberal, Alan Simpson offers the right corrective in labeling him "a religious enthusiast."[15] Among other things, it was Williams's pursuit of one aspect of covenant theology—predestination and the establishment of an unpolluted church—to the exclusion of the others that drove his criticism of the covenant network in Massachusetts.[16] By the 1630s, Massachusetts Puritans were clearly struggling with the question of membership in the covenant.[17] Williams was more than ready to resolve their difficulties by confining covenanting in the fully biblical sense only to the body of examined believers. This excluded the unregenerate and denied corporate covenanting outside the church. It also meant abandoning any church-state partnership. Williams quickly became an enemy of the status quo. But despite admonishment by other clergy, rejection of his land petition for a church within Marblehead Neck, and betrayal by some within his own church (possibly to gain the land petition in spite of him) Williams held fast to his opinions. In 1635 he was exiled from the colony. From 1643 to 1652, he traded polemics with John Cotton, which were then published in London.

Williams employed the hermeneutic of his coreligionists to undermine their civil-religious covenant. Using "typology" theology, wherein Old Testament passages become figures (or types) rather than literal lessons for New Testament believers, Williams argued that the physical punishment for heretics in the Old Testament was only a figure for spiritual punishment experienced under the New Testament.[18] The civil sword of the Old Testament became the spiritual sword of the church, Williams argued. State patronage, the civil sword, would lull the church to sleep. The church advanced through persecution, not protection.[19] In short, Williams was prepared to spiritualize everything, including the corporate covenants found in the Old Testament.

Williams also argued that all nations were alike under the New Testament covenant.[20] Only Old Testament Israel could claim the right to covenant and also persecute dissenters.[21] Williams interpreted the Bible to diminish its more activist political prescriptions.[22] In his epistle dedicatory, Williams wrote the members of Parliament that their duty as Christians was to save souls, but their duty as magistrates was to secure the bodies and goods of others.[23] Deaf to the subtleties of federal theology, Williams argued that Christian ordinances could not convert the people. The ordinances could only civilize them.[24] Christian ordinances would not only fail to convert, but would give people a false sense of blessedness leading to damnation. Citing early church history, he argued that

Roman rulers were not appointed as guardians of the church; this was a task given only to the apostles.[25] Williams did not believe that the enforcement of orthodoxy was prescribed after the coming of Christ. Citing Calvin and Beza to support his case, Williams argued that Romans 12 and 13 dealt only with external matters, not with spiritual matters.[26] Further complicating the civil picture, Williams argued that both the magistrates and the people from whom the magistrates derived their civil authority were capable of doctrinal error. Thus, persecution of heresy could shed the blood of saints.[27] One famous centerpiece of the Cotton-Williams debate was their interpretation of Matthew 13:24–30, the parable of the wheat and tares.[28] This was a long-running debate within Reformed theology.

What makes Williams important, however, is not just his dissent on matters of religious orthodoxy and civil enforcement. Other English Independents more or less agreed with him concerning the pitfalls of religious intolerance. His most significant contribution was to push the civil consequence of soteriology to the point where it challenged the parallel theology of the civil-religious covenant. In the face of arguments that heresy would threaten the spiritual health of believers, Williams retorted that the sovereignty of God's grace would preserve them from error.[29] Conversely, Williams may also have believed in double predestination and reprobation.[30] God's Spirit, Williams argued, did not require the help of the civil magistrate.[31] He charged those who tried to use the civil sword to encourage belief or discourage heresy with practicing Arminianism.[32] Furthermore, Williams argued, mandatory church attendance encouraged hypocrisy and divine condemnation in addition to changing the character of preaching and worship.[33] Unregenerate persons might even have their fate sealed by church attendance, giving them a false sense of security.[34] All of this Williams argued on the basis of divine sovereignty and election.[35] This was the first time that someone within the Reformed tradition had so thoroughly used its own soteriology to undermine its civil theology.

Williams's legacy was the Providence Plantation charter (the Patent for Providence Plantations, 1643), later folded into the Rhode Island Charter given to John Clarke in 1663. Providence Plantation's charter marked a change in religious tone from the royal charters in New England. While the charter acknowledged the religious motivations of its members and the conversion of the Native Americans, it reflected dissent in both Old and New England. It explicitly separated the civil magistrate from religious matters and an established state church. In Rhode Island, civil religion was to be sustained by private religious commitments only. This, the charter assured the Crown, would lead to greater public morality and patriotic commitment.[36] Hence, Williams succeeded in divorcing the civil from the ecclesiastical in a way heretofore not known in England or in America. More important, he did it using the logic of covenant theology.

COVENANT AND SACRAMENT

The New England civil-religious covenantal vision was threatened not only by dissenters such as Williams but also by internal ecclesiastical challenges. Presbyterians had never viewed church covenants in the same way Congregationalists did. Presbyterians were content to allow access to the sacraments based only on a Christian profession free from scandal.[37] For example, Richard Baxter, though technically not a firm Presbyterian, disagreed with Independent John Owen's restrictive admission to communion, and Baxter's Ministerial Associations took a more generous approach. The church-state synthesis was accomplished by this kind of broad participation in worship and sacraments. Presbyterians embraced the parish system of the English church more fully, declining the ecclesiastical purity sought by the Independents or Congregationalists. To the degree that the New England Puritans embraced the Congregational model, they faced a rigorous challenge in administering the sacraments.[38]

For Congregationalists, the church covenants were not just theological or political expressions but, rather, literal compacts by believers who erected a community based on their shared experience of true conversion. The church was the work of the Holy Spirit as discerned by the church leadership. Guarding the visible purity of the churches was ultimately the responsibility of church elders. The vehicle for maintaining the integrity of the members' professions became the cross examination of conversion narratives. One could be a member by baptism, and Congregationalists were paedobaptists (they baptized infants). Full membership—including access to the communion table, baptism for one's children, and voting rights—required a generally unimpeachable demonstration of conversion.[39] When the townspeople of Dedham, Massachusetts, began to organize a congregation in 1637, for example, they needed some means of discerning the saints among themselves. They employed a criterion used by nearby congregations. Candidates would have to demonstrate moral conduct and soundness in doctrine. They would also have to confess the work of grace experienced in their regeneration. Through the 1630s, churches enjoyed high attendance—much higher attendance than in Tudor or Stuart England. After 1645, churches required longer and more personal conversion narratives. To the Congregationalists, this did not undermine the civil-religious covenant. Rather, they believed it strengthened that partnership. Strong and sincere churches meant a coherent, godly, and orderly society together with covenantal blessing. Weak or hypocritical churches meant civil disorder and covenantal sanction.

Presbyterians in particular did not agree with this approach. In the 1640s, Presbyterians in England and Scotland complained that thousands of persons otherwise reputed to be Christians were denied membership in New England churches. Some Presbyterians even suggested that three-fourths of the community were excluded. Discontent worried the Congregational ministers, as evidenced by one minister's comment to John Cotton: "Many [are] murmuring that we come to make Heathens rather than convert Heathens to Christianity."[40] During the 1630s and 1640s, the membership controversy in America was advanced by Presbyterians emboldened by their gains in Britain.

Attendance and membership began to slip in the New England churches.[41] Faced with a rising generation of baptized persons who could not provide a sufficient conversion narrative as adults, the churches had to decide how to address the question of the sacraments—and specifically, baptism for the children of those parents.[42] Ideally, baptism would be administered only to children of regenerate parents, but as individuals struggled with the demands of piety, fewer parents could or would withstand the rigors of cross examination for membership.[43] In Massachusetts, the Half-Way Covenant solution was reached by specially called synods in 1657 and 1662.[44] The Half-Way Covenant allowed the children or grandchildren of full members to enjoy partial membership by baptism. It also enabled baptism to serve as sufficient in qualifying for the civil benefits of church membership.[45]

Because the civil vision was so clearly integrated with the religious vision, the Half-Way solution was a major threat to the "City on a Hill." If fewer persons could give convincing testimony of divine sanctification, what would this eventually mean for public morality and orthodoxy? The civil-religious covenant network relied on every institution fulfilling its proper role, especially the church. The conversion crisis, and the accompanying reformulation of baptism, meant a crisis for covenant theology. Some churches, as demonstrated by the Brattle Street Church's *Manifesto,* would address this problem by distinguishing between adherence to "historical faith" and adherence to "saving faith," and giving preference to the former over the latter in deciding membership.[46] Churches founded in the wake of the Half-Way controversy, such as the Third Church, Boston, included explicit reference to their posterity to keep them from being excluded.[47]

Massachusetts churches struggled with the Half-Way Covenant solution for decades.[48] King Phillip's War (1675–1676) and the smallpox epidemics (1677, 1689, 1702, and 1721) had encouraged revival from both pulpit and pew, but that revival was difficult to sustain. The revocation of the colony's charter in 1684 by Charles II did not help. The Congregationalists lost their formal alliance with the civil magistrate and were therefore forced to maintain the covenant ethos without civil support. Before long, New England Congregationalists essentially surrendered to the partial covenanting measures. Already by 1690, less than one quarter of the Massachusetts churches dissented from the new Half-Way approach to baptism.[49] The Half-Way Covenant had opponents, but sustained a partial solution to an important problem.[50]

It was not long before the question of how to discern conversion also caused a crisis over communion. Prominent in the opposition to the Congregational approach to exclusion was Solomon Stoddard, grandfather of Jonathan Edwards and pastor of Northampton Church.[51] Beginning in 1679, Stoddard recommended a more Presbyterian approach to sacraments, opening the communion table to those who professed belief and lived free of moral scandal.[52] Stoddard wrote in 1700 that the traditional Congregational understanding of church covenants was wrong and shut too many out from church privileges.[53] Stoddard considered the sacrament as a means of grace that was open to all professing Christians participating in the (implicit) national covenant.[54] Furthermore, if one was not in fact converted, the grace available in the sacrament might contribute to conversion. Stoddard was followed in this by most of the churches in the Connecticut Valley, though he was opposed by the Mathers.[55]

Stoddard used an argument similar to the one used in Providence Plantation's appeal for a secular charter. Opening communicant membership would strengthen rather than weaken the church and the clergy, which was important for the preservation of New England's civil-religious covenant.[56] Virtually everyone would be in a parish and baptized, hence under the discipline of the church. George M. Marsden characterizes Stoddard as saying, "Not only were the people under a national covenant, but the church and the people of the nation (or, in this case, a province,) should be, more or less, coextensive. In other words, the essence of a nation should be a true national church."[57] Some of Stoddard's opponents, such as Reverend Edward Taylor of Westfield, Massachusetts, protested on grounds that open access to the sacrament would diminish its importance. Privately, Taylor compared Stoddard's vision with the degeneracy of the Church of England and criticized the implicit Presbyterianism as "Prelacy at best." Increase and Cotton Mather suggested Stoddard had become a Congregational Pope.[58] Increase Mather insisted that the sacrament could not be administered to any who were not in covenant with God.[59] But as with the Half-Way Covenant, the status quo was difficult to uphold. New England Puritans found it difficult to exclude so many and still maintain the framework of corporate responsibility. Over time, Stoddard's approach won the day.[60]

Solomon Stoddard and Roger Williams could not have been more different in their discerning worthiness for recipients of the sacraments. Stoddard prescribed generous inclusion; Williams thought the Congregational approach too generous and therefore led to hypocrisy. (He eventually separated from all denominations.) But Stoddard and Williams unwittingly worked both sides against the middle in undermining the implicit New England covenant. Williams used the Reformed idea of predestination to encourage hyper-separation by individuals and churches from the larger body of professing Christians, to question the civil covenant, and to justify religious toleration; Stoddard appealed to Reformed theology to question the sincerity of conversion narratives—the means by which Congregationalists identified believers for church membership. Converting ordinances and means of grace were not to be avoided on the excuse of being unconverted, Stoddard argued.[61]

Both views implicitly centered on the role of the Old Testament for the church. Both tried to guard the proper place of the church in society and the just claims of Christ's elect. Williams turned the Hebrew polities into spiritual metaphors for the church. He attempted to create a church free of confusion with the broad civil-religious covenant of the Old Testament, believing that the integrated version fostered hypocrisy and threatened sincere piety. What Williams saw as metaphor (the Old Testament civil-religious covenant), Stoddard took literally. Stoddard was literally reviving the Old Testament vision on the grounds that deserving persons might be shut out by scriptural arguments to the contrary. Williams's high view of the covenant meant excluding all but the most evidently deserving. Stoddard's high view of the covenant meant including all but the most undeserving.[62] This was the ethos of the covenant working against itself.

PLURALISM, SECULARISM, AND REVIVALISM

In addition to fighting dissent from within, New England clergy struggled with rising secularism and religious pluralism. The revocation of the Massachusetts Bay Colony charter in 1684 and the Restoration put politics on a different legal footing. Immigration continued. Religious dissent, not originally accommodated by the old covenantal vision, was becoming an unavoidable reality in the late seventeenth century. And the challenge was substantial. Though the New England Puritans were proud of their English heritage, they had come to America with the expressed intent to be ruled by Scripture and those whom God called to lead. This vision was above and beyond the English constitution. If they were to be governed by standing law alone, what would define them as a peculiar and covenanted people? How would they navigate the new freedom given to dissenters?[63] With the exception of the Andros episode (1686–1689), the trend in New England was toward liberty in matters of religion and in other matters more generally. The Massachusetts Bay Province Charter of 1691, which united New Plymouth Colony and Massachusetts Bay Colony, extended the franchise to property owners: from "Freeman" (church member) to "Freeholder" (property owner).[64]

The solution articulated by the Mathers to the challenge of secularism and pluralism diluting the covenant vision was to reestablish the vision on the bedrock of English constitutional law. This pushed things in a more secular direction but did not jettison spiritual goals. In Cotton Mather's 1692 election sermon, he avoided the typological identification with Israel and praised royal governors concerned with secular interests. That praise included an expectation that the ruler should uphold every person's "Right unto his Life, his Estate, his Liberty, and his Family." While the new government was not commissioned by God to promote Congregationalism, it did protect life, liberty, property, self-government in the popular assembly, and the privilege of electing the Governor's Council. Christians should rejoice that there was no taxation without consent and that their worship was unmolested. This sermon echoed a sentiment stated previously by his father, Increase, wherein he praised the Royal Charter as securing "all Christian Liberties, and all English Liberties." Such a commonwealth approach did not entirely abandon the traditional covenantal vision. Mather argued that it was in the context of political liberty that New England was able to pursue its covenantal vision. The people must still lean upon God; it was God's covenantal faithfulness that enabled economic prosperity and political liberty. A fusion of English law and covenant logic became a theme of election sermons for the next seventy-five years. This was not the covenantal vision of the founders, but neither was it a wholesale abandonment.[65]

But while covenant-minded clergy thus found a way to deal with political secularism and religious pluralism, they had much greater difficulty with revivalism, which posed a more subtle and serious threat. Revivalism made policing the borders of the covenant network difficult and created rifts and dissent that threatened to tear the covenanted community apart. Not only did revivalism undermine ecclesiastical hierarchy, it threatened religious orthodoxy. Hence, it was not so much secularism as religious enthusiasm that imperiled the reformers' covenanted approach to life in the world.[66] Revivalism would reach its superlative heights during the Great Awakening (c. 1730–1750). In principle, revival preaching was hardly new in Reformed theology. There had already been an emphasis on "experimental" or "experiential" religion in English Puritans such as Joseph Alleine, Richard Baxter, or John Flavel, who stood on the shoulders of federal theologians such as William Perkins or English preparationists such as Richard Sibbes.[67] There was also a tradition of revival preaching in Scotland and Northern Ireland.[68]

Ironically, revivals were originally intended to strengthen the covenant vision, particularly the part of it that was concerned with righteousness among its members. Concerns about piety and righteousness were to be expected in light of the diminished standards of the Half-Way Covenant and Stoddard's approach to communion.[69] New England churches, beginning in the 1670s, had begun the practice of "covenant renewal" ceremonies as a way of reviving piety among their members and partial (Half-Way) members. The first ceremonies took place under Pastor James Fitch of Norwich, Connecticut. Other covenant renewal ceremonies followed, including those led by John Cotton, Jr., and Samuel Willard.[70]

Publicity became essential to the revival movement, beginning with the account of a 1705 covenant renewal ceremony in Taunton, Massachusetts. Led by Pastor Samuel Danforth, Jr., as a revival of the church's 1676 covenant renewal during King Phillip's War, this ceremony would set a precedent for the later "Great Awakening" when it was cast in the transatlantic journal *Christian History* as a "second Instance" of revival following the 1680 renewals.[71] Renewals came to be known as spiritual harvests, but further blurred the distinction between hypocrisy and sincerity.[72]

Both covenant renewal and revivals were a logical outgrowth of the internal tension of Reformed theology whereby true divine grace and faith must be evident in the believer's life. One could not rely on the alleged "works righteousness" of Rome; instead, the covenanted believer had to experience the "new birth." Revivals would strengthen emphasis on spiritual regeneration and rouse church members from dull piety.[73] They would emphasize the important difference between the visible and invisible churches.[74] As the population increased in the eighteenth century, revivals became an important covenantal function. But they soon grew out of control. This was partly because of geography. Population growth not only forced parish splits and new civil incorporations, it also pushed a new class of persons out to the frontier. Revival served the same function for rural areas that formal and ceremonial covenant renewal did for churches in the cities.[75]

As broad interest in revival and "awakening" grew, clergy lost control of its use. The Great Awakening caused serious splits within churches with a professional clergy and organized governing structure.[76] This was especially true in Anglican areas. Occasional revivals or renewals gave way to *revivalism,* which posed important threats to the standing political order. First, revivalism transitioned many churches and regions from clerical religion to lay religion, which meant that there were no longer designated guardians of the covenant vision.[77] Second, it moved American Christianity from an emphasis on doctrine to an emphasis on piety. Third, it resolved a long-standing tension within Congregational New England. The definition of a church went from its dual role in the national covenant (as a guardian of civil piety and gatekeeper of full civil membership through baptism) to an insulated role as a covenanted community of the converted.[78]

Critics equated revivalism with "enthusiasm," a pejorative term for false and irrational religious experience.[79] Some equated revivalism with libertinism. The threat that critics saw revivalism and enthusiasm posing to law and propriety was perhaps no better (or more humorously) illustrated than by clergyman and itinerant preacher James Davenport. While stocking a fire in March 1743 with books and other "luxuries" that he urged his adherents to burn, Davenport removed his own "plush" pants and threw them into the fire. Thankfully, the fire had not yet been lit, and Davenport was not forced to "strutt about bare-arsed" (as one account wrote). But Davenport's fate was sealed by the fact that his pants had to be rescued by a young woman who (herself alluding to a biblical narrative of covenant failure) told Davenport, "The calf you have made is too big." This broke Davenport's charismatic hold over others and nearly ended his ministerial career. It certainly stifled the radical wing of the revivalist movement.[80]

Americans anticipated the arrival of famous revivalist George Whitefield as either the instrument of God for spiritual awakening or else the instrument for catastrophic disorder.[81] Charles Chauncey, a prominent New England critic of the revivals, denounced Whitefield as a slick promoter. Chauncey engaged in an exchange of polemics with Jonathan Edwards. Edwards generally defended the revivals while cautioning against their excesses. Stephen Williams, another New England–based critic, objected to the itinerant revivalist practice of bypassing duly constituted ecclesiastical structures and preaching directly to the masses. The effect of revivalism on social order and the development of the Middle Colonies was particularly devastating. By 1743, opponents on both sides of the Atlantic formed networks to coordinate their attacks on the revivalists.[82]

As with all the previous controversies concerning baptism and communion, Stoddard was found both front and center in the origins of covenant renewal and revival, having led a number of spiritual harvests and developed an elaborate evangelical theology of conversion.[83] It can be argued, ironically, that the revivalism Stoddard supported actually undermined the de facto national covenant he championed. At the same time that he was embracing a national covenant by opening wide the church doors and the sacrament table, he was also lamenting the loss of heartfelt religion. Stoddard did not see any contradiction between a national covenant (with essentially open communion) and an emphasis on revival. He complained that while fashion, merchandise, and learning had been promoted in the colonies with great zeal, sermons, laws governing morality, and the making of covenants had "miscarried." Stoddard and others also feared the rise of Enlightenment philosophy, Deism, and English latitudinarianism. His solution was to support religious revival. A striking testimony to Stoddard's role in the juxtaposition of the national covenant with true piety is that he was later cited by both proponents and opponents of revivalism.[84] He also paved the way for the revivalism of his grandson and successor, Jonathan Edwards, who indeed may have sealed the fate of the civil-religious synthesis that Stoddard had tried to sustain.

JONATHAN EDWARDS AND THE POLITICAL COVENANT

Jonathan Edwards presented the most articulate and systematic opposition to the inclusive view of church membership and its institutional synthesis of civil and ecclesiastical powers. This meant shifting emphasis away from a nexus of individual, church, and society, back to the cornerstone bond between church and individual. Against the previously broader view of the church covenant that had been prevalent since the Half-Way Covenant, Edwards presented a high standard for full membership. Against the idea that sacraments and preaching could inspire broad civic virtue, Edwards countered any basis of morality other than the Spirit-led morality of the regenerate.[85] He abandoned his grandfather Stoddard's practice of open communion, arguing that sacraments were covenant privileges only for regenerate persons.[86] Edwards was particularly sensitive to the treatment of children under the covenant, believing that they should essentially be treated as unregenerate persons who must seek salvation just as if they were lost in sin.[87] This, together with accompanying controversies about immoral behavior among covenant children, eventually cost Edwards his church in Northampton.[88] Edwards's cousin, Solomon Williams, engaged him in a dispute on the matter. He argued that Edwards confused *entering into* covenant with *keeping* covenant and also that both external and internal covenants were valid (the first not being conditional on the second). Furthermore, the Lord's Supper was not a means of sealing the covenant but instead a profession of one's engagement to fulfill it.[89] Despite Edwards's (or anyone's) best efforts, Williams argued, there remained the undisputed reality of hypocrisy in Christian professions.[90] Here again was the problem of the postlapsarian (post-Fall) condition (an emphatic point in Reformed theology), creating another internal tension within Reformed theology. The same postlapsarian corruption that inspired a narrow view of the church covenant also challenged the mechanism of enforcing it: conversion narratives. If human nature was truly sinful, then was it not capable of manufacturing phony conversion narratives?

In matters of political theology, Edwards did not emphasize the network of social covenants. He held to a commonwealth approach, emphasizing only minimal *salus populi* obligations of civil government. In listing the proper functions of government, Edwards declared that the first function of government was to secure property and protect rights. The next three functions included the maintenance of order, the ensuring of justice, and national defense. In short, government did its job best by preventing an assortment of recurring human evils. The fifth duty of government was to make laws against immorality for the sake of public virtue. The sixth responsibility was to help the poor. The seventh function of the magistrate was to give indirect support to true religion. This meant calling a day of prayer or thanksgiving, though Edwards, in an unpublished sermon on Ezekiel 23:37–39, warned against hypocrisy in such things.[91] Magistrates should not have anything more to do with ecclesiastical matters, nor were persons necessarily qualified for civil service as a result of their personal piety.[92]

Edwards did not abandon the idea of a national covenant altogether, though he modified it substantially. Gerald R. McDermott calls Edwards's doctrine of the national covenant "neither tribalist nor provincial."[93] Edwards remained concerned with national piety and corporate responsibility before God.[94] This is exemplified in a 1729 sermon on Proverbs 14:34: "Sin and Wickedness Bring Calamity and Misery on a People."[95] Edwards still saw New England as being in covenant with God insofar as particular events could be interpreted as acts of covenantal blessing or sanction.[96] In a sermon on II Chronicles 23:16 in 1737, Edwards wrote, "We have been greatly distinguished by God as a covenant people. . . . The land of our forefathers has been a land of such light . . . You are a people that have been distinguished of God as a covenant people for a long time and have been distinguished in the means that God has used with you." But Edwards's view of that national covenant was similar to his view of covenant children. They were neither "confirmed" in their faith nor "excommunicated" for gross desertion of the covenant.[97] This was something of a lame jeremiad, however, when compared with those of the previous century.

Edwards saw the covenant mainly as a device for the church that, if properly constituted and directed, could then inspire civil piety. If there was a civil covenant, it relied entirely on the success of covenantal faithfulness in churches. In 1742, for example, Edwards tried to channel the fading fires of revival into the stability of an elaborate church covenant. This included a day of fasting, prayer, and owning the covenant on March 16, 1742. All members of the congregation over fourteen years of age assented to the covenant. Edwards hoped that this would serve to make Northampton a model town. The Northampton covenant was a formal contract; it catalogued past moral failings, set forth provision for restitution, and required extensive promises for moral behavior in the future. It was a way of institutionalizing the spirit of the revival that would make Northampton not just a model parish but a model civil community.[98] But his overall goal for Northampton failed, and the town became a microcosm of the American experience. Tensions within Reformed theology could not seem to hold the American covenant together.

THE WAR FOR INDEPENDENCE: REVIVING THE COVENANT

During the War for Independence, the covenant enjoyed a resurgence.[99] Colonial Americans largely remained a devout people who saw things in providential terms. Of the twenty-nine sermons published by Massachusetts clergy from 1777 to 1783, twenty-two reminded the listeners of the covenant and called them to virtue and piety.[100] Clergy in the Middle Colonies were also conversant in the use of covenantal political theology.[101] The rhetoric of the War for Independence became a repeat of the politico-theological rhetoric of the Puritan Revolution. At the time of America's war with England, Horace Walpole (fourth Earl of Oxford) is alleged to have said, "Cousin America has run off with a Presbyterian parson, and that is the end of it."[102]

This covenant revival during the War for Independence was not exactly a return to the thinking of the New England forefathers, but there was certainly a thread of continuity. In the 1770s, at least 50 percent of American colonial churches subscribed to key aspects of Reformed theology regardless of denomination.[103] The Book of Deuteronomy, the most politically prescriptive book of the Bible and a narrative of Israelite nationality, is the most cited source in American political writings between 1765 and 1805.[104] Clergy used political sermons and jeremiads to provide leadership and encouragement by framing crises in biblical terms. There is much in the Revolutionary and Founding sermons that one can recognize as covenantal in theme and symbol: moral declension, providential interpretation of history, corporate responsibility, and providential history, if not outright millennialism.[105] Political sermons such as Henry Cumings's *A Sermon Preached at Lexington* have the flavor of a jeremiad.[106] Samuel Cooper's *A Sermon on the Day of the Commencement of the Constitution,* for example, casts the covenant of the "Hebrew nation" as evidence that it was a "free republic" (much like America).[107] Joseph Sewall's *Nineveh's Repentance and Deliverance,* Samuel Dunbar's *The Presence of God With His People,* and Jacob Cushing's *Divine Judgments Upon Tyrants* repeatedly cast divine and human faithfulness in terms of covenants.[108] Samuel Sherwood's *The Church's Flight Into the Wilderness* is a sermon of outstanding millenarian expression. Presbyterian Abraham Keteltas's *God Arising and Pleading His People's Cause* is entirely dependent on themes that were central to Reformed theology, such as election and chosenness, providential history, predestination, and the federal emphasis on virtue. *Defensive Arms Vindicated,* attributed to "A Moderate Whig" (but actually taken from a 1687 sermon by Scottish Presbyterian covenanter Alexander Shields titled *A Hind Let Loose),* was used to defend the duty of American citizens to put up resistance.[109]

It is difficult to cast any particular category of clergy—orthodox or heterodox, Reformed or otherwise—as being entirely in one camp or another in supporting the War for Independence. Generally speaking, many conservative or "evangelical" clergy were patriots, but so were many liberal or skeptical clergy.[110] Anglican clergy are also impossible to generalize; as many as one-third in Virginia and Maryland supported the Revolution. Reformed clergy were often patriots, particularly in New England. But Pennsylvania's German Reformed, for example, were generally silent concerning politics.[111] There were prominent Presbyterian clergy who supported independence, most notably John Witherspoon (signatory of the Declaration of Independence) and William Tennent III.[112] There were prominent Presbyterian exceptions, such as John Zubly in Savannah, who supported resistance against some policies but not revolution.[113] In a 1775 letter, the Presbyterian

Synod of Philadelphia counseled its churches toward loyalty though not without some sympathy for resistance.[114] Support for independence cannot be ascribed to either Trinitarian or Unitarian theology, as evidenced by the unorthodox Jonathan Mayhew. Mayhew, pastor of Old West Church in Boston, was unorthodox in many dimensions of his theology and would today be called a Unitarian. But this did not diminish his reputation as a leading critic of the Stamp Act nor did it mute the impact of his seminal revolutionary sermons. His *A Discourse Concerning Unlimited Submission* was delivered in 1749 and published in 1750 to commemorate (and celebrate) the one hundredth anniversary of the execution of Charles I. Mayhew's 1750 sermon articulated the historic foundation of English liberties and became the first major tract for resistance against the Crown. *The Snare Broken* was published in 1766 to both give thanks for repeal of the Stamp Act and to warn English leaders of the Americans' right to self-preservation.[115]

Many Patriots were driven by the desire not just for political liberty but also for religious liberty. This group included Baptists and other Separates in New England and denominations seeking disestablishment in Anglican strongholds.[116] It also included those who dreaded the export of Anglican bishops from England to places such as New England where Anglicanism was equated with Romanism. American fear of Roman Catholicism was yet another vestige of America's Reformed heritage. While most Protestants at this time still distrusted Rome, Americans inherited the English eschatological context for Rome described in Chapter 7 in which the pope was the Antichrist and the Roman church the Whore of Babylon. This eschatological context was combined with the fact that Americans had fought a Catholic power in the French and Indian War (1754–1763) and the Church of England still reminded New England Congregationalists of Rome.[117]

Many New England clergy in the Reformed tradition broadcast the theology of liberty.[118] Contrary to the thesis that the Revolution was an Enlightenment affair, Alan Heimert makes the argument that traditional clergy were friends of progress, democracy, revolution, and natural rights. But Heimert's thesis has been questioned, and rightly so.[119] Nathan Hatch, in a study of New England clergy, emphasizes the "republican eschatology" that grew up in historical circumstance and its theological modifications after the Great Awakening.[120] Hatch revisits the rhetoric of the "Old Lights" or "Old Sides" (who generally opposed the revivals) as well as the "New Lights" or "New Sides" (who supported the revivals) and carefully examines the evolving eschatology between the Awakening and the Revolution. Some critics have taken issue with Hatch's characterization that there was an intellectual shift in the New England clergy, which, Hatch claims, "saw the expansion of New England's functional theology to include republican ideas as a primary article of faith."[121] Both Harry Stout and Dale Kuehne believe that too little is made of theological content for its own sake in Hatch's presentation.

Stout states, "The more one reads these sermons, the more one finds unsatisfactory the suggestion that ideas of secular 'republicanism,' 'civil millenarianism,' or class-conscious 'popular ideology' were the primary ideological triggers of radical resistance and violence in the Revolution."[122] There were many streams of theological, philosophical, historical, and legal influence such that one cannot discern a shift with any precision. In other words, it is difficult to successfully paint too many clergy with a broad brush.

The great challenge in reading the political sermons of eighteenth-century America is that they can be read from a variety of perspectives. Massachusetts Congregationalist political thought, for example, appears upon first reading to be indebted to a number of different intellectual traditions, including republicanism and Lockean liberalism (though the "Lockean" part is contestable, since Locke's *Two Treatises* was not printed in America until 1773). If one is familiar with the broad tradition of Reformed political theology, it becomes harder to strictly compartmentalize the content of the political sermons as "Reformed," "liberal," "republican," and so on.[123] Given the different ways in which the covenant was used as political theology, one can argue for both liberty and virtue inside a covenantal framework. This is not an either/or proposition. Both virtue and liberty had been prescribed by Reformed political theologians a hundred years earlier in the English Civil War. They did not see these prescriptions in ideological terms. There is flexibility within Reformed political theology which demonstrates both the genius of the clergy and the value of the covenant. This flexibility is not without tension, however. As Kuehne puts it, "What vexed them [Massachusetts clergy] was trying to create a coherent vision of religious freedom and the Puritan desire that religion pervade all of life, including politics." Did the Congregationalist ministers tempt the "corruption" of Calvinism? Or did the covenant remain central? Kuehne states:

> The covenant remained as important to the [Revolutionary New England] Congregationalists as it was to the Puritans, and it continued to form the basis of their political vision. Although the mature Congregationalist constitution may have several similarities with secular republican thought, in the ministers' eyes it was not secular at all. . . . The future would show a failure of the cement to bond, but if these ministers had been forced to choose between their present Constitutional theory and the covenant, they would have reexamined their political theory immediately.[124]

"Republicanism" or "liberalism" in the sermons is not therefore evidence of a deliberate abandonment of the Reformed tradition for secular political philosophy. Arguments for revolution were an extension of the theological heritage of Reformed Protestantism and not an abrupt shift to secular ideology.[125]

The use of "secular" arguments from nature in Revolutionary War political sermons demonstrates nothing conclusive. Arguments from nature—natural law or natural right—were hardly absent or contradictory in Reformed political theology (see Chapter 9). Arguments from natural law, especially for self-defense, were often extensions of Reformed theology more than anything attributable to abandoning theology for political philosophy.[126] Nature had earlier been a tool in debates over church polity, for example. John Wise's earlier defense of Congregational church polity (drawn largely from nature and arguments by Pufendorf, *Vindication of the Government of New-England Churches* [1717]) was indeed met with opposition by the Mathers. But there is no reason to think that his justification from "nature" was the cause of the Mathers' opposition.[127] Stoddard's *Doctrine of Instituted Churches* argued from "the Light and Law of Nature" without controversy over method.[128] Indeed, when the contrarian and controversial Brattle Street Church (also known as the *Manifesto* Church) defended its constitution as being "from the Law of Nature," the church was only responding to the lead of Cotton Mather and the Cambridge Association. They had defended their church covenant by declaring it to be evident from both divine inspiration and "the Light of Nature."[129] Even as far back as 1642, ministers of the Plymouth Plantation had defended capital punishment for "a certain unnatural vice" as consistent with the law of nature.[130] Even if references to nature could be ascribed to some creeping secularism in New England, Reformed clergy in the Middle Colonies certainly retained theistic language in equal or greater measure.[131]

But this is not to say that clergy used theological arguments exclusively. Well-educated clergy could draw successfully from a variety of sources. During the last half of the eighteenth century, and particularly during the Revolution, other political and legal arguments enjoyed propagation alongside the Reformed political theology.[132] Ministers such as Samuel Cooper had no problem including arguments such as those of Locke or Sidney.[133] Ministers would have seen such sources in political sermons as appropriate, given the religious language of both. The same could also be said of appeals to traditional classical sources, familiar to the clergy as part of the classical discourse that came from their education.[134] Long-standing legal arguments provided by Coke or Blackstone were also readily available to most clergy, especially the university-educated Reformed clergy who were well-schooled in these arguments. Republicanism and religious rhetoric became intertwined.[135] Social contract theory is seen only in retrospect as "liberal." New England clergy readily summoned it as consistent with, if not derivative of, their political theology.[136] After all, social contract theory strongly resembled the same argumentation of covenantal political theology that came along a century before Locke or Hobbes.

Being used in the cause of American liberty, with all of its religious overtones, was indeed a glorious and fitting way for the covenant to see its last full engagement on the political stage. This American episode exemplified what Reformed Protestants arguably did best: provide existential teeth and theological grit to arguments for liberty. The covenant proved itself to have a flexible genius in the eighteenth century. But it had also changed from its soteriological and orthodox beginnings and weathered much in the Anglo-American trials of the mid–seventeenth century.

9 Natural Law and Natural Right in Reformed Political Theology

Having summarized the historical theory and practice of Reformed political theology over three centuries, it now becomes appropriate to situate the Reformed Protestants within the mainstream of political theory. It is important to determine how they used natural law and natural right in their thinking, and how they understood related arguments from reason and from nature. Briefly defined, natural law argues that general revelation or nature can reveal to humankind important moral principles, and these principles are universal and knowable by reason alone. The theory of natural right argues that certain universal human rights are found in the "natural" condition of human beings. The natural condition is often cast as an "original position." This original position exists prior to the creation of any formal civil authority. Whatever pre-political rights can be discerned or posited in the original position then prescribe the origin and limits of civil authority. Early modern right theorists such as John Locke advocated fundamental liberty, equality, property rights, and the right of resistance or revolution. Natural rights theorists also cast civil power as a trust, with magistrates seen as fiduciaries of the people.

The contexts of natural law and natural right are important for arguments about historical continuity and discontinuity. Questioning the Reformed tradition's use of nature in its political theology is complicated by a long-standing but mistaken belief that Reformed Protestants are prejudiced against natural law.[1] But both natural law and arguments from reason or experience were readily used by Reformed Protestants, though not always in the same way as by previous Christian traditions. And it is no mere coincidence that modern natural right thinking took root in countries with a strong Reformed Protestant tradition.

In the following discussion of natural law thinking, the main figures will be, from the sixteenth century, John Calvin, Christopher Goodman, John Knox, and Phillipe Du Plessis Mornay, along with one figure from the seventeenth century,

Samuel Rutherford. In the discussion of natural right, the main authors for study are Mornay and Rutherford. Their theological texts advancing proto-natural right positions are Mornay's *Vindiciae, Contra Tyrannos* and Rutherford's *Lex, Rex.* Both of these texts predate Locke, and both have been compared to Locke's works and asserted (probably unsuccessfully) as influences on Locke's thinking. Locke's Puritan father fought as an officer with Parliamentary forces during the English Civil War, and he was probably familiar with these monarchomachic theories at some level. Thomas P. Peardon, in his introduction to Locke's Second Treatise, notes, "It can safely be supposed that Locke was familiar with the celebrated treatise, Vindiciae contra tyrannos, published anonymously in 1579 and republished in Leyden in 1648." Locke notes in a 1681 cataloging of his books that he owned a copy of the *Vindiciae.*[2]

In the case of *Lex, Rex,* evidence of a link to Locke is purely speculative and circumstantial. Rutherford's *Lex, Rex* was published just three years before Locke came to Westminster as a student, and the Westminster Assembly (of which Rutherford was a member) did meet at the same time that Locke was engaged in his studies. Christian apologist Francis Schaeffer captured the imagination of American Protestants when he claimed that Rutherford's imprint on Locke is evident, but Rutherford's only modern biographer, John Coffey, rejects the idea of any clear influence. There is no clear evidence that Locke ever owned a copy of *Lex, Rex.*[3] Nothing can be conclusively demonstrated to argue for a Reformed influence from either of these works on the thinking of Locke, but the similarity of Locke's arguments to the arguments of Mornay and Rutherford is striking.

REFORMERS AND NATURAL LAW

Would a "Calvinist" argue from nature? On the face of it, this is a silly question. It should be expected that the humanist academic training of the reformers would lead them to make natural law a major category of argumentation. It was a category of argumentation going back to the ancients and a root of Western ethics and politics. But shouldn't Reformed theology's emphasis on postlapsarian corruption and the need for electing grace also discourage them from relying on natural law? Perhaps surprisingly, Reformed theology's emphasis on election and divine sovereignty not only enables *but encourages* attention to natural law. Speaking generally of traditional Christian approaches to ethics and politics, reference to the natural world was another means of authenticating divine truth.[4] Furthermore, while it may seem that Reformed theologians' emphasis on the fallen nature of postlapsarian humankind would disincline them from the theory of natural law, the mystery of election and divine sovereignty coupled with the universal need for government put them in the same place as their predecessors. They required some kind of general revelation to inform politics.[5] They could not rely on one source alone (Scripture) when additional sources (from reason or nature) could appeal to a populace of both believing and unbelieving persons. Furthermore, having more than one source enabled a repetition that could more likely persuade a mind corrupted by sin.

The northern European humanism that characterized the thinking of both Protestantism in general and Britain in particular demonstrated considerable respect for classical sources. In almost every case, the humanists' high regard for the Scriptures complemented rather than contradicted their humanism. The Reformed tradition, like the humanist tradition it drew from, was rich and diverse.[6] Margo Todd describes Puritan humanism as "biblical in its apologetic, eclectic in its sources, mundane in its concerns but religious in its goals, practical in its methodology, and activist in its approach."[7] To understand the reformers, one cannot make scholasticism the equivalent of humanism. The reformers were humanists who wanted to break selectively with scholasticism. This selective break did not mean casting off the previous theological or philosophical system entirely (particularly its use of natural law), or breaking with scholasticism on every point.[8]

Given their humanist training, it is not surprising that the reformers turned to natural law as a form of general revelation. Richard Tuck, a prominent historian of natural right, even argues that Calvinists were better humanists than were many Catholics.[9] Theodore Beza, Calvin's successor in Geneva, was regarded by Montaigne as one of the greatest Latin poets of the century. Thoroughly acquainted with classical texts, Beza saw to it that the Academy of Geneva had a classical foundation to its curriculum. He was responsible for a return to Aristotle, personally insisting on this in a letter to Peter Ramus, a French humanist and favorite logician and rhetorician of some Reformed Protestants.[10] Bullinger and Calvin both had a thoroughly humanist training. Even Martin Luther (who was unfairly caricatured for a Wittenberg sermon calling reason the devil's whore) considered classical studies to be essential background for theology. The same Luther who said of the Dutch humanist Desiderius Erasmus, "[He] does not go beyond the light of nature, may like Moses die in the plains of Moab without entering into the promised land of those higher studies that belong to godliness" also said, "I am persuaded that, without a skilled training in literary studies, no true theology can establish and maintain itself."[11] John Coffey describes young Samuel Rutherford's curriculum as "strikingly secular." Rutherford so embraced his humanist and secular education that he could rightly be called a major figure in the development of the natural law tradition. Alexander Taylor Innes calls Rutherford "St. Thomas and St. Francis under one hood."[12]

NATURAL LAW IN CALVIN

John Calvin was a humanist, and the humanism of his education left a deep impression on his work. Christian humanists Erasmus and Jacob Faber Stapulensis Lefevre have even been credited with Calvin's conversion.[13] He was deeply influenced by the Renaissance's attention to both individualism and natural law.[14] One of the humanist legacies he left was the Geneva Academy, an institution whose library was later sought out for purchase by Thomas Jefferson.[15] While Calvin appreciated the fruits of his humanist education, he did assert that there were limitations on human reason. But one must be precise in understanding Calvin here. He was emphatic about the failure of natural reason *alone* to discern either the true nature of God or even what was truly good.[16] He also argued that all theology, apart from Christ, would be fatally corrupted by sin. As he put it, "Therefore all theology separated from Christ is not only confused and empty but also mad, deceiving and counterfeit."[17] But these three points hardly amount to a rejection of reason, humanism, natural law, or philosophy. Nor does Calvin's emphasis on Scripture equate to anything approaching "fundamentalism" to the exclusion of arguments from nature.

To understand Calvin better, one must separate (as much as he will allow) the role of nature in conversion and faith from the role of nature in all other matters. Like other reformers, Calvin believed that the Creation left secular philosophers without excuse if they did not see God's hand and goodness in it.[18] But this does not mean that nature was good only for leaving unbelief without excuse or for providing a redundant revelation.[19]

In his *Institutes,* Calvin makes an important distinction between earthly things and heavenly things. Note especially his reference to politics and its reference to nature:

> By earthly things, I mean those which relate not to God and his kingdom, to true righteousness and future blessedness, but have some connection with the present life, and are in a manner confined within its boundaries. By heavenly things, I mean the pure knowledge of God, the method of true righteousness, and the mysteries of the heavenly kingdom. To the former belong matters of policy and economy, all mechanical arts and liberal studies. To the latter . . . belong the knowledge of God and of his will, and the means of framing the life in accordance with them. As to the former, the view to be taken is this: Since man is by nature a social animal, he is disposed, from natural instinct, to cherish and preserve society; and accordingly we see that the minds of all men have impressions of civil order and honesty. Hence it is that every individual understands how human societies must be regulated by laws, and also is able to comprehend the principles of

> those laws. Hence the universal agreement in regard to such subjects, both among nations and individuals, the seeds of them being implanted in the breasts of all without a teacher or lawgiver.[20]

In his dedicated discussion of politics at the conclusion of the *Institutes,* Calvin argued forcefully for natural law and against the Anabaptist adoption of the Mosaic Law for civil polities.[21] So while Calvin was skeptical about the role of nature and traditional philosophy in reaching to spiritual things, he did not extend that skepticism to earthly things and to politics in particular. Those subjects could certainly be informed by secular sources. Calvin frequently cited classical authors (including Cicero, Homer, Aristotle, Plato, and others) when outlining the civil magistrate's responsibilities. He also commends the degree of truth evident in secular writers, asserting that their wisdom should "teach us how many gifts the Lord has left in possession of human nature, notwithstanding of its having been despoiled of the true good."[22] There is an important difference between reason ruling the soul for earthly things and reason ruling the soul for heavenly things. Natural law can have more than one function. For example, Calvin clearly believed natural law greatly inferior to divine law for moral instruction to Christians. But regarding the earthly subjects' touching of all persons, natural law had great legitimacy and value.

Calvin's distinction between earthly and heavenly things is often lost on scholars. Ralph Hancock, for example, seems confused by Calvin's discussions of reason and sin. Hancock insists on imposing categories of investigation that Calvin would neither recognize nor accept. Hancock writes, "Calvin's quite frequent appeal to natural law, despite his consistent emphasis on the depravity of nature, has long presented an obstacle to efforts to provide a complete and coherent account of Calvin's political teaching."[23] That statement tells us more about modern interpreters than it does about Calvin.

Calvin refers to the natural law every place that moral questions are treated in his theology.[24] This does not mean that Calvin always agreed with his medieval predecessors on the precise use of moral law in prescribing morality. But his disagreement was not with the content of the natural law. Rather, Calvin's disagreement with medieval predecessors concerned man's ability to pursue the good apart from divine grace. Reformers agreed with their medieval predecessors on man's knowledge of the natural law. Where they disagreed was in the natural ability to obey it. Conscience, according to Calvin, is more a function of the intellect than of the will.[25] That is, it was more readily known than obeyed. This is where lapsarian theological distinctions become most important, though Reformed teaching on the conscience did not remain static with Calvin.[26]

NATURAL LAW IN GOODMAN AND KNOX

Even Goodman and Knox, though extremely covenantal and scriptural in their political thinking, appealed to natural reason. They both believed it could be called upon to demonstrate some plain points of political theory. Speaking of the case of Mattathias's rebellion against the Syrian Greeks in the second century BC, Goodman wrote: "Yea and if there were neither example nor Scripture to prove his fact; yet would natural reason compel every man to allow the same, as most Godly. And that therein he did nothing but his duty, which thing was approved in the judgment of that age, and as a lawful fact and monument write and left to be read by all posterity, the law of nature so directing their judgments."[27] Mattathias seems an odd choice for a Protestant such as Goodman to choose, given that his history is found in the Books of the Maccabees (a book not included in the Protestant Bible). Goodman argues that his case is not to be referenced because it is in a canonical book, but rather because it is a case that demonstrates armed resistance to be justified by both reason and Scripture.

Knox also relied on reason to reinforce clear points from Scripture. Like other Reformed Protestants, he looked to Scripture and to the Church Fathers, but he also cited quite a few sources outside the Bible.[28] He references Aristotle and Cicero, Themistius and Democritus.[29] This is not to say that Knox was equally comfortable trafficking in both types of sources.[30] But Knox was ready, willing, and able to argue that demonstrations of his political prescriptions were not confined to Scripture.

NATURAL LAW AND NATURAL RIGHT IN MORNAY

Mornay's *Vindiciae* also did not shy away from secular sources that drew on nature and experience. His language is perhaps the most secular of the sixteenth-century Reformed writers' rhetoric, appealing as he was to moderate Catholics in France.[31] *Vindiciae, Contra Tyrannos* is so dependent on secular sources that it is easy to overlook its dependence on biblical theology. Indeed, Mornay's covenant scheme is presented in such a generous and cosmopolitan manner that scholars continue to debate the precise consequence of theology in it.[32] But while Mornay is comfortable with an eclectic variety of sources, he also distinguishes what is demonstrated (that is, taken from Scripture) from what is merely confirmed (that is, taken from nature, law, or authoritative pronouncement) or supplemented (that is, from custom).[33] In other words, the secular sources are used not with parity to Scripture but rather to supplement or confirm. This broad arsenal of sources is characteristic of Mornay's other writing. Paul T. Fuhrmann echoes John T. McNeill in calling Mornay a founder of modern ecumenicity.[34]

Mornay calls on a broad array of sources to work in the defense of liberty, including the assertion of certain natural rights. The *Vindiciae* is divided into four questions concerning civil government, and the third question provides the greatest evidence of natural right language in Mornay. The question is directed to tyrants—those whom Mornay described as "deaf unto the voice of that law which is grounded upon reason."[35] Mornay argues that "the people establish kings, puts the scepter into their hands, and who with their sufferages, approves the election."[36] Mornay also casts the people as intermediary for God, emphasizing natural equality and popular sovereignty. He casts political power as a fiduciary power, just as the early modern natural rights theorists did.[37] Mornay argues that the "whole body" of the people is above the king, and he readily cites many "sacred and profane" examples to demonstrate his point.[38] And like Rutherford, Mornay saw the power of consent that lies in the people as undiminished by time or succession.[39] Mornay's acceptance of hereditary monarchy—conditional on its being an "elected system"—would strike most moderns as archaic.[40] But it must be remembered that even a natural rights icon such as John Locke did not disapprove of hereditary monarchy or consider it inconsistent with natural right or popular consent.[41]

Mornay's pre-political persons are described as equally free and consenting to government for the sake of some advantage not yet found in nature. In a passage that could have been written by any natural right philosopher a century later, Mornay says, "In the first place every one consents, that men *by nature* loving liberty, and hating servitude, born rather to command, than obey, have not willingly admitted to be governed by another, and renounced as it were the privilege of nature, by submitting themselves to the command of others, *but for some special and great profit they expected from it.*"[42] And in passages that Quentin Skinner finds indicative of modern natural right language, Mornay dwells at length on the importance of civil justice applied to person and property.[43] Mornay includes a defense of private property, asserting against kings that "Every man loves and cherishes his own."[44] Citing both the Old Testament and classical histories, he asserts that property is the foundation of government, an idea that is found generations later in the natural right arguments of Locke and Rousseau. Mornay states, "When, therefore, that these words of mine and thine entered into the world, and that differences fell amongst fellow citizens, touching the propriety of goods, and wars amongst neighboring people about the right of their confines . . . kings were created in the first ages; to wit, to administer justice at home and to be leaders in the wars abroad."[45]

Mornay's text prefigures seventeenth-century natural right constitutionalism: The law is king, and the king is not the source of law. Mornay even calls law the "soul" that animates the king.[46] The king is accountable to both justice and divine law.[47] The people are equally accountable to the law.[48] Referencing Saint Augustine,

Mornay argues that those who enjoy political rule are similar to husbands or fathers only insofar as they *serve* those that they command.[49] Mornay's argument here is very traditional and goes back even to Plato: To command is to serve.[50] The king's power over life and death is tied to his responsibility for the "benefit and profit of the public state."[51] To submit to a cutthroat as king is to deny the benefit of political association and to undermine the whole point of political association.[52]

Mornay is emphatic that resistance to tyranny is just. Mornay defines tyrants, eligible for "suppression and expulsion," as those who threaten the minds, souls, bodies, or estates of the people.[53] His first argument for resistance is drawn from natural law and self-defense of life and liberty.[54] This is not simply the common argument of Mornay's era, that religious oppression justifies resistance. Emphasizing the role of government for secular purposes as well, Mornay writes, "Whereby it plainly appears, that not for religion only, but even for our country and our possessions, we may fight and take arms against a tyrant."[55]

Political ideas associated with modern "natural right" include asserting that liberty and equality are ordained by nature, the civil magistrate is a fiduciary, government is the creation of popular consent, property rights provide a core motivation for civil society, and the right of active or violent resistance to tyranny. All these positions can be discerned in Mornay, who also provides one of the most explicit and detailed presentations of covenantal political theology. Mornay's *Vindiciae* demonstrates that what is considered by many a largely "modern" and "secular" argument is quite at home in the covenantal political theology of the sixteenth century.

NATURAL LAW AND NATURAL RIGHT IN RUTHERFORD

Among Reformed theologians, we perhaps find the most generous and ecumenical view of natural law and natural right in Samuel Rutherford. Coffey notes that in the course of his works Rutherford refers to over seven hundred different authors: "Spanish Jesuits, rabbinical commentators, Greek and Latin Fathers, classical philosophers, contemporary Protestants, medieval scholastic theologians, and of course, the sixteenth-century Reformers . . . roughly divided into five broad categories: classical, patristic, medieval, post-Reformation Catholics, and Protestants."[56] The list includes authors that were important for the late-medieval development of natural right theory: Aquinas, Gerson, Suarez, Almain, Ockham, and Mair.[57] Like many of his fellow reformers, Rutherford was well-schooled in Aristotle and even cited him as an authority against Thomas Hooker in their disputations over church government.[58] He did not share the Ramist preoccupations of some of his Reformed contemporaries. As Coffey put it, "It is hard to find much trace of Ramist logic in his work."[59]

Rutherford also followed the lead of George Buchanan in defending Presbyterianism using a natural law argument. Some might view this use of natural law as a betrayal of the Reformation, a turning away from orthodoxy on postlapsarian reason.[60] To the contrary, such use of natural law was certainly consistent with the orthodox position, not only among Scottish Presbyterians but also among other seventeenth-century Reformed Protestants.

Federal theology not only made natural law binding on all men and a vehicle for articulating political theory, but also was often a necessary precursor to the divine law and spiritual conversion. This view stood in direct opposition to Rutherford's opponents, including Antinomians and the Anabaptists. Each, Rutherford believed, held a contemptuous and heretical disregard for created things as spiritual vehicles. He went so far as to equate disregard of nature to the ancient heresy of Manichaeism and cast it as a threat to social order.[61]

Rutherford gives priority to Scripture but braids it with secular sources.[62] His approach in the case of politics is summarized early in *Lex, Rex:* "What is warranted by the direction of nature's light is warranted by the law of nature, and consequently by a divine law; for who can deny the law of nature to be a divine law?"[63] Both regenerate and unregenerate had moral power to submit to superiors, though the divine law made the conscience more subject to political authority.[64] To acknowledge the abuses of intellect did not constitute a categorical argument against its use. Rutherford was working against a contemporary gradual divorce of reason from a theocentric and covenantal framework and foresaw in Hugo Grotius, for example, a move toward a political theory essentially free of theological presuppositions.[65]

As with Calvin, one understands Rutherford by recognizing the contexts in which he is speaking of nature and reason; when speaking of righteous and authentic Christian conduct, his discussion of nature must give way to grace. Thus, when speaking of it in an ethical sense, Rutherford speaks of nature as at once both fallen and broken; it is corrupted by sin.[66] But nature remains unbroken and sinless in its metaphysical constitution. This includes things as God made them in their nature. Created things still require grace, but not the same grace necessary to redeem from sin.[67] Rutherford concludes, as Calvin does, that Word and Spirit must work together in conversion. The Word is reasonable, but it requires Spirit. The Spirit moves only through the Word.[68] But as with Calvin, one must separate heavenly from earthly things in order to understand Rutherford's use of natural law and reason. Rutherford's approach was also not unlike the ones taken by the American Puritans. Natural law could inform earthly matters quite handily, but had to give way to grace and the sanctification that came with spiritual regeneration and conversion.[69] But conversion is not the same as politics.

An examination of Rutherford's *Lex, Rex* reveals a strong concordance with the themes of modern natural right: natural liberty and equality, government by consent, magistrates as fiduciaries, the right of resistance, and an emphasis on property rights. For Rutherford, the origin of civil power is both divinely ordained and natural. It is ordained insofar as God is the author of human nature. But, contra modern natural rights interpreters such as Richard Tuck or Leo Strauss, God's being the author of political power in no way undermines the idea that individual persons are the authors of civil power.[70] Rutherford wrote:

> All civil power is immediately from God in its root; in that, 1st, God hath made man a social creature, and one who inclineth to be governed by man, then certainly he must have put this power in man's nature: so are we, by good reason, taught by Aristotle. 2d, God and nature intendeth the policy and peace of mankind, then must God and nature have given to mankind a power to compass this end; and this must be the power of government. . . . As domestic society is by nature's instinct, so is civil society natural *in radice,* in the root, and voluntary *in modo,* in the manner of coalescing. . . . [I]t is natural that they join in a civil society.[71]

The phrase "inclineth to be governed by man" in no way denies natural equality. The political state is preceded by a state of nature with only domestic (familial) power, not civil power: "Now, the people were a people many years before there was a government, (save domestic)."[72] For Rutherford, this state of nature is a state of both freedom and equality.

Contrary to the criticism that reformers supported a divine-right-of-kings approach to civil government, Rutherford asserts something very "Lockean" at the outset of *Lex, Rex:* "If all men be born equally free, as I hope to prove, there is no reason in nature why one man should be king and lord over another. . . I conceive all jurisdiction of man over man to be as it were artificial and positive, and that it inferreth some servitude whereof nature from the womb hath freed us"; also, "Princedom, empire, kingdom, or jurisdiction hath its rise from a positive and secondary law of nations, and not from the law of pure nature."[73] Later he argues, "Man is born by nature free from all subjection, except of that which is most kindly and natural, and that is fatherly or filial subjection."[74] No one is born either a king or a subject.[75] The end of all laws is the safety of the people and not simply the will of the king. Without this "intrinsical worth," the king cannot put his stamp on the law.[76]

Rutherford's jurisprudence is not rooted in a theory of Divine Command but instead in a study of how natural inclinations reflect divine intent. On this point, Rutherford is indistinguishable from other natural rights theorists. Men submit to civil law because of their natural inclinations toward self-love and self-preservation.[77] It is in human nature to be political and to form political societies. This instinct comes not from any divine intervention. The desire to be in a political society comes from what natural right theorists would agree are men's "natural right" inclinations, self-preservation and ownership.[78] Both rights are obliged by natural reason, which Rutherford calls "God's court."[79] Property plays an important part in self-preservation. The establishment of government, freedom, and equality requires the safety of one's material goods as means of self-preservation and resource to defend against tyranny. Echoing Mornay's discussion of property as the basis for government, Rutherford states, "It is morally impossible that there should not be a distinction of *meum et tuum,* mine and thine; and the decalogue forbidding theft, and coveting the wife of another man . . . doth evidence to us, that the division of things is so far forth (men now being in the state of sin) of the law of nature, that it hath evident ground in the law of nations." Private property is rooted in the law of nature and the basis of community, Rutherford argues. A tyrant is defined as one who would take the proper goods of his subjects as if they were his own.[80]

Rutherford's interplay of nature and divine appointment in establishing political society is not nearly as simplistic as Tuck or others might suggest.[81] Rutherford presents a thoughtful evaluation of the relationships among human law, natural law, divine law, and eternal law. Human law is the product of political association, necessitated by the inconveniences of the state of nature. The natural law, defined as men's reason, drives man to political society. This is all part of the eternal law, operating through the natural law and supplementing it by the divine law. The power of the government is from God but mediated by the people; it is the same power that they held in the state of nature. "The king is said to be from God by way of naked approbation; God given to a people power to appoint what government they shall think good, but instituting none in special in his word."[82] Rutherford later argues, prefiguring Locke and his natural rights theory, that civil power not only comes from but also devolves back to the people.[83] It is therefore God's plan that the people are the essential creators of political rule which itself is necessitated only by political agreement—a kind of proto-social contract.

For Rutherford, liberty is a gift of God because it is a gift evident in nature. The people cannot surrender what they did not have by natural law or divine grant, a right to destroy themselves.[84] In other words, the people cannot make a suicide pact by consenting to tyranny. Rutherford's list of abuses in I Samuel 8 includes both material and spiritual tyranny. If Rutherford had not initially posited (what we view in hindsight as) a "Lockean" state of nature, he could be seen to be winding up at the same absolutist conclusions as Suarez or Thomas Hobbes. But unlike Suarez, Rutherford argues that the natural right of persons cannot be surrendered to absolute political rule. This has to be kept in mind when interpreting Rutherford's argument that the community "resigneth" their power to civil rulers. Rule requires consent, necessitated by man's natural liberty and equality. Rutherford notes, "As a man may not take away his liberty without his own consent, so can he not, without his own consent, give his liberty to be subject to penal laws under a prince, without his own consent."[85] Should the king betray his trust, the people are no longer bound to obey. There is no obligation to stand by a "bad bargain" as there is in Suarez or Hobbes.[86] Rutherford wrote, "A power to destruction was never given, nor can it, by rational nature, be given. . . . A people free may not, and ought not, totally surrender their liberty to a prince, confiding in his goodness."[87]

More than forty years before Locke published *Two Treatises on Government* (1689), Rutherford articulated ruling as a "fiduciary" responsibility with an accompanying doctrine of resistance.[88] To betray the responsibility that the ruler has toward God and man, mediated through the will of the people, is to be a tyrant. And on this question, Rutherford echoes Bullinger. Tyranny is not from God.[89] Rutherford's citizens are free to withdraw their consent and also to resist. The same God who mediates rule through the people is also capable of contesting political rulers through acts of the people.[90] Rutherford demonstrates no equivocation on the subject of resistance. To live under tyranny is to lose the benefits sought by leaving the state of nature in the first place. Tyranny is anarchy, and worse than the anarchy of nature.[91]

Like his Reformed predecessors, Rutherford did not interpret Romans 13 to command unconditional political obedience. This should be noted by modern scholars who, when they discover Protestants who assert a biblical right to disobedience, attribute it to some philosophical takeover by a secular, natural right tradition.[92] But no Reformed Protestant presumed St. Paul to command unconditional obedience (as previous chapters have demonstrated). Rutherford, even more than other Reformed Protestants, goes to great lengths in parsing Romans 13. His argument is a crucial step in the development of resistance theory. Rutherford wrote, "It is evident from Rom xiii. that all subjection and obedience to higher powers commanded there, is subjection to the power and office of the magistrate *in abstracto,* or, which is all one, to the person using the power lawfully, and that no subjection is due by that text, or any word of God, to the abused and tyrannical power of the king."[93] Rutherford is saying that by establishing political authority for good, God denies the license usurped by tyrants. He directs his reader to the phrase "of God" in Romans 13:1. The meaning of this phrase denies the tyrant any legitimate claim to rule against the express commands of God. Rutherford follows Bullinger's lead:

> Tyranny being a work of Satan, is not from God, because sin, either habitual or actual, is not from God: the magistrate, as magistrate, is good in nature of office, and the intrinsic end of his office, (Rom. xiii.4) for he is the minister of God for thy good; and, therefore, a power ethical, politic, or moral, to oppress, is not from God, and is not a power, but a licentious deviation of a power; and is no more from God, but from sinful nature and the old serpent, than a license to sin.[94]

There is no natural authority in the tyrant who denies men the benefit of political society for which they left the state of nature. Nor is there divine authority in the tyrant, having denied his responsibility to do the good implicit in anything done "of God." To act by violence and without law denies civil magistry altogether. Hence, to resist the tyrant is not to resist God at all. Rather it is to assert God's law against the tyrant.[95]

Against the notion (advocated by some) that tyranny is a deserved punishment of God, Rutherford offers plain logic. If Christians are meant only to suffer under tyranny, then no recourse to end their suffering could be biblically justified. The scourge of tyranny, while certainly painful, would obligate passivity and willful suffering. There could not be any biblical remedy to avoid it, not even self-exile. If tyranny were the deserved punishment of God, to escape it would be the same as escaping the justice of God. Against those who cite tyranny as ordained of God in the first place and therefore requiring passivity in the face of it, Rutherford asks if the Israelites were to lay down their arms and pray to God in the face of the Assyrians or if famine is to be met with prayer rather than industrious bread production.[96]

It is cases such as Rutherford and Mornay that should force scholars to reexamine their assertions about a discontinuity between political theology and political philosophies calling on nature, natural law, or rights derived from an original position. Prominent Reformed political theologians were not only prepared to call on both arguments from nature and secular sources. They may have had some hand in informing the "Enlightenment" traditions that supposedly grew up entirely ex nihilo in the very countries where Reformed political theology dominated political thinking.

10 The Reformation in Retrospect

REDISCOVERING COVENANTS

Reformed Protestant Hebraism, emphasizing the Old Testament patriarchs, circumcision, and covenants, was a means of recasting the Christian's relationship with God. Calvin and Bullinger and other sixteenth-century reformers were looking at the same biblical text as their Roman Catholic predecessors, but their construction of a new theological continuity stretching back to the Hebrew patriarchs convinced them they had rediscovered biblical truths both ancient and foundational. This not only justified their reforming effort, it gave that reforming effort a powerful symbol and device. The covenant, as a symbol, provided a moral ethos that could define the new theological community of Reformed Protestants on a par with the Old Testament's chosen people. As a device, it cast salvation largely in legal terms consistent with northern European humanism and its emphasis on law.

When viewed as an imposition or a demand, the covenant asserted the sovereignty of God to do with His creatures as He saw fit. This was consistent with Reformed Protestant theology, which emphasized divine holiness, justice, and mercy. When viewed as something more akin to a contract both voluntary and conditional, it recognized that the sovereignty of God did not negate the responsibility of persons. Thus, the covenant preserved the rights of God and man.

Reformed Protestantism understood that the biblical narrative is not a story of puppets or of push-pull cause-and-effect. It is a story of redemption, and redemption follows failure. The Bible's patriarchs and leaders proved capable of great deceits and betrayals. Christ's parables tell of stony ground, unfaithful servants, prodigal sons, and barren fig trees. This recounting of failures enabled reformers to talk about the covenant of salvation as both bilateral and unilateral at the same time. God defined terms and in some mysterious way enabled believers to persevere to the end, but He also called on them to heed and hearken to terms, leaving persons without excuse.

The covenant became a perfect tool for politics. The terms of salvation appeared almost contractual. Why should not the order, justice, and rewards of the civil magistrate work in much the same way? The covenant made divine attributes accessible and applicable, resembling the power of civil authorities. God established *order* at creation, the same kind of order established by civil law. God's *justice* is manifest from the Fall until Judgment Day, and civil magistrates execute justice as well. God's *rewards* are bestowed graciously and powerfully, but not without terms of performance. If divine authority could be fit to conditional terms of rewards and punishments, the civil magistrate could have no better model. Liberty and order were thus complementary.

The covenant was both liberating and challenging. It enabled new understandings of freedom and equality. It respected individualism but always in the context of duties and community. All men and women found themselves under the same terms of redemption, the same economy of salvation. The covenant asserted the importance of the individual conscience. But while the covenant offered many advantages over secular political philosophies, it also imposed many difficult demands. As a covenant of salvation, persons were always called to terms that required divine grace, and this grace was found in a community deliberately called out of the world. Demands of moral improvement and separation, coupled with the desire to appropriate the mysterious means of grace, introduced unprecedented challenges into politics.

REFORMING POLITICS

Whether the Reformation was a restoration, as the reformers insisted, or it was a revolution, as its opponents insisted, it resulted in a re-formation of politics. This re-formation had a significant impact on Anglo-American political theory. Protestant reformers were first motivated primarily by what they viewed as corruption of authority in both the political and the ecclesiastical realms. They responded to that corruption by calling for moral reformation of the use of authority. Insofar as the Bible cast authority as a delegated trust from God, power had to be used in accordance with biblical prescriptions and proscriptions. Though the idea of righteous resistance to tyranny did not begin in the Reformation, there was something radically innovative in this new re-formation of politics.

Every Christian, especially magistrates, became a watchman against the abuse of authority. At first, the Protestants resisted the abuse of papal authority, but they soon directed their polemics at the legal abuse of civil authority as well.

As arguments progressed, the right of resistance and revolution became a duty. Some reformers even cast the origins of civil society from the standpoint of an "original position," long before this was done by well-known political theorists such as Hobbes, Locke, or Rousseau. Civil government and political society was not cast as something created by the will of God alone or by some organic process. Rather, it was something that came from the will of God as expressed and activated by human nature and the consent of the people. Though the idea of political consent did not begin with the reformers, their articulation of consent as a covenant gave the idea new life and opened the door for secular and less demanding social contract theories.

The reformers proved conservative even in the midst of their political revolution, however. They retained much of the political theory that came before them. As humanists in the commonwealth tradition, the principle of *salus populi* remained an important foundation of Reformed Protestant political theory. Varying accommodations were made for natural law and reason as tools to legitimate political orientation and argument. Reformed Protestant implementation of the biblical narrative was often done through the lens of standing legal institutions and jurisprudence, though religious enthusiasms distorted that use to varying degrees in the Wars of the Three Kingdoms.

All reformers agreed that politics succeeded when it enabled faithfulness on the part of both ruler and the ruled. Faithfulness consisted in three things: religion, morality, and political authority. Religious faithfulness minimally required a broad civil and social adherence to Protestant orthodoxy, perhaps with some narrow toleration for other believers. It also required a close civil-ecclesiastical partnership, prophetic witness to civil rulers by the clergy, punishment of heterodoxy, and close attention to true piety and religious sincerity in churches. Moral faithfulness required attendance to the moral prescriptions of the Bible. It was accomplished most often by the grace imparted in worship, preaching, and sacraments. Only secondarily was it accomplished by civil sanction against immorality. When these two kinds of faithfulness, religious and moral, were secured so far as the postlapsarian condition would allow, providential promises of blessing would follow. The third category of political faithfulness was the one on which the other two depended. Not only must the civil polity be rightly conceived (implicitly or explicitly through the covenant); it also must have its authority rightly bounded as a delegation from God. Neither the civil magistrate nor the people could misuse the authority or the right that had been delegated to them. All authority, magisterial or popular, had to be properly bounded. Abuses of power were violations of covenant faithfulness. Abuses or neglect would not only bring a disordering of political (or ecclesiastical) societies, it would invite providential sanction. Resistance thus took on a moral dimension. Believing watchmen were to stand guard against abuse of power on the part of rulers or complicit acquiescence on the part of the people.

Faithfulness in all three areas brought liberty, and covenantal political theology is centered on liberty. One could be cynical and argue that this liberty was incomplete in the British and early American practice. After all, most reformers did not believe in wide tolerance for religious dissenters. Church attendance, justified under the covenant of works or preparation theology, was often required. Admittedly, the reformers were not classical liberals. Nor would they have seen eye to eye with proto-liberals who followed them in the Enlightenment or the Republic of Letters. But the reformers merit criticism largely in hindsight. The reformers' emphasis on liberty is an important voice in the rhetoric and theory of modern political development. Though there were other voices for liberty in the sixteenth century, none could claim influence as great as Reformed Protestantism. It was under the leadership of Reformed Protestants that some of the best innovations of modern politics took root. This includes the separation of church and state (which began with Calvin's assertion of independent church discipline), moral condemnation of tyranny as abuse of a popular trust, and the accompanying doctrine of resistance.

VARIATIONS IN COVENANTAL POLITICS: DISAGREEMENTS AND TENSIONS

No political tradition of consequence, the covenant tradition included, is monolithic. The covenant can be seen as a conceptual device, much like the original position or social contract device in liberalism. It can also be seen as a symbol. All devices and symbols can be troublesome in their interpretation and application. Furthermore, diversities of biblical hermeneutic and systematic theologies underlying covenants account for variations and tensions. The covenant provided a comprehensive and corporate vision of society. In some ways this was not much different from the medieval vision of society wherein church and state worked together to attend to all aspects of the human life and soul. The reformers' break with Rome ended a unified Christendom on the medieval model, but retained a catholic outlook nevertheless. The new comprehensive Reformed vision was inspired by their view of corporate accountability under the covenants. Societies, and the corporate bodies that comprised them, were in a covenant with God. This was not because every member of the society subscribed to the Christian faith. Nor was the "invisible church" (the body of true believers) the basis of the covenant, at least in the beginning. Moral faithfulness, even if only to the universal terms of the human conscience, was the minimum that God expected. Pagan societies could operate according to the wisdom of nature, but that wisdom was only barely adequate. Much more was expected of those to whom God had given His revealed Word. God had great things in store for faithful societies. Many clergy applied this argument to America and Britain, implicitly if not explicitly. Only the more radical Separatists such as Roger Williams dissented from the application of that Hebrew covenant to their own societies.[1] (The assertions of covenant continuity in Bullinger's *De Testamento* survived for at least a century.) But even when Williams rejected covenant continuity with Abraham, this was arguably done on Reformed grounds too. Williams was simply denying the civil component of that continuity with Abraham.

In the medieval conception of society, faithfulness to God was accomplished through faithfulness in church attendance and sacraments. So long as there was broad subscription to these practices, there was wide latitude for secular society. The reformers, dissenting from the Roman church, took a much different view of grace and faith. Catholics were criticized by the reformers for eclipsing true faith with "works."[2] Reformers emphasized preaching and a modified liturgy to complement the sacraments. The final question to be sorted out in Anglo-American Reformed practice was whether the church was to primarily serve members of the covenant of grace or members of the covenant of works or both. The answer to this question determined how the church would mirror ancient Israel.

Independents, Congregationalists, and Presbyterians in the seventeenth century did not always take all their cues directly from Calvin or Bullinger and the sixteenth century. But Calvin and Bullinger along with Martin Bucer, Peter Martyr Vermigli and others began the Reformed Protestant debate over sacraments and church discipline. Independents and Congregationalists, more so than Presbyterians, emphasized the importance of faithfulness and sincere profession among those persons constituting the church. Only within a sincere and pious church, made purer by the discerning eye of elders and clergy, could true piety be enabled. True piety would enable moral and religious faithfulness in the society at large. But would the parish model, which was more attractive to Presbyterians, tempt confusing tares with wheat? This remained a tension in Independent and Congregationalist political theology as they strove to accommodate the covenant of grace while guarding the purity of the church. Political society remained, by definition, in covenant with God. Most Independents and Congregationalists implicitly still believed this; only the more radical Separatists explicitly denied it. But the terms of that covenant depended largely on the faithfulness of churches and their members. Heresy still had to be avoided and church attendance encouraged.

Presbyterians took the covenant of works more seriously insofar as they focused on national faithfulness across the lines of both church and society. They could not have believed that the covenant of works would result in salvation. At best, the futility of works could be used by God to direct one to the perfect covenant of grace in His economy of salvation. But salvation was not the only point of the covenant of works. It served to order societies and was no less part of God's wise providence. Thus, Presbyterians viewed society as a hybrid of faithfulness to both the covenant of works and the covenant of grace. Faithfulness to the covenant of works was accomplished more through the parish model of the church. Presbyterian use of the federal scheme also allowed for a wider secular sphere. Political theory and jurisprudence were free to draw from secular British traditions, including natural law and common law. This openness to secular arguments makes the Presbyterians and some American Congregationalists seem more mainstream and modern from our perspective. But Presbyterian insistence upon religious intolerance was also a feature of the parish model. Independents could insist on toleration, not so much because they respected differences but because toleration became the logical conclusion of their desire to separate from obligatory union with other churches.

THE LEGACY OF THE COVENANT IN ANGLO-AMERICAN POLITICS

The covenant enjoyed the zenith of its power in the seventeenth century as variations of Reformed theology predominated in Britain and America. It met harsh resistance after the Restoration in Britain because of its association with the execution of Charles I. But even before its eventual demise in Britain, tensions between Presbyterians and Independents revealed some of the problems inherent in applying the covenant symbol to politics.

American Puritans (mainly Congregationalists) were not directly caught up in the crucible of the British civil wars and enjoyed much more freedom to explore the covenant, but this freedom did not preserve it. Rather, the Americans were freed merely to become further entangled in the internal tensions of Reformed political theology and to face crucibles of their own. They struggled to define the appropriate and successful church-state partnership that could adapt to demographic changes and theological challenges. Ironically, this struggle initiated the Great Awakening and essentially ended the traditional ecclesiastical-civil covenant in America while trying to revive its original spirit of morality and community. The covenant was revived during the American War for Independence, but essentially faded from explicit political thinking thereafter. Even the great piety of Americans could not save the covenant.

Insofar as covenants lie at the root of modern constitutionalism, one might argue that the covenant idea lingers in the greatest of constitutions, composed in Philadelphia in 1787. Perhaps the covenant idea can also be found in the Declaration of Independence or state constitutions, or in the American invention of modern federalism.[3] America's covenantal legacy also lingers in presidential proclamations, holiday proclamations, political rhetoric and even a contemporary jeremiad tradition.[4] The lessons of the covenantal tradition are certainly not forgotten altogether.

Despite its failures, the covenant device has proved to be surprisingly flexible in many respects. It impressively introduced and sustained biblical political concepts and gave them an important role in the development of modern politics. It was also able to survive its own radical inclinations much longer than might have been predicted. Radical interpretations were moderated by the reformers' appreciation of commonwealth and natural law. Temptations toward millenarianism and revivalism (as outgrowths of covenantalism) were thwarted mainly by measured opposition to "enthusiasm," together with the Reformed humanism. In the American case, for example, one finds in John Witherspoon both a determined patriot and an opponent of revivalism.[5] These kinds of multiple routes for political theology had the effect of keeping the covenant grounded in prudent application.

There is also an internal logic in covenantal political theology that limits the grant and use of political power. These internal limits led to some interesting consequences during the English Civil War, for example. Independents used their Reformed theology (applying divine sovereignty over salvation) to argue against the imposition of Presbyterianism. Presbyterians used their Reformed theology (applying the covenant of works) to argue against the radical implications of Independent jurisprudence. Each had the effect of blunting the radicalism of the other. Without this kind of built-in restraint, the covenant probably would have been associated only with its more radical interpretations and abandoned altogether sooner.

Part III

PART III

11 Contemporary Perspectives on Covenanting

Several modern scholars of political theory have studied the prospects of covenants for contemporary politics. Eric Voegelin argued the covenant to be an important but precarious political symbol. Daniel Elazar argued for the continuing relevance of political covenanting. David Novak has taken the most exclusive view of covenanting, leading to the most narrow contemporary application for covenants. All three authors prove helpful in determining a proper perspective on covenanting in the twenty-first century.

ERIC VOEGELIN

Rather than create separate categories of philosophy and religion as his contemporary Leo Strauss did, Voegelin argues that both philosophy and religious texts can provide insight into the tension man feels as a spiritual being. There are no dichotomies between philosophy and religion, or between reason and revelation, in Voegelin's arguments. All serve to address man's participation in the mystery of being. All are equally legitimate sources for understanding man's spiritual condition.

Voegelin presents the biblical covenant (*berith*) with Israel as being one of the symbols in history that relieve the anxiety of being, which is common to all persons.[1] The biblical covenant resembles the existential tension of man himself, who finds himself in the Metaxy, a term Voegelin uses to describe existence between the divine (God) and the mundane. Within Voegelin's framework, the struggle of Israel is representative of the struggle of all who are tempted to seek the Promised Land in time and this present world.[2] Israel was, as Voegelin put it, "a people that moved on the historical scene while living toward a goal beyond history."[3] The idea of being a "chosen people" asserts a qualitative leap and conversion in resolving the tension inherent in the Metaxy. The idea is one particular response to the revelation of divine being. But Voegelin argues that only Jeremiah and to some degree Amos fully articulate the true meaning of the theophany, or conversion, effected by the covenant. Yahweh is the universal God of history. He is not, Voegelin argues, a God to be negotiated with or to be appropriated for Israel's pragmatic purposes.[4]

The covenant becomes a Rosetta Stone for understanding the history of the Israelite theopolity, with even the pragmatic and mundane events of the polity having symbolic meaning as either fulfillments of, or defections from, the covenant order.[5] Voegelin says of the covenant and other Israelite symbols that they have a "baffling structure" but remain enduring symbols in politics.[6] They inform, Voegelin says, the first stirrings of theocratic consciousness, continuing through the end of Christian imperial culture.[7] They are also, according to Voegelin, revived to Gnostic effect in the crisis of the Reformation and the modernity that follows.

Voegelin describes two focal points in the Israelite theopolity: the creation of community through the covenant (obedience to divine instructions) and political organization necessary for pragmatic existence (existence in history).[8] When Christians later confronted these necessities in their own theological symbolism, they eventually divided them into church and state, which remained largely separated even through the crisis of the Reformation. Through the efforts of Christ in the Sermon on the Mount, of Saint Paul, and of Saint Augustine, the church rarely confused the social order with the Kingdom of God.[9] At the time of the Hebrew theopolity, the challenge of this covenant symbol was not yet tested or refined. It was, Voegelin says, "ambiguous and fraught with dangers of derailment."[10] In some ways, this political and spiritual tension enabled an important lesson in the history of order. Voegelin says of Israel, "For the first time men experienced the clash between divinely willed and humanly realized order of history in its stark brutality, and the souls of the Prophets were the battlefield in this war of the spirit."[11] Only later would profane existence be better translated into the *civitas Dei* of Saint Augustine.[12]

In Israel's case, Voegelin argues, the problem is centered on the establishment of the monarchy. He states, "As soon as the monarchy was established and had adjusted itself to the internal and external exigencies of politics, it became obvious that the new social order did not correspond to the intentions of the Covenant." The failures of the monarchy enabled the rise of the prophets. And with the prophets arose what Voegelin calls "Yahwism."[13] That is, if it had not been appropriated for political gain or had not fallen prey to "externalization" (pragmatic concerns) by the monarchy, the covenant would not have necessitated prophetic clarification. Like most political symbols within the Metaxy of human existence, the covenant required spiritual openness. Pragmatic appropriation of the symbol doomed the monarchy but also inspired the jeremiad-driven symbolization of the prophets. The legacy of the Hebrew theopolity is the message of the Prophets, universalized and rescued by Christianity, as "life of the spirit and the life in the world."[14] As the Hebrew monarchy wound to a close, the prophets asked who would carry their historical order into the future. Beginning with the eternal covenant alluded to by the Davidic monarchy, this becomes the "Messianic problem"—the central question of Christianity.[15]

The prophetic symbols remain loaded with the problems of balancing the transcendent with the pragmatic.[16] It was hard, Voegelin argues, to get beyond the "terrestrial sense" of the symbolism revealed at Mount Sinai.[17] The Decalogue and the Sinaitic covenant were not, Voegelin insists, "a catechism of religious and moral precepts."[18] Such an interpretation externalizes the substance of divine order, tempting destruction of the delicate balance between Israel collectively and the people individually. Interpreting the Sinaitic covenant as an externalization of divine order replaces communal life with ritual observance.[19] To paraphrase the prophetic message, God desires mercy or loyalty, and not sacrifice. What the covenant revealed and the terms it specified were not a contract that men could define for themselves; nor was it an agreement between equals.[20] Instead, the covenant is best understood as something to be absorbed into the souls of "those who listen to the call."[21] This life of the spirit is existence in community, but it cannot become a pragmatic formula for political community. The pragmatic formula encourages the very thing that the Decalogue forbids—human self-assertion. Hosea and Amos were prophetic voices against the false institutionalizing of the covenant revelation. Though they could not forestall the death of Israel, they communicated the provisions of the covenant as a key symbol. Voegelin states,

> The insight that existence under God means love, humility, and righteousness of action rather than legality of conduct was the great achievement of the prophets in the history of Israelite order. Even though their effort to disengage the existential issue from the decalogic form did not lead to expressions of ultimate, theoretical clarity, the symbols used in their pronouncements leave no doubt about the intended meaning.[22]

Given the ambiguity of their symbols, Voegelin argues, the prophets had remarkable success in disengaging the existential meaning of the Decalogue from their opposition's merger of divine and human order.[23]

Where the prophetic appeal failed, including appeals to the standards of the Book of the Covenant or the Deuteronomic Torah, it offered a "compact" rather than "differentiated" view of the Decalogue. Compact appeals did not adequately differentiate the "existential and normative issues" of the Sinaitic covenant.[24] This compact appeal could have been improved, Voegelin argues, had the prophets had at their disposal the positive Platonic-Aristotelian vocabulary of *arête* or the Heraclitian theory of faith, hope, and love.[25] More serious than the compact appeal is what Voegelin identifies as a line of "magic" in some prophetic efforts, particularly those of Isaiah; this is what Voegelin also calls "metastatic faith."[26] Voegelin first explores the problem of metastasis in the context of the prophets, although he argues that the problem was inherent in the very beginnings of the Mosaic founding of the theopolity. Briefly summarized, a metastatic faith attempts to transcend mundane existence and to appropriate a symbol (such as the covenant) against reality. This is done largely through "eschatological, mythical, or historiographical phantasy."[27] It is a form of pragmatic rebellion against the divine ground of being (God). Pragmatic rebellion is a serious charge by Voegelin, and he used this charge against religious and secular movements that he characterizes as Gnostic and heretical.[28] Whereas secular movements would resolve the tension of historical order by sweeping and bloody acts, the prophets looked to the revealed will of God. This, Voegelin says, is the difference between metastatic nightmares and metastatic dreams.[29] For the most part, Israel was tempted by metastatic dreams rather than the bloody revolutions of metastatic nightmares.

Just as Voegelin criticized the Hebrews who immanentized the transcendent qualities of the covenant, he warns against immanentizing Christian revelation. Voegelin's own summary of Christianity emphasizes the priority of mystery.[30] In *The New Science of Politics,* he argues, "Uncertainty is the very essence of Christianity. The feeling of security in a 'world full of gods' is lost with the gods themselves; when the world is de-divinized, communication with the world-transcendent God is reduced to the tenuous bond of faith, in the sense of Heb. 11:1, as the substance of things hoped for and the proof of things unseen."[31] Voegelin castigates those who claim certainty in such matters, casting certainty as a corrupted and heretical claim to knowledge in the face of uncertainty. This criticism applies particularly to those who claim their knowledge to have political import. Writing eloquently of the existential Christian experience and the temptation toward what he calls Gnosticism, Voegelin says, "The life of the soul in openness toward God, the waiting, the periods of aridity and dullness, guilt and despondency, contrition and repentance, forsakenness and hope against hope, the silent stirrings of love and grace, trembling on the verge of a certainty which if gained is lost—the very lightness of this fabric may prove too heavy a burden for men who lust for massively possessive experience."[32]

Voegelin argues that the metastatic dreams of the Hebrew prophets become metastatic nightmares in the Reformation. Voegelin directs sharp criticism at covenantal politics, citing the Puritan Revolution as a case study of "Gnostic" politics—an attempt to create a new reality. The Reformation, he argues, is a "successful invasion of Western institutions by Gnostic movements."[33] He calls Calvin's *Institutes* "the first deliberately created Gnostic koran."[34] While Voegelin's critique of Puritanism simply repeats many of Richard Hooker's criticisms, he sees the movement in much more critical terms than Hooker.[35] In short, because Puritanism's assertions destroyed the careful metaphysical balance of Christianity, Puritanism brought about the destruction of the public order.[36] Voegelin goes so far as to associate Puritanism with communism, national socialism, and Hobbes's authoritarian state.[37]

For Voegelin, the Reformation was not only catastrophic in its destruction of the social order; it contributed nothing to the development of political theory. He says of the monarchomach trend that it merely worked with fragments from previous literature with varying degrees of skill.[38] Of all the leading political theologians of the Reformation, Voegelin believes that none is a great ordering mind.[39] He is critical of both Calvin and Luther; he attributes the Reformation largely to Luther's own personality and reserves for him his harshest criticism.[40] Voegelin characterizes the whole sixteenth century as "singularly barren with regard to work of intellectual distinction in politics" (excepting Jean Bodin).[41] Whatever political ideas the reformers did offer had already been argued, Voegelin believes.[42] Johannes Althusius's *Politica,* written in the covenant tradition, was a "slight step" that would lead to a secularized system of natural law.[43] Voegelin's verdict on the *Vindiciae, Contra Tyrannos* and its use of the Hebrew covenants is that while its arguments serve their purpose to provide a scriptural rather than a natural law, its details are conventional rather than original.[44]

DANIEL ELAZAR

Whereas Voegelin's critique rejected any particular relevance for political covenants beyond vague existential symbolism, Daniel Elazar has advanced their contemporary importance by putting them at the root of federalism, constitutionalism, republicanism, and political culture.[45] His studies consider the entire history of covenanting, beginning with the Hebrew peoples and extending into contemporary pseudo-covenants, treaties, and trade agreements.[46] Elazar contrasts political covenanting, classified as strong or weak, with organic or hierarchical political arrangements and those founded on conquest, natural law, or natural right.[47] He concludes that political covenanting is exceptional and unsurpassed among political theories in its ability to fulfill political goals of liberty, equality, and justice. But it has also undergone substantial changes that can cause one to question the covenant's contemporary relevance.

In Elazar's schema, covenants exhibit important and distinctive components.[48] All of these elements are important because they emphasize covenantal politics as *relational.* He notes, "[A]ll covenantal political understanding revolves around similar questions of obligation and consent, free will, self-government, and political order—in other words, how are the relationships of humans one to another and to this universe and its transcendent power established and maintained so as to preserve both order and freedom, equality and opportunity, neighborliness and distinctiveness, liberty and law?"[49]

Elazar describes political covenanting as serving three important functions, which distinguish it from hierarchical or organic political orientations: as a form of political conceptualization and mode of political expression; as a source of political ideology; and as a factor shaping political culture, institutions, and behavior. Political covenanting is unsurpassed in its reconciliation of power and justice, a reconciliation enabled by unique political and social traditions.[50] A covenant is therefore more than an institutional or legal formulation; it becomes, in short, a political and social worldview.[51] Without this worldview, Elazar argues, certain institutional dimensions of constitutionalism cannot succeed. These dimensions of constitutionalism include the separation of powers, limited government, a jury system, and true federalism.[52]

Covenants limit the authority of civil magistrates and set the bounds on what is constitutional. The task of civil magistrates is to lead by example in fulfilling the terms of the covenant. Magistrates are to implement justice and mercy, protect virtue against vice and appropriately guard against heresy. They ignore this calling at their own peril. Unlike other theories of political origin, there is a clear resistance theory inherent in covenantal political thought.[53] The people, or their appointed "lesser magistrates," may remove a ruler by force of arms.[54] The very idea of constitutionality is derived from political covenanting, Elazar argues.[55] Judging the constitutional propriety of legislation is the modern secular version of testing what the covenantal tradition called federal liberty.[56]

Elazar looks to a Reformed Protestant, John Winthrop, to define his terms. Elazar defines federal liberty as "the freedom to freely hearken to the law."[57] This stands in contrast to natural liberty, which is a liberty to do whatever one wants. Natural liberty is freedom to do evil as well as good and is incompatible with authority.[58] Thus, natural liberty is a liberty that is lawless and incompatible with political life. Federal liberty is ever mindful of political society and its need for morality and law. This distinction, Elazar argues, is at the root of our modern idea of what is "constitutional." To make a judgment of what is constitutional requires more than merely perusing a constitutional text; one must determine what is compatible with the preconditions of the civil society's political order and what is not. Constitutionality is thus judged by the terms of previous covenants, together with the general moral guidance of the natural law.[59]

Elazar argues that there are two forms of covenanting: strong and weak. While strong (orthodox and explicitly religious) political covenanting is no longer practiced, weaker forms of political covenanting remain. Weaker forms are evident in modern constitutionalism or in theories of social contracting. Weaker political covenanting may emphasize morality or community, but lacks the explicit theological and divine component. Elazar's distinction raises important questions. Given the intensely religious basis evident in historical political covenanting, can one even speak of an evolving "covenant" at all? At what point in the "evolution" of political covenanting does covenanting cease to be recognizable as covenanting?

Elazar tries to discern the precise impact of political covenanting on modern constitutionalism by creating categories drawn from the language used in the early history of Anglo-American constitutionalism: covenant, compact, and contract. Each term represents a different kind of political agreement. Covenants and compacts are asserted to be historically more prevalent than contracts and also more constitutional or public in character. As reciprocal instruments, covenants and compacts bind their parties "beyond the letter of the law." Contracts tend to be private devices and not the public documents that political theorists allude to when they generalize the foundations of constitutionalism as "social contract theory." Covenants, even more so than compacts, introduce a morally binding dimension above the legal dimension.[60] Covenants are also distinguished from compacts and contracts by the belief that God is a guarantor of, or a direct party to, the relationship between parties in the covenant. Compacts do not explicitly include a divinely transcendent dimension and instead rely on mutual pledges and a secular legal grounding. Modern constitutions are no longer made with God but instead "under God."[61] In this respect they are more like compacts than covenants. Contracts are distinguished primarily by their private and strictly legal nature.[62] Contracts also do not emphasize morality for their members beyond legal and minimally moral reciprocity.

Covenants, compacts, and contracts all seek liberty for their members, but each articulates its own relationship between liberty and morality. At the one extreme, covenantal liberty has a strong and binding communal nature, particularly under divine law. At the other extreme, contracts tend to emphasize positive law and individualistic notions of liberty.[63] Elazar argues that these two features of contracts—secularism and individualistic freedom—make it difficult for contracts to command moral unity or coherence.[64] Covenants, more so than compacts or contracts, articulate the moral adherence necessary for representative government. This was particularly the case in America.[65] The ways in which these three devices (covenant, compact, and contract) parallel, intersect, intertwine, or dominate one another have important political consequences. They approach the moral and legal bases of society in different ways, which results in various political conceptions.

Elazar is certainly on to something valuable in theoretical terms, but the precise interpretive application of his covenant-compact-contract taxonomy is limited, so it is more valuable as a theoretical tool than as a means of interpreting historical documents. The test of Elazar's taxonomy, especially if one is going to use it as a tool for developing a theory of constitutional evolution, is to check whether his historical subjects can be said to agree with him in the usage of these terms. If such agreement cannot be established, and in many cases it probably cannot, the theoretical distinctions may still hold. But as a means of interpreting historical documents, Elazar's taxonomy has limited value. One could not come to a particular document or time, for example, and impose Elazar's definition on an author's choice of the term "compact" over the term "covenant" and determine that the intent was to avoid theological significance. In the case of Hobbes, for example, one could hardly presume that the use of the term "covenant" was intended to signify a political agreement of traditional moral and theological significance.[66] And, as David Weir points out in his exhaustive study of colonial "covenants," explicit religious content is often only implied, and sometimes it is absent altogether.[67]

Despite these obstacles, Elazar's work has conceptual value. His discussion of the divine or theological component of the covenant is also helpful but imprecise, however. He seems to think the moral consequence that results from the divine party's participation may even be more significant than the divine party itself. The transcendent power subscribing to this covenant requires that human freedom be understood as federal liberty, not natural liberty.[68] Federal liberty emphasizes freedom within the boundaries of community and moral responsibility. Elazar notes, "The omnipotent Deity, by freely covenanting with man, limits His own powers to allow humans space in which to be free, only requiring of them that they live in accordance with the law established as normative by the covenant."[69] Federal liberty calls all partners to public and private adherence to both social norms and divine moral prescriptions.[70] This liberty binds the community together and transcends what may otherwise be only minimal moral obligations prescribed by legal, contractual, or private agreements. Without moral reformation, no true covenant is possible. This explicit moral dimension, Elazar argues, qualifies covenantal politics as a political theology.[71] But is the divine component necessary for the moral component? Again, Elazar does not give a definite answer.

Perhaps some answer can be derived from returning to Elazar's distinction between "weak" and "strong" covenanting. In areas where strong and explicit covenantalism once ruled the political landscape (as in the British and American cases), there now exist only the weakest forms of covenantalism. These are reflected in modern formulations of constitutionalism. Can one then say that political covenanting has been lost, or simply that it has been modified? Any answer to this question must first determine what distinguishes strong covenantalism from weaker forms of covenanting. One must also examine the historical reality of how this change from strong to weak covenantalism took place. Are the historical benefits of the covenant maintained by contemporary consensual politics even if the argument for consent has changed?

Elazar addresses these questions with both hope and skepticism. He offers a persuasive argument for the survival of covenantalism when contrasted with competing models of political organization. Consent and law on the covenantal model, not a classical model, is perhaps the healthiest surviving element of premodern politics. The covenant, argues Elazar, builds a bridge between the premodern and postmodern epochs and may even provide the origin and basis for much of modern political theory, including constitutionalism. This bridge is discernible not only in institutions but also in political culture. As evidence for this claim, Elazar cites the success enjoyed by modern constitutionalism in countries with a Reformation covenantal tradition versus those dominated by contrasting political or religious traditions.[72]

Elazar argues, "As constitutionalism has spread, covenantalism seems to have retreated."[73] The change is most evident in the loss of explicitly religious language in modern constitutionalism. This can be called the "secularization" of the covenant. At first, God was seen as a party to the political covenant. Then, God was seen as the overseer of the covenant, though not a direct party. Finally, in the weakest expression of a divine covenant, the human parties to the covenant were seen to possess a power or an end consistent with the divine will. Elazar respects the practical difficulty of articulating God's direct participation in a pluralistic culture. But he still insists that some remnant of this expression must endure in order for the traditional functions of covenanting to remain.

If the essential "theological" quality of covenanting is its moral rather than its divine component, can the moral component survive without the divine component? Perhaps as a legacy or tradition, Elazar seems to argue. "There seems to be little question that the full power of the covenant grows out of a political theology emphasizing the first perspective, that of covenant as having its ultimate source in the will of God."[74] Even where secularization persists, a "residue of religious commitment remains a powerful force and magnet shaping political culture and behavior."[75] Only in France, Elazar argues, has a truly secular model of consent emerged. Even so, one must still press the question and ask how long covenantal culture and behavior can survive in a "contractual" political regime.

Elazar recognizes that the loss of the divine partner may represent both progress and failure. A secularized covenanting process may enable a broader acceptance and use of consensual politics, but it does not satisfy the same needs that a religious approach does.[76] So, while Elazar is not suggesting a return to Hebrew or Reformed covenanting, the divine party to the covenant must be made more explicit again. But Elazar is unclear as to how this is to be done. He does assert that he is not arguing for a return to the "old-time religion," as he puts it, but rather for a return to what brought about the religious devotion in the first place, and to what gave religious devotion its compelling character.[77] Again, what Elazar means here is unclear. He seems to mean a sense of shared moral purpose among partners to the covenant. This is not the full purpose and expression of the covenant, because it avoids the divine lawgiver, but it is more "orthodox" than simply emphasizing consent without a moral dimension. Better to focus on the purpose of the covenant, its moral expression, than simply its method, which is consent. Full covenanting must be true to both purpose and method. Elazar argues that one can be covenantal in method but without the corresponding belief in God. But to say this misses the proper purpose, as Elazar has defined the covenant.[78] The loss of explicitly religious language and understanding undermines a cornerstone of covenanting, which is its shared purpose and vision.

This invites an important question, which is implicit in Elazar's analysis. Can similar vision and purpose be recovered in a secular age? And once again, Elazar is unclear. He suggests that civil societies can be reinvented on a basis similar to a covenant.[79] But he does not clearly spell out what this means. To complicate the question, Elazar notes that while the call for moral reformation was a source of the covenant's original vision, it was also the cause of its downfall. Elazar argues that Reformed Protestantism valued liberty and equality but achieved them through institutions that were "insufficiently broad or free" or else demanded an impossibly high standard of behavior that the vast majority of people could not achieve. Thus, it was left for a secular "new science of politics" to selectively use the anthropology of Reformed Protestantism and to implement an implicitly covenantal approach.[80]

Was the new science broadening the covenant for the sake of its survival, however, or was the new science terminating the covenant's essential qualities in order to replace it with a fundamentally new formulation of consent? It would seem that losing the calls to both moral reformation and divine partnering should signify the end of the covenant. With the loss of moral reformation comes a reformulation of the functions of government. Reformulation caused covenantal commonwealths to become civil societies and later, social contracts.[81] The purpose and function of the state changed when the two essential elements of strong covenanting were lost. If the practical consequences of covenanting are lost, then how can one say that the covenant endures in any form?

Of the new "compact" or contract theory, Elazar is at once both generous and critical. He sees compacting and contracting as being within the covenantal *tradition,* but yet being distinct from covenanting primarily by their secular nature. Elazar suggests that the covenant did not become lost altogether, but that essential elements became integrated into new theories of civil society.[82] This civil society was not without covenantal elements.[83] In this, Elazar may be referring to the preservation of moral concord in the contracting regimes. He cites the modern proliferation of democratic republics as demonstration of the triumph of covenantal principles now secularized.[84] Republicanism is, he argues, the triumph of consent common to all variations of covenanting: covenant, compact, and contract. Historically, Elazar is correct. Democratic societies have been formed on both compacting and covenanting (and even contracting) theories. But consent is simply the lowest common denominator of covenanting traditions contrasted with organic or hierarchical forms of organization. In order to argue the triumph of covenantal political thought, does one have to reduce it to its lowest common denominator of consent alone? Also, does one have to accept Elazar's claim that political theories are distinguished according to the categories of being organic, hierarchical, or consensual (covenantal)? This appears to be a beggar's approach to the problem.

Overall, Elazar's writing makes one both optimistic and pessimistic for the future of the covenantal tradition. Even though the covenantal commonwealth is largely forgotten in the new liberal democracies, he argues hopefully, "The covenantal foundations remain and manifest themselves in those polities even in unexpected ways in every generation."[85] Part of this manifestation is evidenced in the new language of political theory: *foedus, pactum* or *pactio, confederatio, contractus,* and *consocentio.* Part of it is found in the theme of "deliverance" that can be seen in both covenantal theology and social contract theory.[86] Part of it is to be found in the understanding of rights only as liberties integral with justice and moral duties.[87] Part of it is found in the moderate egalitarianism that is characteristic of modernity's rejection of organic and hierarchal arrangements.[88]

However much these themes may or may not reflect a covenantal past, their new articulators no longer explicitly recognize that ancestry, however.[89] And what is more, there are seemingly new formulations of civil society that contest or reject altogether the covenantal traditions. In the end, it seems as though a covenant without transcendent divine or moral elements ceases to be a covenant at all. Elazar states, "When covenantal arrangements have been reduced to mechanism they offer much less to the people who use them. Often they degenerate to window dressing."[90] Nevertheless, Elazar argues, the descendants of these covenantal societies will probably continue to succeed. It may sound as if Elazar is essentially making a pragmatic argument here, but his understanding of human nature is informed explicitly by political theology. Sacrifices of natural liberty enable greater federal liberty under God.[91] As long as that foundation remains, then liberty remains. When this theopolitical foundation is *completely gone,* Elazar argues, then political liberty will go with it.[92] He believes that the acknowledgment of divine authority and a vision of a moral political community are the catalysts rather than the enemies of liberty.[93] The quest for politics is, for Elazar, fundamentally a quest for meaning, and this meaning is possible only under God's direction.

DAVID NOVAK

David Novak provides a two-tiered application of the biblical covenants to politics. He argues that only two biblical cases are pure covenants (*ha-berit*): the Noahide covenant and the Sinaitic covenant. The Noahide covenant is made with mankind. It is the assurance of justice to all persons.[94] The Sinaitic covenant is made with biblical Israel. Both are everlasting.[95] Any further covenants, whether made with or between Jews or not, require one of these two covenants as a deliberate foundation.[96] The Noahide covenant, although a valuable legal and moral tool, is quite different from the covenant at Sinai. Whereas the Sinai covenant established a covenanted community by direct revelation, the Noahide covenant is an indirect revelation that merely serves as a common guarantee of human justice. It is akin to what philosophers have called natural law. But however valuable the Noahide law, it is not sufficient to establish either a community or a relationship with God.

Novak argues that it is only through direct revelation from God that communal history and its corresponding festivals are established. And Elazar argues that communal history and festivals are the basis for true community. General human experiences and natural law cannot serve as the basis of history and communal celebration. Celebration and history require particular experiences of a particular people. This particular history often includes miracles.[97] Experiencing and interpreting those miracles, Novak argues, distinguishes the universalizing scientific (Enlightenment) cosmology from the particular and historical biblical cosmology. Novak sees in the biblical miracles revealed and relational qualities. They become the voice of God.[98]

For a biblical demonstration of the Noahide covenant serving only as a legal and moral (and political) device but not the establishment of a community, Novak cites the inter-human covenant between Abimelech and Abraham in Genesis, in which Abimelech and Abraham joined as political equals forming a bilateral pact or trust. The covenant negotiated between them determined the conditions that enabled them to live in peace with one another.[99] They shared a universal moral law though they do not share the same theology.[100] But Abraham could not covenant with the king of Sodom because of his kingdom's excessive sin.[101] (They shared neither common morality nor theology.) Novak argues that in cases such as Sodom or the Hittites, Abraham can only arrange commercial transactions.[102] Thus, while the universal Noahide covenant makes lawful relations possible and is important for political and social relations, it is not enough to establish full community.[103]

One cannot force one's way into a Sinai-type covenant without divine election. Novak is quick to remind the reader that the Sinai covenant was made with one particular people in "local experience and practice." It is ultimately meant for all mankind, as indicated by the promise to Abraham in Genesis 12:3. But the inclusion of all peoples will come only by God's doing in the messianic age.[104] Any attempt at universal language or community apart from direct revelation or election becomes idolatry—a "self-divinization of the people" like the one at Babel.[105] Any attempt at a human "monoculture" of redemption will lead to enslavement or extermination.[106] The all-inclusive national covenant is initiated only by divine election, not by inter-human agreement or evangelism. For now this limits true covenants to Jews, though gentile monotheists share some theological commonality (according to Novak).[107]

Novak also closes off any possibility for speaking of covenants as evolving into more inclusive social contracts (as Elazar suggested). Novak associates covenants only with the biblical narrative, whereas social contracts are the phenomena of democratic polities.[108] Novak argues that covenants and social contracts can coexist, but must be considered in proper priority as political formulations.[109] Contracts, the broader and more inclusive tool, are to work in the service of covenants.[110] Novak argues that this is because the regime under which one lives is not one's ultimate destination.[111] Religious association and community take ontological and historical priority over one's citizenship.[112] One is a member of a particular community before one is a citizen.

This is an important difference between Elazar and Novak. Whereas Elazar addresses the covenant as a potentially universally accessible political device, a method for legal institution and political conceptualization, Novak confines the covenant strictly to the biblical covenants. Elazar articulated a theory of the covenant in an inclusive way, making the covenant's function similar to that of a social contract or constitution. For Elazar, the covenant (or contract or constitution) sets the terms of political obligation within the community. Novak is asking about the place of a biblical covenant in a larger political society that will not or cannot covenant.

Novak's insistence that covenants take priority over social contracts emphasizes ontological priority and Novak's own convictions as a Jew. But it also enables him to also make a substantive demand that any functioning social contract respect its members. Novak argues that in any social contract, not just one in which Jews are participating, it is important to see that only "full" persons are capable of agreeing to a social contract. These are persons who first "reside" (in the fullest sense) in communities, primarily religious communities. There must be respect for preexisting historical and ontological identities in any political arrangement.[113] Properly understood from the necessary perspective of communities, we are "persons," not "individuals."[114] Although rights are exercised legally by "individuals," the moral context for those rights is learned in original communities. Morality comes from communities, which cultivate and nurture the individual and put individual rights in perspective.

This argument for the priority of covenants has some similarity to what Elazar emphasizes (that morality is an essential part of any covenant), but remains substantially different. When Elazar argues that a covenant precedes a contract in the case of some constitutions, he is referring to the moral vision that the covenant sets in view for the subsequent contract. The larger community may then have both a covenant and a contract, with the former preceding the latter. Elazar argues that this is the case in the American Declaration of Independence, which set the moral tone for the Constitution.[115] In Novak's case, the covenant is something that a particular community has within the social contract of the larger civil polity.[116] The covenant certainly precedes the contract (as in Elazar), but it also takes clear priority. In Elazar, they are complementary rather than competing against each other. In Novak, a community has its own covenant and is then viewed as participating (as a community) in the political society. Though Novak never uses the term "federal," that is essentially what his political vision is. Communities preserve their integrity even while subscribing to larger political units.

The Noahide covenant (that is, society based *only* on natural law) has additional limitations. While it may provide essential social prohibitions (against crime or other injustice, for example), it is not sufficient for what Novak calls "deep cultural existence."[117] This can only come from the Mosaic Torah. The failure of the Noahide law is not that its morality is insufficient to restrain or encourage a just or orderly human society. Rather, the Noahide covenant does not fulfill the deepest human communal needs. It cannot serve as anything other than a formal and abstract guide.[118] Understood merely as "natural morality," it does not constitute any real community in the world, nor can it effectively limit the power of the state.[119] Justice and order are necessary but not sufficient for real community.

This argument of Novak's is a significant justification for covenantal political theory; individuals in society seek not only law but also a community. The deepest community is founded in a common morality, but morality must provide more than restraint. Restraint is necessary for liberty, but too much restraint threatens liberty. To preserve liberty against the overextension of the civil law and magistrate requires more than moral prohibitions. It requires that the claims of community be considered prior to the demands of political society. This requires a delicate balance of enforcement using both legal institutions and personal interaction in communities. When legal enforcement is too much, impersonal institutions displace personal interaction. When enforcement is too little, protective institutions are eclipsed by personal interaction. Imbalance can subvert God's authority. Novak argues, "Only when God's authority is presented in the covenant do the lesser authority of society and the lesser authority of the individual person find their rightful places respectively and their rightful correlation one with the other."[120] This was a key point in the triumphs and failures of

Protestant political theory under covenant theology. From the earliest tensions within Zurich and Geneva, the Reformed Protestants had to decide where the respective authority and jurisdictions of the church and state began and ended.

An additional problem of a community founded only on the Noahide covenant or natural law is that it is tempted into misunderstanding the priority of civil society. When civil society is understood to come directly from a state of nature, justice is sought but community is not. The Hebraic alternative places the life mediated by the Torah in between a state of nature and civil society; it recognizes civil society not as the fulfillment of rights already known in the state of nature but, instead, as something that comes only after real moral community has been established. We do not leave the state of nature and enter into civil society; we leave the state of nature to enter communities that then exist inside of civil society. This serves to protect the rights of both God and His people.[121] The Hebraic alternative also moderates justice with the virtues of community.

The Noahide covenant fails to create community also because it provides only negative commands. It sets limits and provides boundaries, but is not inherently relational.[122] A community is created only through positive commandments that are expressions of love. Thus, while the Noahide law can guard against disorder and provide the minimal boundaries for a society, it cannot become the basis for a community. A community must provide more than "thou shall not." Covenantal political theory is concerned with much more than order or simple justice, for it includes a belief in the possibility of community. Its positive commands (fulfilling duties to others) are addressed to persons who are linked with one another through communal identity and revelation.

The biblical contribution of the Sinaitic covenant as a model community can help to resolve differences between so-called liberals and communitarians.[123] Novak argues that liberalism emphasizes rights to a fault while communitarians emphasize duties to a fault.[124] In his opinion, this notion of "rights" has a place in the Jewish political tradition, though not as moderns have articulated them.[125] The biblical approach keeps the person from becoming an idol or falling into a trap of subjective autonomy. Novak argues that rights must be rooted in duties to others, including God. Rights are means to a dutiful end. What is more, loving one's neighbor cannot be reduced to just not doing him harm.[126] Love is both horizontal, toward others in the covenant, and vertical, toward God.[127] Unlike minimalist social contract thinking, which extends goodwill and tolerance for the sake of safety, the covenant is the way of shalom.

Non-covenantal theories of natural right are insufficient because they lack the context of a voice or a relationship. A covenantal view of rights emphasizes that God is the basis of authority over all rights and duties, rather than either the individual (autonomy) or the community (heteronomy) being the basis of authority. It is from God that one learns to love.[128] It is also in response to God that one expresses one's love for others.[129] It is our inequality before God that emphasizes our equality with one another.[130] It is God's rights that stand at the root of any "rights talk." Covenantal rights are based on God's primordial right as the Creator. God's right has no duty underlying it but, rather, creates our duties, and those duties create our rights. The duties that God asks, His covenantal claims, are the basis of His response to persons. By doing our duties and respecting God's claims on us, we respect God's right. This gives legitimacy and dignity to our rights, Novak argues. Rights are gifts of God in the context of the covenanted community.[131]

12 Lessons for Religion and Politics Today

For Voegelin, the covenant is a symbol that both reveals the tension inherent in human existence and transcends political or moral appropriation. For Elazar, the covenant is a peerless and flexible device underlying modern constitutionalism, federalism, and social contracts. For Novak, the covenant appears as both symbol and device only for communities sharing a revelatory tradition and not for civil society. If we accept Voegelin's proscription against its appropriation, the covenant remains a revealing but inaccessible symbol in the history of political order. If we accept the optimistic reasoning of Elazar and decide that covenantalism may be alive and well in secular constitutions, we risk losing the distinct contribution of a divine partner and accompanying transcending moral obligations. If we accept Novak's critique of the Noahide covenant and rely only on the Sinai covenant, we risk losing the possibility of applying the covenant to any communities beyond biblical communities. And we lose the value of the covenantal ethos for civil society as a whole. What should we say to these three presentations of covenanted politics?

REDEEMING THE COVENANT

The covenant reveals what Voegelin calls the Metaxy of human existence: the fact that humankind is suspended between divinity and the mundane. Because the covenant addresses the challenges of humankind's special status as the *Imago Dei,* it is what I called in Chapter 2 a political theology par excellence. The covenant summons with a moral call that transcends selfishness and cynicism. Its exacting treatment of authority warns us of the tyranny of political expediency. The covenant exalts the highest fulfillments of community and morality. It calls us not merely to conform to what is right but also to establish relationships and communities around what is just and good. Establishing these relationships and communities summons the qualities of our nature that are divine, those rightly emphasized by the jeremiads of the biblical prophets. We must not trade those transcending principles of justice and goodness for cynical and utilitarian goals of realpolitik or the deceptive visions of political demagogues and messiahs.

In criticizing the Hebrew use of the covenant, Voegelin argues that the greatest misuse of the covenant symbol was to make Yahweh a God for the pragmatic purposes of Israel, rather than a universal God of history. Voegelin's argument must be read as a warning against appropriating any symbol in such a way as to allow a nation to see itself as the culmination of history. This is precisely what went wrong when Reformed Protestants went from a prophetic to an apocalyptic eschatology during Cromwell's Commonwealth. In the case of the Britain, the result of apocalyptic exceptionalism was theological suicide for the covenant tradition there.

The American use of the covenant was not so tragic. By the time of their War for Independence, Americans had succeeded in building levees against the theological spillover of millenarianism and chiliasm that had doomed the covenant in Britain. The American Founders called upon another aspect of Reformed theology, the limitations of the postlapsarian condition, to curb the excesses of Gnosticism lest the chosen people think themselves called to something other than the mansions of heaven. As Ellis Sandoz casts it, this was a republic for sinners rather than for saints.[1] Realistic acknowledgment of postlapsarian (fallen and imperfect) human nature carried on into the Constitution and its distrust of centralized power. As the so-called "father of the Constitution," James Madison, argued, self-interested human nature would not and could not be miraculously cured. Rather, it was to be used in the service of limiting power. Men were not angels. They were ambitious and factious, and that fact must be acknowledged and then harnessed in the service of liberty.[2]

Voegelin's admonishment serves as a warning against the appropriation of salvation to politics. The call of the covenant is more clearly discerned during the spiritual openness caused by crises of liberty. This is demonstrated in covenanting episodes both ancient and modern and in the endless replaying of the Exodus narrative throughout history. When the covenant is recalled in politics, it must be used only to restore the liberty that has been lost. Anything more ambitious than the restoration of liberty leads to messianic ideology and tempts peoples to political excesses that come from believing themselves "chosen." Beyond the restoration of political liberty, the covenant points only to a spiritual end, the *Civitas Dei*, the City of God. This was the great challenge for the Israelites, for the early church, and for those who revived the covenant later in Europe, England, and America.

If the covenant symbol is ever to be recovered in politics, its end must be clearly established from the beginning. This requires a proper approach to history, and a proper approach to authorizing, interpreting, and mediating the covenant. If the goal of covenanting is some messianic end beyond the defense of liberty, then politics and the state become deformed. The civil magistrate is not, and cannot be, a messiah. Politics cannot bring heaven to earth. It cannot resolve or close the Metaxy of human existence and make the mundane heavenly or the heavenly mundane. This was the challenge to Britain on the eve of the regicide and further civil war, when the country was driven to bloodshed, from metastatic dreams to metastatic nightmares. It has been a recurring challenge to Americans, once described by Abraham Lincoln as the Almighty's "almost chosen people."[3]

The abuse of the covenant comes from those who falsely claim a mediatory power equal to the biblical prophets. The biblical covenants were administered by the offices of persons whom Scripture claims were divinely raised up for unique events in time and place. We can find common ground with their spiritual and political crises. But we cannot presume to have the authority of the biblical prophets and, ourselves, seek political solutions to spiritual problems. Spiritual problems require spiritual solutions, which must now come at the level of community rather than political authority or legal institution. If the repair of spiritual deformation requires a revival of the prophetic voice, even the rhetoric of the jeremiad, so be it. But this prophetic voice must come from the community and its members. Mediating the covenant cannot be delegated to the civil magistrate. This is where we find the greatest errors in the Reformed Protestant experience. They were not errors so much because they offend our modern pluralistic sensibilities but, rather, because they contradicted the spirit of the covenant, limited its efficacy, and shortened its days as a political symbol.

It is more urgent than ever, because we live in an era of Gnostic ideologies, that we do not allow the abuse of the covenant symbol to deform our politics. What was always tempting because of the Metaxy of existence is doubly tempting in an era when ideological politics tempts political redemption. The modern prophets of the covenant must have enough discernment to see liberty as the historic *sine qua non* of the covenant. It is on occasions of liberty against tyranny that the covenant symbol is recalled in history. This means that the prophets of the covenant must continue to stand against contemporary abuses of politics and to look to communities for the fulfillment of our noblest desires and virtues. The abuses of religious politics cannot be replaced by the abuses of ideological and Gnostic politics.

PRESERVING THE COVENANT IN AN ERA OF SECULARISM

Preserving the covenant within communities would not only be consistent with the prescription of a modern covenantal theorist such as David Novak but also with an older one such as Johannes Althusius, who described political society as a federal network of private associations.[4] In order for covenanted communities to persevere, there must be an appropriate relationship between them and civil society. Civil society cannot become so ideologically intolerant that religious communities become opponents. Nor can religious communities be tempted by the kind of political exceptionalism that challenged liberty in times past. The solution to this question draws our attention to a long-standing problem but one that has become increasingly ideological on the political side and Gnostic on the religious side. It is the challenge of secularity and secularism. "Secular" is not a diabolical term invented by modern atheists, as some pious persons might fear. It is a medieval term that respects a division between earthly and heavenly matters. This division was respected by Reformed Protestants such as John Calvin or Samuel Rutherford (as illustrated in Chapter 9).

The concept of secularity goes back to the roots of Christianity. When asked about taxes for Caesar, Jesus urged his interrogators to distinguish between what belonged to God and what belonged to Caesar. He also said, "My kingdom is not of this world."[5] Can any contemporary nation claim to be the people of God and thereby assert the promise of II Chronicles 7:14? "If my people who are called by my name humble themselves, and pray and seek my face and turn from their wicked ways, then I will hear from heaven and will forgive their sin and heal their land." Or would it be more fitting to instead assert Proverbs 14:34? "Righteousness exalts a nation, but sin is a reproach to any people." Both of these are covenantal expressions insofar as they exhort corporate responsibility and plead for moral faithfulness. Both have the tone of a jeremiad. Both speak of God's role in the destiny of nations. But the first claims an exceptional relationship for the nation that the second does not.

Rightly understood, secularity requires not only that religious communities not co-opt the larger social contract but also that the social contract not discourage religious or theological expression. Bigotry against religious communities is now justified by theories of minority tolerance, public reason, or jurisprudence that would have been unrecognizable even several decades ago. "Accommodation" too often means the loss of religious liberty. Every public record or event is increasingly scrubbed clean of all things theological. Hypersensitivity becomes the order of the day, and judges wrestle with ever more creative and convoluted interpretations of legal rights that defy natural rights. Freedom *for* religion becomes replaced by freedom *from* religion.

The answer to the survival of the covenant among communities depends on a longstanding social challenge: the appropriate domain of what is "secular." Novak offers an insightful contrast between *secularity* and *secularism.* For him, secularity is finite or neutral. It does not look to any particular community for legitimization.[6] It is consistent with the biblical covenant and the Talmudic principle that "the law of the state is the law."[7] Secularity respects biblical revelation, but limits its application in public norms.[8] It respects religious persons but seeks accommodating negotiation. Secularism, by contrast, is an ideology that seeks to coopt real communities.[9] It sees human-made law as not only necessary but also sufficient for human fulfillment. Secularity can accommodate and respect covenanted communities. Secularism cannot. Civil society under secularism attempts to replace the sacred realm by becoming the sacred realm itself.[10]

The philosophical anthropology of secularism is flawed. It denies that communities precede society. The democratic polity depends on the nurture and socialization capacity of its communities. Persons exist in communities before they can exist in societies. Their happiness depends on those communities enjoying a certain degree of autonomy—together with respect—from society at large. When human nature is thought to be rooted first in civil society, there is no real place for community.[11] One makes room for real society only by making room for communities.[12] The problem with oppressive public ideologies such as secularism is that they see this original orientation toward communities as something to be overcome rather than something to be cultivated.[13]

When religious communities are respected and intact, there is hope for true and neutral secularity because these communities have a religious need for that public space. Every religious community desires to preserve public space for themselves, but realize that this cannot be to the exclusion of others.[14] This suggests a federal, and therefore covenantal, solution to a human problem. This means decentralizing, dispersing and moderating authority.

How will morality and law be negotiated between covenanted communities and the rest of the civil polity? The kind of communities spoken of here—those able to covenant—are defined by their moral ethos. The civil polity also requires a moral ethos. A successful social contract for the civil society at large will address the task of social morality through both theology and philosophy—not through just one or the other. After all, moral principles do not originate in society at large. They come from the respective traditions and communities within a society, which are then coordinated through philosophical reasoning. Theology is used to articulate the norms within a particular tradition and community. Philosophy, particularly "natural law," is used to enable intercultural dialogue.[15] The Noahide covenant, natural law, is not able to construct a community, but it is able to reconcile the differences and agreements among communities. It is able to provide the moral basis of civil society only.[16] If theological communities believe that divine law reveals nothing for *political life* that is not already known by natural law, they have nothing to lose by having this dialogue with the larger society in terms of natural law. If they do not believe natural law to be minimally sufficient for civil law, they must then wrestle with all the aforementioned challenges of the Reformed Protestants in merging their religious community with the civil order.

THE IMPORTANCE OF THE COVENANTAL ETHOS

Why preserve the covenant at all in political life? While it has served as a powerful symbol for moral reformation and liberty in the face of moral decline and the abuse of political power, any justification of it must extend further. The covenant represents more than a "Thou shalt not" to tyrants and moral depravity. The ultimate contribution of the covenant is to enable the kind of community that fulfills the highest aspirations of politics and human nature while we remain in the Metaxy. As with the covenants described in this book, this enabling begins with a call or a hearkening. The covenant's terms are not negotiated, but its benefits must still be sought and won. We must decide if we will hearken to this particular call of the covenant.

Covenants stand for community and against both individual autonomy and moral expediency. As social philosophies, autonomy and expediency present both an epistemological problem (truly perceiving what one's self-interest is) and a motivational problem (acting outside of what one perceives to be one's self-interest). While it is true that decisions can be made in the interests of both self and community without conflict, as Cicero argued in *De Officiis,* casting the dichotomy this way emphasizes Elazar's salient contrast between a contract and a covenant. A contract creates something with the consent of parties presumed to act only upon expediency. A covenant binds its parties with predefined terms that go beyond the foreseeable horizons of expediency.

Unlike a contract, which presumes to create things *ex nihilo,* covenants call us to things that precede and transcend us. It is no mere coincidence that covenants are therefore associated with communities whose traditions cannot be created out of nothing: the marriage covenant, the church covenant, the oath of citizenship. These communities and traditions precede and transcend us with the wisdom of obligations descending from time out of memory. Just as a covenant binds parties beyond the letter of the law, it also creates something larger than the sum of its members. When the parties to a marriage, a church, or a nation join a covenant, they answer a call to something they did not create.

No covenant is under the precise control of the covenanting parties. They are invited into it—perhaps even bound to it—by divine call. They can decide whether to hear its call by adhering to its terms, but they do not create that to which they are called. Nor do they define the terms of participation. One could even draw a link between covenants and the traditional meaning of vocation. Consistent with the Latin root of the word *vox*, one is *called* to one's vocation. This is true in the classical sense, as exemplified in the Hippocratic Oath, and in the broader biblical sense. Those who bind themselves by oath to the profession of medicine take on obligations they did not define. The same is true of secular or sacred vocations in Christianity or Judaism.

One does not have absolute freedom in a covenant. But if one thinks of liberty as more than the desire or calculation at the end of one's nose, then what is defined as "covenant liberty" is indeed the only sustainable kind of liberty for a community. It is, as both Elazar and Winthrop defined it, federal liberty, the freedom to do what is according to our nature as a member of a community.

We live in community to understand what human beings want to know and to serve the noblest goals that human persons can pursue. What are these noble goals, however? Are we called to join in community with others only for the "love of wisdom"? Here we may call on Aristotle again. There are three things that motivate action: perception, intelligence (*nous*), and desire.[17] Without desire, understanding and perception will not move us to act. It is on this point where the philosophical tradition should learn from the biblical tradition. There is beauty in classical philosophy's superlative picture of love, Plato's *eros.* There is compelling pragmatism in modernity's minimalist love, Hobbes's desire.[18] But both must give way to love cast in the biblical tradition. The end of human community ought not to be simply the love of wisdom but also the wisdom of love, as Emmanuel Levinas has eloquently argued.[19] Rightly understood, community is defined by the ethics of responsibility. This is the heart of the covenant.

It is no coincidence that the biblical tradition is marked by its emphasis on both love and covenanting and on the relationship between the two. Love is not simply the foundation of the covenant. It is the basis of the sweetest human relationships and therefore of all things political. The prophet Hosea asserts that God desires mercy and not sacrifice.[20] Christ repeats this, adding that love (*agape*) is the sum of the law and that love distinguishes his disciples.[21] Saint Paul argues that the greatest of the virtues is love.[22] The federal liberty of the covenant requires us to transcend the love of self. The model of love is divine love, and covenant love begins with the love of God rather than the love of self.[23] God is *chesed* in the biblical tradition, what some English Bibles translated as "loving-kindness." The ultimate end of this loving-kindness is shalom, meaning peace and wholeness. Shalom is the great contribution of the covenant tradition, and the possibility of loving-kindness in communities holds out hope for a truly humane political order.

Notes

CHAPTER 1: INTRODUCTION

1. I do not use the term in any way connected with Carl Schmitt or his book *Politische Theologie* ("Political Theology").

2. Theology: θεός–λόγος.

3. This is denoted, for example, by particular denominational categories within Protestantism. Congregational and Presbyterian, for example, are different forms of ecclesiastical polity.

4. In *The Myth of American Individualism: The Protestant Origins of American Political Thought,* Barry Alan Shain delights in relaying two anecdotes from works by Samuel Eliot Morison and David Hacket Fischer in which Revolutionary War veterans were asked of their familiarity with authors such as Locke, Paine, or Sidney and why they joined the fight. The veterans could not recall familiarity with any of these authors. One cites having read only religious material (Bible, catechism, hymns) and the almanac. Shain, *Myth of American Individualism,* 79. Also cited by Patricia U. Bonomi, *Under the Cope of Heaven: Religion, Society, and Politics in Colonial America,* 5.

5. For example, see Philip Schlesinger and François Foret, "Political Roof and Sacred Canopy? Religion and the EU Constitution."

6. Proponents of a radical political Islam often oppose the West on contradictory grounds, and these reflect our own inconsistencies. Radicals are unable to decide if our worst crime is to be ambivalently secular or to stand as heir to medieval Christendom and its conflicts with the Islamic world.

7. Classical liberal arguments which emphasize the liberty and equality that radical Islam denies may be themselves largely rooted and supported, if not sustained, by a certain kind of biblical political theology. This argument is enjoying resurgence. See, for example, Greg Forster's *John Locke's Politics of Moral Consensus,* Kim Ian Parker's *The Biblical Politics of John Locke,* or Jeremy Waldron's *God, Locke and Equality: Christian Foundations in Locke's Political Thought* for examples of theological or biblical content within the development of Locke's proto-liberalism.

8. René Descartes, for example, proposed to construct epistemological foundations from whole cloth, in his *Meditations on First Philosophy* and *Discourse on the Method.* While Descartes is rightly influential, he cannot be said to have constructed his argument from whole cloth (by which I mean that there can be no dependency on prior thinking

of any kind). He remains dependent on many historical arguments, traditions, and methods.

9. This is not to imply that all good things began with the Reformation. See Brian Tierney's *The Idea of Natural Rights: Studies on Natural Rights, Natural Law and Church Law 1150–1625,* or Annabel Brett's *Liberty, Right and Nature: Individual Rights in Later Scholastic Thought,* for example. But many important ideas did not come to fruition in articulation or practice until they were forced to do so by the crucible of the Reformation. The tradition under discussion in this book comes deliberately out of the Protestant Reformation. Most of those who articulated and advanced these ideas saw them as part of a new (Protestant) tradition rather than just the modification of an older tradition.

10. A brief sampling of anthologies, surveys, and textbooks demonstrates the problem. Leo Strauss and Joseph Cropsey's *History of Political Philosophy* dedicates one chapter to Luther and Calvin together and one chapter to Richard Hooker alone. J. S. McClelland's *A History of Western Political Thought* devotes no space to Luther, and less than a page to Calvin and Knox. John H. Hallowell and Jene M. Porter's *Political Philosophy: The Search for Humanity and Order* lists Hobbes, Locke, and Rousseau under "Calvinism" in the index but gives no space to Luther or Calvin in the text. Donald Tannenbaum and David Schultz's *Inventors of Ideas: An Introduction to Western Political Philosophy* does devote eleven pages to Luther and Calvin in a chapter entitled "The Religious Basis of Modern Political Thought." Dante Germino devotes one chapter collectively to Luther, Calvin, and Hooker in *Machiavelli to Marx: Modern Western Political Thought.* William Ebenstein and Alan O. Ebenstein devote none of their chapters to the Reformation in *Introduction to Political Thinkers.*

11. Leo Strauss addresses the challenge in *The Rebirth of Classical Political Rationalism,* 270. John G. Gunnell says of Strauss, "He would eventually conclude that 'no one can be both a philosopher and theologian' and that revealed divine law and rationally discerned natural order present fundamental alternatives which can be neither transcended nor synthesized." John G. Gunnell, "Strauss before Straussianism: Reason, Revelation, and Nature," 65. See also extended discussions in Heinrich Meier, *Leo Strauss and the Theologico-Political Problem,* and Steven B. Smith, *Reading Leo Strauss: Politics, Philosophy, Judaism.*

12. Leo Strauss, "Jerusalem and Athens: Preliminary Reflections," 221. This is another fine essay for understanding Strauss's discussion of faith and reason, revelation and philosophy.

13. For an interpretation of Strauss's treatment of Calvin, see Daniel Tanguay and Christopher Nadon, *Leo Strauss,* 33–36.

14. Richard Hooker is the only theologian mentioned outside the Roman Catholic tradition. Leo Strauss, *Natural Right and History,* 163–65.

15. Leo Strauss, "The Living Issues of German Postwar Philosophy."

16. John Adams, *A Defense of the Constitutions of Government of the United States of America, Against the Attack of M. Turgot, in His Letter to Dr. Price, Dated the Twenty-Second Day of March, 1778,* vol. 3, ch. 1, cited in *The Political Writings of John Adams,* ed. George Carey, 6:224–25. Regarding the authorship of the *Vindiciae, Contra Tyrannos,* see George Garnett, "Editor's Introduction," lv–lxxvii.

17. The general point is that common people were driven more by religious ideas than by "Great Books." The significance of this for politics is made quite prominently in Shain's *Myth of American Individualism.*

18. Alexis de Tocqueville, *Democracy in America,* I.i.2, 32.

CHAPTER 2: DEFENDING POLITICAL THEOLOGY

1. David Novak, *The Jewish Social Contract: An Essay in Political Theology,* xiii.

2. In this case "humanist" means a tradition calling on classical education. It is not meant in the ideological sense that began in the French Revolution.

3. The complications of this are demonstrated by debates over the role of Christianity in John Locke's philosophy, for example.

4. Luke 10:27, Leviticus 19:18. There is an intentional irony here, given the role of Christian morality in the formulation of Kant's ethical philosophy and his famous categorical imperative.

5. See, for example, Andrew R. Murphy, *Conscience and Community: Revisiting Toleration and Religious Dissent in Early Modern England and America;* John Marshall, *John Locke, Toleration, and Early Enlightenment Culture;* Chris Beneke, *Beyond Toleration: The Religious Origins of American Pluralism.*

6. John Locke, *Letter Concerning Toleration,* in Ian Shapiro, ed., *Two Treatises of Government and A Letter Concerning Toleration,* 230.

7. Ibid., 215.

8. The atheist may certainly believe in virtue, but one cannot appeal to those beliefs (in tolerance, for example) as one would appeal to a Christian in the name of a *Christian* virtue.

9. See, for example, Eric Voegelin, *The New Science of Politics: An Introduction,* 107–32, and *Science, Politics and Gnosticism,* 83–114.

10. Stephane Courtois et al., eds., *The Black Book of Communism;* Paul Hollander, ed., *From the Gulag to the Killing Fields: Personal Accounts of Political Violence and Repression in Communist States;* Richard Pipes, *Communism: A History.*

11. Marx and Engels state, "There are, besides, eternal truths, such as Freedom, Justice, etc., that are common to all states of society. But communism abolishes eternal truths, it abolishes all religion, and all morality, instead of constituting them on a new basis; it therefore acts in contradiction to all past historical experience." Karl Marx and Friedrich Engels, *The Communist Manifesto,* 242.

12. What is often emphasized in Ludwig Feuerbach's *Essence of Christianity* is his critique of religion as a projection. What is not often emphasized is that Feuerbach saw this critique as necessary for ushering in a progressive future enabled by atheistic solidarity.

13. In Jean-Jacques Rousseau's powerful metanarratives of human development, *Discourse on the Arts and Sciences* and *Discourse on the Origin and Basis of Inequality among Mankind,* there is no role for religion. See also *The Social Contract,* book 4, chapter 8 for his creation of a "civil religion."

14. See, for example, Charles Norris Cochrane, *Christianity and Classical Culture: A Study of Thought and Action from Augustus to Augustine;* George Kennedy, *Classical Rhetoric and its Christian and Secular Tradition from Ancient to Modern Times;* Everett Ferguson, ed., *Backgrounds of Early Christianity.*

15. Etienne Gilson, *God and Philosophy,* 6–8, 17.

16. Ibid., 21. One cannot avoid the problem by speaking of "nature." It is the very imprecision of this word that led to the ancient distinction between matter and the gods, or between *phusis* and *nomos.* The Greeks were more attuned to these difficulties than we are today.

17. Ibid., 22.

18. Aristotle, *Physics* VIII.1, 5, 6; *Metaphysics* XII.1, 6–9.

19. We create this imperative as a result of logical argument within ourselves. See X.7–8 of the *Nicomachean Ethics.* We should mimic the gods because the gods are perfect. But there is no relationship with these gods; one mimics them in Greek fashion, that is, one would pattern oneself after them just the same if they were figures in a frieze.

20. These lesser gods are moved by the beauty and excellence of the unmoved mover, but this is still a kind of mechanical and necessitated motion. They are not moved by affection or devotion, as are willing persons, as existential beings.

21. *Nicomachean Ethics* 1177b26–1178a5, 1178b25–30. One cannot say that we "share" it, only that we mimic it.

22. Deuteronomy 6:4; Gilson, *God and Philosophy,* 38–40.

23. "*DIEU d'Abraham, DIEU d'Isaac, DIEU de Jacob non des philosophes et des savants*" (the GOD of Abraham, the GOD of Isaac, the GOD of Jacob and not of the philosophers and sages). This was written in Pascal's conversion narrative, now called his *Memorial,* originally sewn into the lining of his jacket and found after his death.

24. Plato, *Euthyphro,* 10a.

25. Josef Pieper, *The Silence of St. Thomas,* 54–56.

26. Gilson, *God and Philosophy,* 72.

27. Ibid., 68.

28. Pieper, *Silence of St. Thomas,* 29–38.

29. Plato, *Republic,* lines 380–83. Plato's metaphysics would make the Incarnation either impossible or a form of deception.

30. John 1:14.

31. Romans 8:20–22.

32. Mark 16:19, Luke 24:51, Acts 1.

33. John Calvin, *Concerning the Eternal Predestination of God,* 185. Calvin notes, "I say nothing more than every believer experiences in himself, though my words fall far short of the reality." John Calvin, *Institutes of the Christian Religion,* I.vii.5.

34. Calvin, *Institutes,* IV.xvii.32 (hereafter cited parenthetically in the text). I am indebted to Tim McClain for this citation.

35. Charles Partee, *Calvin and Classical Philosophy,* 39.

36. John Calvin, *Calvin's New Testament Commentaries,* 5:211. Partee, quoting this passage and commenting on the matter, notes, "There is no chapter in Calvin's writings which deals with experience by itself, but he often uses experience as a descriptive term in connection with Scripture and faith and even, as above, with reason. Thus the appeal to experience identifies an epistemological position which surpasses reason and in which Scripture and faith find confirmation. Calvin does not develop this insight in a technical way, but it serves an important function in his thought." Partee, *Calvin and Classical Philosophy,* 36.

37. René Descartes, Dedicatory Epistle for *Meditations on First Philosophy,* 47.

38. Friedrich Nietzsche, *The Gay Science,* book 3, section 125.

39. It should not be presumed that this chapter's argument agrees entirely with Voegelin. A careful reader will note that my understanding of revelation is more narrowly defined than Voegelin's, though my broader definition of theology is akin to his broader definition of revelation.

40. Jean-Paul Sartre, *Existentialism Is a Humanism.* Because he discerns the intimate relationship between the traditional concept of "essence" as the source of intelligibility

and the act of God's Creation, Sartre denies both God and essentialism in order to enable freedom. If man has an essential quality, he is bound to act in a manner consistent with it. But this would deny him the freedom Sartre is asserting. Persons have no essence. Thus, Sartre makes the philosophical maneuver of asserting absolute free will while simultaneously denying any eschatological or essential moral imperative that should guide the use of that will. Sartre and Camus, more than most contemporary atheists, realized the great need of man to understand things in existential terms.

41. Kevin J. Vanhoozer, ed., *The Cambridge Companion to Postmodern Theology;* Graham Ward, *Barth, Derrida and the Language of Theology;* John Milbank, Catherine Pickstock, Graham Ward, eds., *Radical Orthodoxy: A New Theology;* Jean-Luc Marion, *God without Being: Hors-Texte;* John D. Caputo and Michael J. Scanlon, eds., *God, the Gift, and Postmodernism;* James K. A. Smith, *Introducing Radical Orthodoxy: Mapping a Post-secular Theology.*

42. Robert Bellah, *The Broken Covenant: American Civil Religion in Time of Trial,* 167.

43. Aristotle, *Politics,* 1276b16–1277b30.

CHAPTER 3: THE BIBLICAL BACKGROUND TO COVENANTING

1. Daniel J. Elazar, *Covenant and Polity in Biblical Israel,* 57–58.

2. Ibid., 180. No particular political regime appears required by the biblical covenants. Israel goes from a confederation of nomadic tribes under Moses to a government of settled tribes under Joshua, who carries out the provisions of the Torah in the new Hebrew nation. They then go from a government of settled tribes to a confederal government under the Judges to a federal system under Samuel and Saul. The final regime is a federal monarchy under David and his successors. It is notable that there is no hereditary political leadership. Only the priesthood had hereditary leadership.

3. See, for example, Michael Walzer's lecture "Where Were the Elders?"

4. Gordon M. Freeman, *The Heavenly Kingdom: Aspects of Political Thought in the Talmud and Midrash,* 43–44; Zacharias P. Thundyil, *Covenant in Anglo-Saxon Thought: The Influence of the Bible, Church Fathers, and Germanic Tradition on Anglo-Saxon Laws, History, and the Poems* The Battle of Maldon *and* Guthlac, 77; Dennis J. McCarthy S.J., *Old Testament Covenant: A Survey of Current Opinions,* 3; Elazar, *Covenant and Polity,* 65, 68–69.

5. For a good treatment of this, see Joshua Berman, *Created Equal: How the Bible Broke with Ancient Political Thought.*

6. Thundyil, *Covenant in Anglo-Saxon Thought,* 77; McCarthy, *Old Testament Covenant,* 3. It is not known why the Septuagint chose the rather unusual *diatheke* (testament) to translate the Hebrew *berith* (covenant). McCarthy, *Old Testament Covenant,* 1.

7. There is, not surprisingly, prominent use of the term in the letter to the Hebrews. Thundyil, *Covenant in Anglo-Saxon Thought,* 83.

8. McCarthy, *Old Testament Covenant,* 4.

9. Rolf Rendtorff, *The Covenant Formula: An Exegetical and Theological Investigation,* 3, 57.

10. Controversies regarding the concept of election and its political significance will be taken up later in the book in the context of the Reformation.

11. Noah is obviously included in this last covenant, but it is not a particular covenant with Noah. See David Novak, *Natural Law in Judaism,* 39–40.

12. Elazar, *Covenant and Polity in Biblical Israel,* 82–83. Novak, citing Proverbs 21:30, emphasizes that justice does not stand above God himself, as implied by Grotius, Kant, or perhaps Plato. Novak, *Natural Law in Judaism,* 42–43. For a Reformed perspective on this, see Heinrich Bullinger's *Decades,* where he approvingly cites a definition of law from Cicero's *De Legibus* I.6 ("an especial reason, placed in nature") but then adds, "And verily the law is nothing but a declaration of God's will, appointing what thou hast to do, and what thou oughtest to leave undone. The beginning and cause of laws is God himself" *(Decades* II.1, 193).

13. All quotations are taken from the English Standard Version unless otherwise noted.

14. The same could also be discerned from Exodus 34:12 or Deuteronomy 7:2, where the Israelites are warned against making covenants with "the Amorite, and the Canaanite, and the Hittite, and the Perizzite, and the Hivite, and the Jebusite."

15. Jacob schemes with his mother to obtain Isaac's deathbed blessing (Genesis 27), though Esau is said to "despise his birthright," trading it to his brother for food in Genesis 25:29–34.

16. Elazar, *Covenant and Polity,* 147.

17. Michael Walzer, *Exodus and Revolution.*

18. Elazar, *Covenant and Polity,* 187–88.

19. Freeman, *Heavenly Kingdom,* 4.

20. This corporate promise of blessing and cursing is emphasized in many places: for example, Leviticus 26 or Deuteronomy 28.

21. Elazar, *Covenant and Polity,* 213.

22. Joel S. Kaminsky, *Corporate Responsibility in the Hebrew Bible.*

23. All levels of society are admonished by Jeremiah, for example (see Jeremiah 2).

24. See Freeman, *Heavenly Kingdom,* 50.

25. Ibid., 43, 48.

26. An example of conscience-based disobedience and resistance is found in the response of Samuel and the people to Saul's rash oaths and impiety (I Samuel 14 and 15).

27. Compare II Samuel 7:9–12 with Genesis 12:2, 15:18; 17:8, 14:20, 22:17.

28. George Wesley Buchanan, *The Consequences of the Covenant,* 1, 60.

29. Heinrich Bullinger, *The Decades of Henry Bullinger,* ed. Thomas Harding (hereafter cited parenthetically within the text as *Decades).*

30. See Psalms 47, 93, 96, 97, 99, 145; Buchanan, *Consequences of the Covenant,* 59–60.

31. For the repeated quotation of Psalm 110 in the New Testament, see Matthew 22:44, Mark 12:36, Luke 20:43, Acts 2:35, Hebrews 1:13, Hebrews 10:13. G. Sujin Pak's *The Judaizing Calvin: Sixteenth-Century Debates over the Messianic Psalms* provides an overview of the Protestant reformers' disagreeing interpretations of the messianic psalms.

32. See Matthew 3:2, 4:17, 10:7; Mark 1:15; Luke 1:32–33, 4:43, 8:1, 9:2, 11, 60, 10:9, 11.

33. Buchanan, *Consequences of the Covenant,* 72.

34. Deuteronomy 30:15–20; Amos 5:4–6; I John 3:13–14; Philippians 1:21. See Buchanan, *Consequences of the Covenant,* 111.

35. Buchanan, *Consequences of the Covenant,* 143–44.

36. Ibid., 113, 116, 135.

CHAPTER 4: FOUNDING COVENANT THEOLOGIES

1. Consistent with what Friedman calls the "Strassburg-Basel-Zurich school of Hebraica," Calvin, for example, favored an active but moderate use of rabbinic commentators, calling on them particularly in questions of lexicology or grammar. Michael Servetus, by contrast, used the Jewish sources for far more than philological guidance. David L. Puckett, *John Calvin's Exegesis of the Old Testament,* 53, 57; Jerome Friedman, *The Most Ancient Testimony: Sixteenth Century Christian-Hebraica in the Age of the Renaissance Nostalgia.* For a discussion of Luther's concern over the use of Jewish and rabbinic sources by Bucer and other German Reformed Protestants, see Stephen G. Burnett, "Reassessing the 'Basel-Wittenberg Conflict': Dimensions of the Reformation-Era Discussion of Hebrew Scholarship."

2. John Von Rohr argues that the neglect of covenants in Roman Catholic theology reinforced the Reformed theologians' sense that they were reviving the message of the Early Church and restoring the purity of biblical Christianity. John Von Rohr, *The Covenant of Grace in Puritan Thought,* 1. Regarding medieval precedent, see Peter A. Lillback, *The Binding of God: Calvin's Role in the Development of Covenant Theology,* 29–57.

3. Calvin, for example, begins his *Institutes* with a defense of similar doctrines by the Church Fathers. Prefatory Address no. 4, 10–13. Bullinger prefaces his *Sermonum decades quinque* (commonly translated simply as *Decades)* with a summary of early creeds and councils. Bullinger, *The Decades,* Preface, 1–35 (hereafter cited parenthetically in the text by book, chapter, and page number). Also see David Wright, "Heinrich Bullinger and the Early Church Fathers."

4. For a study of the debate over Calvin's use of Hebrew Scriptures and the charge of his judaizing, see Pak, *The Judaizing Calvin.*

5. Friedman, *Most Ancient Testimony,* 182.

6. John Coffey, *Politics, Religion, and the British Revolutions: The Mind of Samuel Rutherford,* 158.

7. See disputes recorded in the Acts of the Apostles or the letter to the Galatians, for example. See also the discussion of the continuity and discontinuity with the Hebrew covenants discussed in the letter to the Hebrews.

8. Comparing Catholics to Jews, for example, Calvin wrote, "The whole discussion [in Romans 5:6] was occasioned by the pride and vain-glorying of the Jews, who, by claiming the name of the Church for themselves, would have made the faith of the Gospel dependent on their pleasure; just as in the present day the Papists would fain under this pretext substitutes themselves in place of God" *(Institutes,* III.xii.4, 215).

9. Puckett, *Calvin's Exegesis,* 1–24.

10. Geneva will be considered "Swiss" for purposes of this narrative, though it was not officially a full partner of the Swiss Confederation in the early decades of the Reformation.

11. George M. Ella argues that Bullinger was the greatest correspondent of the Reformation. *Henry Bullinger: Shepherd of the Churches,* 306–7.

12. Ibid., 41–42.

13. Philip Benedict, *Christ's Churches Purely Reformed: A Social History of Calvinism,* 59–60.

14. Ella, *Henry Bullinger,* 171, 172, 176. Ella argues that by 1550 Bullinger had far outpaced Calvin in publications. Benedict argues that by the 1540s Calvin had outsold Bullinger and continued to do so thereafter. Benedict, *Christ's Churches,* 91.

15. Ella, *Henry Bullinger,* 170–71.

16. Daniel Bolliger, "Bullinger on Church Authority: The Transformation of the Prophetic Role in Christian Ministry," 165. The subject of covenant continuity was asserted by Zwingli and Johannes Oecolampadius around the same time, though without the same focus, depth, or effect. Lillback, *The Binding of God,* 82–85.

17. Heinrich Bullinger, *A Brief Exposition of the One and Eternal Testament or Covenant of God,* trans. Charles S. McCoy and J. Wayne Baker, in *Fountainhead of Federalism: Heinrich Bullinger and the Covenantal Tradition.*

18. Lillback, *The Binding of God,* 110.

19. Bullinger, *Decades,* III.vi, 169–77.

20. Commonly translated as *Institutes of the Christian Religion.*

21. Zwingli and Oecolampadius called them "Catabaptists."

22. J. Wayne Baker, "Church, State, and Dissent: The Crisis of the Swiss Reformation, 1531–1536."

23. Bullinger, *Brief Exposition,* 125.

24. Ibid., 128.

25. Ibid., 113.

26. Ibid., 115.

27. Ibid., 114.

28. Andries Raath and Shaun De Freitas, "From Heinrich Bullinger to Samuel Rutherford: The Impact of Reformation Zurich on Seventeenth-Century Scottish Political Theory"; Emidio Campi, "Bullinger's Early Political and Theological Thought: Brutus Tigurinus," 198; J. Wayne Baker, *Heinrich Bullinger and the Covenant,* 104–5.

29. Bullinger, *Brief Exposition,* 112.

30. Ford Lewis Battles, *Concordance to Calvin's Corpus Reformatorum 1559 Edition of the* Institutes, cited in Lillback, *The Binding of God,* 126–27.

31. Bullinger, *Brief Exposition,* 128.

32. Von Rohr, *Covenant of Grace,* 53; Michael McGiffert, "*The Covenant of Grace in Puritan Thought* by John von Rohr." For a comparison of Calvin with fellow reformers and Thomas Aquinas on the subject of predestination, see David Steinmetz, *Calvin in Context,* 141–56.

33. See Leviticus 26 or Deuteronomy 11, for example. A word search within the King James Bible for "hearken" yields 233 results. See also Elazar, *Covenant and Polity,* 70–71.

34. Abraham or Joseph serve as examples that balance both divine sovereignty and human responsibility, and there are other, similar cases of responsibility and sovereignty. See David J. A. Clines, "Predestination in the Old Testament."

35. Von Rohr, *Covenant of Grace,* 31.

36. Leonard J. Trinterud, "The Origins of Puritanism"; Baker, *Bullinger and the Covenant.* For refutation, see Lillback, *The Binding of God;* Cornelius P. Venema, *Heinrich Bullinger and the Doctrine of Predestination. Author of "the Other Reformed Tradition"?* 17–33; Lyle D. Bierma, "Federal Theology in the Sixteenth Century: Two Traditions?"

37. Baker, *Bullinger and the Covenant,* 193–98. For a short overview of responses to Baker's thesis, and Bullinger's use of the covenant in his theology, see Emidio Campi, "Current State and Future Directions of Bullinger Research," 13–17.

38. Von Rohr, *Covenant of Grace,* 25; Baker, *Bullinger and the Covenant,* 1–26.

39. Lillback, *The Binding of God,* 128–34.

40. John Calvin, *Calvin's Commentaries,* I:452.

41. Ibid., I:449.

42. John Calvin, *Calvin's New Testament Commentaries,* 8:253.

43. Peter A. Lillback, "The Early Reformed Covenant Paradigm: Vermigli in the Context of Bullinger, Luther, and Calvin," 75–80.

44. In *De testamento,* Bullinger says very little about election, simply calling God's joining with "miserable mortals corrupted by sin" a mystery. Bullinger, *Brief Exposition,* 104–5.

45. John Calvin, *Catechism 1538,* Section 13.

46. Calvin's *De aeterna* was written in response to three prior controversies. In 1551, Jerome Bolsec had argued that Calvin's doctrine of predestination made God the author of sin.

47. Calvin, *Eternal Predestination of God,* VIII.5, 123.

48. Calvin, *New Testament Commentaries,* 8:202–3.

49. Calvin, *Eternal Predestination of God,* VIII.5, 121.

50. Ibid., 124.

51. Venema, *Heinrich Bullinger,* 71–100; W. Peter Stephens, "Predestination or Election in Zwingli and Bullinger." Originally written privately by Bullinger in 1564, the Second Helvetic Confession was widely adopted thereafter by Reformed Protestant churches in Scotland, Hungary, France, and Poland.

52. Campi, "Current State and Future Directions," 13.

53. See also John 6:44, 45; I Corinthians 2:14. The fact that Bullinger draws on the famous three virtues articulated by Saint Paul further demonstrates his recurrent theme of covenant continuity.

54. William G. Naphy, "Calvin's Geneva," 45–46.

55. Calvin's own views on predestination were certainly considered controversial within the Reformed community, both near to and far from Geneva. See Benedict, *Christ's Churches,* 103–4.

56. Bolsec was eventually exiled. He got his revenge with his slanderous 1577 biography, *Vie de Calvin.* Bolsec later returned to the Catholic Church and was also numbered among "libertines." This obviously did not help his later reputation within the Protestant community.

57. Venema, *Heinrich Bullinger,* 57–63; Stephens, "Predestination or Election," 325–26.

58. Bullinger also worried about the effect of the doctrine on the "simpler sort" *(Decades,* IV.iv, 185, 187).

59. See also Deuteronomy 10:16, Jeremiah 4:4, Acts 7:51.

CHAPTER 5: REGIME, DISCIPLINE, AND RESISTANCE

1. The cities of Bern, Freiburg, and Geneva entered into an alliance on February 8, 1526. This alliance was necessary for Geneva to stay in the German-Swiss confederacy and out of French control. It also meant that civil authorities in Bern could obstruct some of Calvin's desired reforms in Geneva. The Bern-Geneva union lasted until 1556. Naphy, "Calvin's Geneva," 25-31, 33-35.

2. Calvin could even be called a prophet without honor in his own country. Calvin's successor, Theodore Beza, asserted in a letter to John Knox that the growth of the Reformed community owed more to French immigration than to successful evangelism. Laing, *Works*

of John Knox, 6:563, cited in Ella, *Henry Bullinger*, 46.

3. Baker, *Bullinger and the Covenant*, 108–10, 114.

4. This is also evident from Calvin's use of civil authorities in the controversies with Bolsec or Servetus, for example.

5. Martyr compared Edward VI to Josiah. Peter Martyr to Rudolph Peter Gualter, June 1, 1550, Letter CCXXIX, in Hastings Robinson, trans. and ed., *Original Letters Relative to the English Reformation. Written during the Reigns of King Henry VIII, King Edward VI, and Queen Mary: Chiefly from the Archives of Zurich*, 2485; Calvin refers to only one king, Josiah, in his January 1, 1551, letter to Edward VI, Letter CCCXXXVI, ibid., 707–11.

6. Torrance Kirby, *The Zurich Connection and Tudor Political Theology*, 34–35.

7. Baker, *Bullinger and the Covenant*, 100.

8. I. John Hesselink, *Calvin's First Catechism: A Commentary*, 161–62.

9. Ella, *Henry Bullinger*, 185.

10. Ibid., 186–97.

11. Hesselink, *Calvin's First Catechism*, 162.

12. Naphy, "Calvin's Geneva," 31.

13. Ella, *Henry Bullinger*, 121–23.

14. Letter C, in Hastings Robinson, trans. and ed., *The Zurich Letters (Second Series) Comprising the Correspondence of Several English Bishops and Others with Some of the Helvetian reformers during the Reign of Queen Elizabeth*, 2:252.

15. English Presbyterian William Cartwright later asserted the same thing and insisted that this would in no way diminish temporal authority. See John Ayre, ed., *The Works of John Whitgift*, D.D., 1:20.

16. Ella, Henry Bullinger, 170; Bruce Gordon, "Introduction: Architect of Reformation," 28; Baker, *Heinrich Bullinger and the Covenant*, 90, 118; Letter C, Robinson, ed., *Zurich Letters*, 2:252–53. During later Presbyterian controversies in England, Bullinger's close associate Rudolph Gualter was very wary of church discipline.

17. Raath and De Freitas, "Bullinger to Rutherford," 856.

18. Calvin, *Catechism 1538*, Section 32.

19. Ibid.

20. Ella, *Henry Bullinger*, 239.

21. Bullinger has an extensive condemnation of auricular confession *(Decades*, IV.ii, 80–93). Calvin attacks auricular confession as used by Roman Catholics in his commentary on Matthew 18:18. Calvin, *A Harmony of the Gospels, Matthew, Mark and Luke*, in *New Testament Commentaries*, 2:231.

22. W. Kolfhaus, "*Der Verkehr Calvins mit Bullinger*," 37, cited in Ella, *Henry Bullinger*, 405n40.

23. Calvin's first edition praised monarchy, consistent with his appeal to King François. Diarmaid MacCulloch, *The Reformation*, 190.

24. Letter CCCLII, Robinson, ed., *Original Letters*, 2:745–47.

25. Christopher Goodman, *How Superior Powers Ought to Be Obeyed*, 75–76.

26. Campi, "Bullinger's Early Political and Theological Thought," 197–98.

27. J. Wayne Baker, "Covenant and Community in the Thought of Heinrich Bullinger," 23.

28. Letter XV, Robinson, ed., *Zurich Letters*, 2:34–36.

29. Calvin, *Catechism 1538*, Section 33, 33.

30. Douglas F. Kelly, *The Emergence of Liberty in the Modern World: The Influence of*

Calvin on Five Governments from the Sixteenth through the Eighteenth Centuries, 28–29.

31. Hancock questions whether Calvin's endorsement of resistance by the lesser magistrates cannot also be understood as an endorsement of private action. He characterizes the relationship as follows: "God has given certain men power over other men, but even private men must withdraw obedience from God's supposed representatives when this would require disobedience to God himself. Thus God's ordination does not finally remove the political responsibility of each individual." Ralph C. Hancock, *Calvin and the Foundations of Modern Politics,* 73. There is something to this, but the argument is better rooted in Calvin's argument for conscience.

32. Sermon XXIX on 1 Samuel in Charles Raynal and John Leith, eds., *Calvin Studies Colloquium,* 66, cited in Kelly, *Emergence of Liberty,* 29. This stands in contrast even to the *Institutes.* There he suggested a covenantal reasoning based on reciprocity of duties, but withdrew it. Calvin suggests that perhaps Christians may not be obliged to obey the civil authority over them if the representatives of that civil authority do not fulfill their duties. But he discourages this reciprocity-based view of disobedience, arguing that one must always look to his own duties rather than to "inquire into the duties of one another" (*Institutes* IV.xx.29, 673). Judging from his sermons on I Samuel, he may have changed his mind.

33. Joan Lockwood O'Donovan, *Theology of Law and Authority in the English Reformation,* 106.

34. Calvin, *Catechism 1538,* Preface, 4.

35. Ibid., 3.

36. Ibid., 4–5, 1, 3.

37. These are reprinted in John Calvin, *The Covenant Enforced: Sermons on Deuteronomy 27 and 28.*

38. James B. Jordan, "Editor's Introduction," xxxiv.

39. Heinrich Bullinger, *Anklag und ernstliches ermanen Gottes Allmaechtigen* (1528), quoted in Baker, *Bullinger and the Covenant,* 103, 104.

40. Stephens, "Predestination or Election," 333.

41. Baker, *Bullinger and the Covenant,* 49.

42. Ibid., 108–10, 114.

43. Ibid., 159, 161.

44. Ibid., 90–92.

45. Raath and De Freitas, "From Bullinger to Rutherford."

46. In his twenties, Calvin studied law under two distinguished professors, Pierre Taisan de l'Étoile and Andrea Alciati.

47. Coffey argues that much of what he wrote had been argued not only by previous Calvinist writers but also by the conciliarists and Spanish Thomists. But his integration of their arguments results in radical conclusions not normally drawn within the constitutionalist tradition. Coffey, *Politics, Religion,* 158.

48. Samuel Rutherford, *Lex, Rex or The Law and the Prince,* 119.

49. Quentin Skinner, *The Foundations of Modern Political Thought, Volume Two: The Age of Reformation,* 234–37.

50. This phrase, together with an allusion to biblical warfare ("An Appeal to Heaven") was put on some battle standards during the American War for Independence. Bonomi, *Under the Cope of Heaven,* 215. Ellis Sandoz provides background to this important phrase ("Resistance to tyrants") in *The Politics of Truth and Other Untimely Essays,* 204n6.

51. W. Stanford Reid, "John Knox's Theology of Political Government."

52. Roger A. Mason, "Introduction," xi.

53. John Knox, *The Appellation of John Knox,* 103–5; Mason, "Introduction," xix–xxi.

54. John Knox, *The Debate at the General Assembly, June 1564,* 192–97; Mason, "Introduction," xxiii–xxiv.

55. Paul T. Fuhrmann, "Philip Mornay and the Huguenot Challenge to Absolutism," 46–47.

56. Philippe Du Plessis Mornay, *Vindiciae, Contra Tyrannos,* 1–12.

57. John T. McNeill states, "It was in Calvinism that a uniformly representative polity appeared." See *The History and Character of Calvinism,* 411.

58. Rutherford, *Lex, Rex,* 6.

59. Rutherford, *Lex, Rex,* 45–46.

60. Goodman, *Superior Powers,* 19–20.

61. McNeill, *History and Character of Calvinism,* 414–15. In France, for example, Hotman and Mornay focus on the estates, believing these to be the representatives of the people.

62. Winthrop S. Hudson, "Theological Convictions and Democratic Government," 232–34.

63. Philippe Du Plessis Mornay, *Vindiciae, Contra Tyrannos,* 49.

64. Goodman, *Superior Powers,* 66–67.

65. Knox, *The First Blast of the Trumpet against the Monstrous Regiment of Women,* 29–30.

66. Knox, *Appellation,* 86; see also John Knox, *The Copy of a Letter delivered to the Lady Mary, Regent of Scotland,* 57–58.

67. Knox, *First Blast,* 25–26.

68. Ibid., 43.

69. Knox, *Appellation,* 95.

70. Goodman, *Superior Powers,* 72.

71. Ibid., 71, 72.

72. Ibid., 44.

73. Ibid., 4–5, 8–10, 12, 16–17, 26.

74. Ibid., 69.

75. Ibid., 55–56.

76. Ibid., 28–32.

77. Mornay, *Vindiciae, Contra Tyrannos,* 116–33.

78. Ibid., 45–46.

CHAPTER 6: THE LEGACIES OF GENEVA AND ZURICH IN ENGLAND AND SCOTLAND

1. Letter CCLXXXIII, Robinson, ed., *Original Letters,* 2:618.

2. Joseph C. McLelland, "The Second Book of Common Prayer," and "Translator's Introduction."

3. Ella, *Henry Bullinger,* 309–10; Kirby, *Zurich Connection,* 29. Later editions of Bullinger's *Decades* were often bound and sold with his irenic essay written during the 1560s controversy over worship ritual and vestments. The essay urged clergy to conform rather than desert the pulpit.

4. Diarmaid MacCulloch, "Heinrich Bullinger and the English-speaking World," 931.

5. Bruce Gordon, *The Swiss Reformation,* 304.

6. Ayre, ed., *Works of William Whitgift,* 2:588. By this time, however, the English clergy had been divided by two sharp controversies. Whitgift himself had no contact with Bullinger, and his drawing on Zurich to discourage nonconformity was arguably cynical and utilitarian. By 1586, Whitgift had become an opponent of the Puritans, and it was the Puritans who would deliberately carry the covenant ethos forward. Any prior association of Bullinger with Whitgift by this time, however misleading because Whitgift and Bullinger had not been friends or correspondents, would blunt Bullinger's influence among English Puritans.

7. Andrew Pettegree, *Marian Protestantism: Six Studies,* 3–4.

8. Francis Bourgoyne wrote to Calvin on December 4, 1550, "Our Josiah, the king of England, made most courteous inquiry of me concerning your health and ministry. . . . He sufficiently declared both by his countenance and his words, that he takes a great interest in you, and in every thing belonging to you." Bourgoyne urges Calvin to write to him "such a letter as would add spurs to a willing horse." Robinson, ed., *Original Letters,* Letter CCCXLVI, 2:730. In a letter to King Edward dated July 4, 1552, however, Calvin frets about being troublesome to him and mentions only occasional correspondence. He includes a friendly—but vague—encouragement to him as a Christian king and encloses a recent exposition on Psalm 87. Ibid., Letter CCCXXXVII, 2:714–15.

9. MacCulloch interprets the congratulatory letters of Calvin and Jan Laski as "patronizing advice to a young female." MacCulloch, *Reformation,* 281. Elizabeth urges the Swiss cantons to intervene on Geneva's behalf in 1583 and 1590 (after Calvin's death), but there is no notable correspondence between her and Calvin. Letter CXXXV, Robinson, ed., *Zurich Letters,* 1:333–36; Letters CXXXII, CXXXIII, 2:315–19.

10. Letter XV, Robinson, ed., *Zurich Letters,* 2:34; Wulfert DeGreef, *The Writings of John Calvin: An Introductory Guide,* 86.

11. Kirby, *Zurich Connection,* 25–41.

12. See, for example, John Hooper's affectionate and appreciative letters to Bullinger in Robinson, ed., *Original Letters,* 1:33–44, 48–67, 69–95, 99–101, 102–6. In this particular volume, there are more than one hundred letters written to Bullinger and only a handful written to Calvin. See also MacCulloch, "English-speaking world."

13. Hooper to Bullinger, December 11, 1554, Letter XLVIII, Robinson, ed., *Original Letters,* 1:105.

14. Gordon, *Swiss Reformation,* 303.

15. Ella, *Henry Bullinger,* 367, 371–74, 385, 389; Kirby, *Zurich Connection,* 1.

16. English translation of 1572, *A confutation of the Popes bull which was published more than two yeres agoe against Elizabeth the most gracious Queene of England, Fraunce, and Ireland, and against the noble realme of England: together with a defence of the sayd true Christian Queene, and of the whole realme of England.*

17. Gordon, *Swiss Reformation,* 301.

18. Stephen Brachlow, *The Communion of Saints: Radical Puritan and Separatist Ecclesiology, 1570–1625,* 27–30.

19. For discussion of Calvin and Reformed soteriology by conformists, and agreement on the truly "Calvinist" soteriology of the English church, see Peter Marshall, *Reformation England, 1480–1642,* 126–30. His discussion relies too much on the controversial thesis of Kendall, however, which argues too great a disagreement between Calvin and later "Calvinists." One testimony to the influence of Reformed soteriology in the Church of

England is provided in 1614 by one of its former clergy, Benjamin Carier, a former fellow of Corpus Christi College and earlier a chaplain to Bishop Whitgift and King James. Carier protested that the *Institution* (as Calvin's *Institutes* was then called) was still "the only current divinity in court and country." George Hakewill's official response in 1616 acknowledged the "Calvinisme" of the English church and traced it to Saint Augustine. Benjamin Carier, *A Treatise written by Mr. Doctour Carier,* 10–14, and George Hakewill, *An Answere to a Treatise Written by Dr. Carier,* 285–91, both cited in Nicholas Tyacke, *Anti-Calvinists: The Rise of English Arminianism c. 1590–1640,* 5–6.

20. The objection was more the politics than the soteriology. Marginal notes of the Bishop's Bible included predestinarian soteriology, as Tyacke points out in *Anti-Calvinists,* 2.

21. MacCulloch, *The Reformation,* 298–99.

22. Dale Walden Johnson, "Marginal at Best: John Knox's Contribution to the Geneva Bible, 1560."

23. Peter Martyr Vermigli, *To the Most Renowned Princess Elizabeth, by the grace of God Queene of England, France and Ireland.*

24. John Knox, *Works,* II, 174, cited in Horton Davies, *Worship and Theology in England: From Cranmer to Baxter and Fox, 1534–1690,* 47. Spelling is updated. I have taken the liberty of modernizing spelling in other quotations as well.

25. O'Donovan, *Theology of Law,* 109–10.

26. Letter LII, Robinson, ed., *Zurich Letters,* 2:131.

27. Letter LIX, ibid., 152.

28. Letter LII, ibid., 128.

29. Clarke Kellar, *Scotland, England, and the Reformation, 1534–1561,* 163–64, 180.

30. O'Donovan, *Theology of Law,* 94.

31. Ibid., 110–21.

32. Letter LXXV, Robinson, ed., *Zurich Letters,* 1:176–77.

33. In a letter dated June 11, 1568, Bishop Grindal thanked both Bullinger and "the people of Geneva" for their "quiet posture of affairs" in the controversy in which two hundred persons separated from their own ordained clergy and ministry of sacraments. Letter LXXXII, Robinson, ed., *Zurich Letters,* 1:201–2.

34. Letter XLIX, Robinson, ed., *Zurich Letters,* 2:, 117–20.

35. Letter LXXV, ibid., 1:176.

36. An English translation can be found in Kirby, *Zurich Connection,* 222–33, in Ella, *Henry Bullinger,* 413–20, and in Appendix Letter III, Robinson, ed. *Zurich Letters,* 1:345–53.

37. Appendix Letter III, Robinson, ed., *Zurich Letters,* 1:351–52.

38. Ibid., 348.

39. Ibid., 349.

40. Ibid., 354.

41. Anonymous, *An Admonition to the Parliament.*

42. O'Donovan, *Theology of Law,* 127.

43. Brachlow, *Communion of Saints,* 24, 29–30, 35–37.

44. Letter C, Robinson, ed., *Zurich Letters,* 2:251.

45. Letter XCVIII, ibid., 241–42.

46. Ibid., 242.

47. Letter CXXIII, ibid., 1:311.

48. See Gualter's letters to Bishop Cox, Letters XCIV, C, ibid., 2:225–35, 249–54; Kirby,

Zurich Connection, 3.

49. In 1590, Beza defended the right of presbyteries to excommunicate in *De vera excommunicatione et Christiano presbyterio.* But he had begun to attack the English church polity as early as 1566. See Gordon Donaldson, *The Scottish Reformation,* 188–90. Beza's letters are contained in W. H. Frere and C. E. Douglas, eds., *Puritan Manifestoes. A Study of the Origin of the Puritan Revolt. With a Reprint of the Admonition to Parliament and Kindred Documents, 1572,* 43–55; and Letter LIII, Robinson, ed., *Zurich Letters,* 2:127–36.

50. Letter LIII, Robinson, ed., *Zurich Letters,* 2:128–29.

51. Kirby has argued that Bullinger's influence on the conforming side of the controversy undermines any assertion that the English Reformation was a "theological cuckoo in the nest," an "egg" of Protestant theology inside a Roman Catholic "nest." Kirby, *Zurich Connection,* 203–20, esp. 219–20. See also Diarmaid MacCulloch, *The Later Reformation in England, 1547–1603,* 29, cited in Kirby, *Zurich Connection,* 219.

52. Ayre, ed., *Works of John Whitgift,* 3:496–97.

53. Robinson, *Zurich Letters,* 1:33, 138, 156; Kirby, *Zurich Connection,* 25. It might come as a surprise to some that both Jewel and Whitgift, both ready to praise Bullinger—a Reformed theologian—were responsible for Richard Hooker's *Of the Laws of Ecclesiastical Polity.* Jewel was Hooker's patron at Corpus Christi College in the late 1560s and 1570s. Whitgift appointed Hooker to write this defining work of Anglicanism in 1593. It attacked the Puritan dissent and deliberately and methodically moved the Church of England away from its dissenting theologies. Not only is it ironic that the Reformed influence of Calvin, Bullinger, Bucer, Martyr, and Laski on the Church of England is now largely forgotten, but also that Hooker's *Laws* were rather inconsequential at the time they were written. No Puritans thought it necessary to respond in print until at least 1599. Kirby, *Zurich Connection,* 4; MacCulloch, *Reformation,* 378.

54. Cartwright echoed his co-religionists when he wrote, "The prince and the civil magistrate hath to see that the laws of God, touching his worship, and touching all matters and orders of the church, be executed and duly observed, and to see that every ecclesiastical person do that office whereunto he is appointed, and to punish those which fail in their office accordingly." Quoted in A. F. Scott Pearson, *Church and State: Political Aspects of Sixteenth Century Puritanism,* 30; see 29–35 for a fuller discussion of Cartwright's prescription for the civil magistrate.

55. Ibid., 20–21.

56. Ibid., 15.

57. Peter Lake, *Anglicans and Puritans? Presbyterian and English Conformist Thought from Whitgift to Hooker,* 50.

58. Ibid., 34–37; Letter C, Robinson, ed., *Zurich Letters,* 2:252.

59. John Selden and others carried this debate into the Westminster Assembly. Chapter 30, Section IV of the *Westminster Confession* asserts the right of church officers to excommunicate. But given the lingering Erastian sentiment, this chapter was not ratified by English Parliament.

60. Lake, *Anglicans and Puritans?* 58.

61. Ibid., 36–42.

62. Robert Browne, *A Book which sheweth the Life and Manners of all true Christians.*

63. Brachlow, *Communion of Saints,* 157–202.

64. Even the English Baptists who rejected the paedobaptist tradition of the Reformed Protestants would use the Separatist church polity and thereby adopt covenantal themes of Reformed theology in the late sixteenth century. Ibid., 50–54, 151–56.

65. Perry Miller, *The New England Mind: The Seventeenth Century,* 365–431; Perry Miller, *Errand Into the Wilderness,* 48–90.

66. From a philological standpoint, it would appear that there should be no difference between the terms "federal theology" and "covenant theology," and scholars sometimes use them interchangeably. The root of the word "federal" comes from the Latin *foedus,* which was often translated from the Hebrew *berith* or Greek *diatheke* (testament). A precise understanding would use the term "federal theology" to refer to the later theological innovation of the "covenant of works," for federal theology argues that there are two covenants in Scripture. The first covenant was a prelapsarian (pre-Fall) covenant made with Adam. This is what federal theologians called a "Covenant of Works." Because Adam is seen as a "federal" head of the whole human race, it is a covenant still binding on all men even after Adam's fall. The second covenant is a "Covenant of Grace." It is made with Jesus Christ, who is presented as a "second Adam," and also therefore a federal head. Christ, as a second Adam, keeps the original prelapsarian covenant of works and takes upon himself the penalty associated with it. Redemption is applied from Christ's atonement and applied to the redeemed. Von Rohr, for example, uses them almost interchangeably, preferring to emphasize similarities rather than differences. In his work on covenantal political theory, Daniel Elazar also refers to covenant theology as "federal theology" without distinguishing the theological differences between federal theology and covenant theology.

67. Weir, *Origins of the Federal Theology,* 22, 99–114; William K. B. Stoever, *"A Faire and Easie Way to Heaven": Covenant Theology and Antinomianism in Early Massachusetts,* 81–83.

68. Lyle D. Bierma, "Covenant or Covenants in the Theology of Olevianus?"

69. Weir, *Origins of the Federal Theology,* 115–52; Stoever, *"A Faire and Easie Way to Heaven,"* 84; Gaius Jackson Slosser, "Origins," 17.

70. Samuel Rutherford, *The Covenant of Life Opened, or, A Treatise of the Covenant of Grace.*

71. For the continuing relevance of the moral law under the covenant of works, see Stoever, *"A Faire and Easie Way to Heaven,"* 90–93.

72. William Ames, *Conscience with the Power and Cases thereof: Divided into Five Books,* I.ii.3–5; Lynne Courter Boughton, "Choice and Action: William Ames's Concept of the Mind's Operation in Moral Decisions," 196; Lee W. Gibbs, "The Puritan Natural Law Theory of William Ames," 45–52, 54–57.

73. Weir, *Origins of Federal Theology,* 6.

74. Norman Pettit, *The Heart Prepared: Grace and Conversion in Puritan Spiritual Life,* 48–85.

75. MacCulloch, *Reformation,* 378–79; R. T. Kendall, *Calvin and English Calvinism to 1649,* 52–54, 56, 58, 60–61, 67–76; George L. Mosse, *The Holy Pretence: A Study in Christianity and Reason of State from William Perkins to John Winthrop,* 48–87.

76. Van Asselt and Stoever suggest that insofar as Melanchthon may have been a proto-founder of federal theology, natural law was an essential part of it from the beginning. See Willem J. Van Asselt, *The Federal Theology of Johannes Cocceius (1603–1669),* 326–27, 331–32; Stoever, *"A Faire and Easie Way to Heaven,"* 82.

77. Weir, *Origins of Federal Theology,* 27.

CHAPTER 7: COVENANT, REVOLUTION, WAR, AND ESCHATOLOGY

1. For a discussion of whether these wars should be called "revolutions," see John Morrill, "Introduction."

2. Margo Todd, "The Problem of Scotland's Puritans," 175.

3. Coffey, *Politics, Religion,* 17–25.

4. Todd, "Scotland's Puritans."

5. Margaret Steele, "The 'Politick Christian': The Theological Background to the National Covenant," 46–48.

6. Roger A. Mason, *Kingship and the Commonweal: Political Thought in Renaissance and Reformation Scotland,* 8–138; J. H. Burns, *The True Law of Kingship: Concepts of Monarchy in Early-Modern Scotland,* 19–92; Quentin Skinner, "The Origins of the Calvinist Theory of Revolution."

7. Letter C, Robinson, ed., *Zurich Letters,* 2:251.

8. Letter CXXX, ibid., 312–13.

9. MacCulloch, *Reformation,* 370.

10. Regarding the ecclesiastical demands of the Presbyterians, see Bishop Cox's letter to Rudolph Gualter dated February 4, 1573, Letter CVII, Robinson, ed., *Zurich Letters,* 2:279–82.

11. Ayre, ed., *Works of John Whitgift,* 2:263–64.

12. Dudley Fenner, *Sacra Theologia;* Lake, *Anglicans and Puritans?* 57.

13. Pearson, *Church & State,* 61.

14. P. Hume Brown, *George Buchanan, Humanist and Reformer: A Biography,* 269–71.

15. For an excellent overview of the scholarly debate about what motivated Laud and Charles, see Marshall, *Reformation England,* 194–205.

16. John Morrill, "The National Covenant in Its British Context," 6; Allan I. MacInnes, *Charles I and the Making of the Covenanting Movement, 1625–1641.*

17. Steele, "The 'Politick Christian.'"

18. John Knox, *Summary of the Second Blast of the Trumpet,* 128.

19. Rutherford, *Lex, Rex,* 39.

20. Thomas Hobbes said that Manwaring "preached his doctrine." A. P. Martinich, *A Hobbes Dictionary,* 9.

21. Morrill, "Introduction," xxiii.

22. George Milligan, *The English Bible: A Sketch of Its History,* 86.

23. Rutherford, *Lex, Rex,* 54–62.

24. Ibid., 1, 3, 6, 25.

25. Ibid., 54.

26. Ibid., 54.

27. Ibid., 59.

28. Ibid., 72–77.

29. Ibid., 26.

30. Ibid., 136–43.

31. Ibid., 152–59.

32. Ibid., 33.

33. Lawrence Kaplan, *Politics and Religion during the English Revolution: The Scots and the Long Parliament, 1643–1645,* 151–58.

34. *The Presbyterians Not Guilty of the Unjust Charge of being concerned in the murther*

of King Charles I; also Article 3 of the Solemn League and Covenant.

35. Of the covenanting tradition, Steele notes, "Renewal of such covenants was a well-established ritual with no less than thirty-one extant documents of this type dating from the Reformation, the earliest known being the Duns Covenant of 1556 which was drafted on John Knox's return from exile on the Continent." Steele, "The 'Politick Christian,'" 45–46.

36. Ibid., 54.

37. Ibid., 44.

38. Archibald Johnston, *Diary of Sir Archibald Johnston of Wariston,* 1:308, 408; cited in ibid., 49.

39. For a confirmation of Scottish monarchial allegiance, see ibid., 55–56.

40. MacInnes, *Charles I,* 166–77.

41. Steele, "The 'Politick Christian,'" 45.

42. Ibid., 58.

43. W. D. J. McKay, *An Ecclesiastical Republic: Church Government in the Writings of George Gillespie,* 5.

44. William Lamont, *Godly Rule: Politics and Religion, 1603–1660,* 110.

45. McKay, *Ecclesiastical Republic,* 270.

46. George Gillespie, *Aaron's Rod Blossoming,* cited in ibid., 9–40.

47. One prominent example includes Thomas Goodwin, *Zerubbabel's Encouragement to Finish the Temple.*

48. John F. Wilson, *Pulpit in Parliament: Puritanism during the English Civil Wars 1640–1648,* 174–75.

49. Joseph Caryl, *The Nature, Solemnity, Grounds, Property, and Benefits of a Sacred Covenant Together with the Duties of Those Who Enter into Such a Covenant,* 7, 18–29, quoted in ibid., 171.

50. Examples include Thomas Hill, *The Trade of Truth Advanced,* and Herbert Palmer, *The Necessity and Encouragement, of Utmost Venturing for the Churches Help.*

51. Cornelius Burges, *The First Sermon Preached to the Honourable House of Commons now assembled in Parliament at their Publique Fast,* 57, quoted in Wilson, *Pulpit in Parliament,* 201.

52. Herbert Palmer, *The Glasse of Gods Providence;* John Strickland, *Mercy rejoycing against Judgment.*

53. Wilson, *Pulpit in Parliament,* 183–89.

54. Ibid., 195.

55. Lamont, *Godly Rule,* 13–15.

56. J. G. A. Pocock, *The Machiavellian Moment: Florentine Political Thought and the Atlantic Republican Tradition,* 31–48. See Chapter 11 for a discussion of Voegelin's concept of "metastatic faith" as applied to the Puritans.

57. Lamont, *Godly Rule,* 7–9.

58. Avihu Zakai, *Exile and Kingdom: History and Apocalypse in the Puritan Migration to America,* 16–22. Luther rejected any attempt at dating the apocalypse and also rejected chiliasm. But he did interpret Revelation 20 as part of church history rather than a future eschatological history. This meant that both ecclesiastical events (such as the papacy's war on Protestantism) and political events (such as the Turkish advance to Vienna) were part of the "last things." See Carter Lindberg, "Eschatology and Fanaticism in the Reformation Era: Luther and the Anabaptists," 269–71.

59. Zakai, *Exile and Kingdom,* 25.

60. Lamont, *Godly Rule,* 22–23; George Yule, *Puritans in Politics: The Religious Legislation of the Long Parliament, 1640–1647,* 30–32.

61. Zakai, *Exile and Kingdom,* 26–31.

62. William Haller, *The Elect Nation;* Noel Henning Mayfield, *Puritans and Regicide: Presbyterian–Independent Differences over the Trial and Execution of Charles (I) Stuart,* 43–52; Wilson, *Pulpit in Parliament,* 173.

63. Zakai, *Exile and Kingdom,* 31–37.

64. Lamont, *Godly Rule,* 23, 25, 41–43.

65. Wilson, *Pulpit in Parliament,* 215–23; Theodore Dwight Bozeman, *To Live Ancient Lives: The Primitivist Dimension in Puritanism,* 198–217.

66. Brachlow, *Communion of Saints,* 84.

67. Zakai, *Exile and Kingdom,* 37–46.

68. Wilson, *Pulpit in Parliament,* 208–9.

69. Ibid., 198–99.

70. It should be noted that apocalyptic ideas continued even into the Restoration and were not confined to the revolution or the commonwealth periods. See Warren Johnston, "The Anglican Apocalypse in Restoration England."

71. It is important to note that these categories (Presbyterian/Independent/Congregational) are best applied in retrospect. They were not always clearly defined or heavily utilized at the time.

72. For examples of how the Genevan eschatology made its way into England and Scotland, see Crawford Gribben, *The Puritan Millennium: Literature and Theology, 1550–1682.*

73. Wilson, *Pulpit in Parliament,* 223–30; Geoffrey F. Nuttall, *Visible Saints: The Congregational Way, 1640–1660;* Leo F. Solt, *Saints in Arms: Puritanism and Democracy in Cromwell's Army;* Tai Liu, *Discord in Zion: The Puritan Divines and the Puritan Revolution, 1640–1660.*

74. G. P. Gooch, *The History of English Democratic Ideas in the Seventeenth Century,* 127.

75. Richard Sibbes, *Works of Richard Sibbes,* vol. 7. Sibbes died in 1635 and therefore had no role in the Revolution. Thomas Goodwin, *Zerubbabel's Encouragement.* Goodwin is also thought to be the author of *A Glimpse of Sions Glory,* a prominent millennial sermon.

76. John Owen, *Ebenezer: A Memorial of the Deliverance Of Essex County, And Committee. In Two Sermons.*

77. Bozeman, *Ancient Lives,* 217–36.

78. John Cotton, *The Powring Out of the Seven Vials or an Exposition, of the 16 Chapter of the Revelation, with an Application of it to our Times* and *An Exposition Upon the Thirteenth Chapter of Revelation.* For the idea of the exodus to America as a literal exodus from the judgment of God, see Zakai, *Exile and Kingdom,* 63–65; Bozeman, *Ancient Lives,* 237–62. See also Francis J. Bremer, "The Defense of Regicides: John Cotton on the Execution of Charles I."

79. Thomas Hooker, *A Survey of the Summe of Church Discipline.*

80. Hugh Peters, *God's Doings and Man's Duty;* Hugh Peters, *A Word for the Army and Two Words to the Kingdom.*

81. William Dell, *The City Ministers Unmasked;* Peter Sterry, *The Comings Forth of*

Christ; John Owen, *The Shaking and Translating of Heaven and Earth.*

82. Mayfield, *Puritans and Regicide,* 112.

83. Goodwin, *Zion's Glory,* 79.

84. Wilson, *Pulpit in Parliament,* 231–32.

85. Mayfield, *Puritans and Regicide,* 101.

86. William M. Lamont, *Puritanism and Historical Controversy,* 145.

87. Goodwin, *Zerubbabel's Encouragement,* 118; John Cooke, *King Charles's case or, an appeal to all rational men, concerning his tryal at the High Court of Justice.*

88. Mayfield, *Puritans and Regicide,* 186.

89. Thomas Goodwin, "Epistle to the Reader," *Innocency and Truth Triumphing Together,* 9, 89, 134, quoted in ibid., 187.

90. Mayfield, *Puritans and Regicide,* 82; Lamont, "Introduction," x. It bears mention that Baxter had an abiding interest in eschatology and the millennium, but this flowered long after the civil war. See William M. Lamont, *Richard Baxter and the Millennium: Protestant Imperialism and the English Revolution.*

91. Robert Baillie, *Letters and Journals of Robert Baillie,* 2:313; Wilson, *Pulpit in Parliament,* 228; Lamont, *Godly Rule,* 112. Chiliasm was considered a heresy by most of the church, particularly the reformers, because it interpreted Scripture to require a one-thousand-year literal rule (on earth) by Christ. It was associated with radicalism and violence throughout church history.

92. Samuel Rutherford, *A Survey of the Summe of Church Discipline.*

93. Alexander Henderson, *A Sermon Preached to the Honorable House of Lords.*

94. John Lightfoot, *A sermon preached before the honorable House of Commons.*

95. Thomas Hayne, *Christs Kingdome on Earth, opened according to the Scriptures. Herein is examined what Mr. Th. Brightman, Dr. J. Alstede, Mr. I. Mede, Mr. H. Archer, The Glympse of Sions Glory, and such as concurre in opinion with them, hold concerning the thousand years of the Saints Reign with Christ, and of Satans binding;* Thomas Hall, *A confutation of the Millenarian Opinion;* Katherine Firth, *The Apocalyptic Tradition in Reformation Britain 1530–1645.*

96. Brachlow, *Communion of the Saints,* 118–23.

97. Mayfield, *Puritans and Regicide,* 186–92. Mayfield's analysis is insightful, but he places too much emphasis on a nature-grace dichotomy in Calvin. My corrective is in Chapter 9.

98. Larzer Ziff, *The Career of John Cotton: Puritanism and the American Experience,* 187–88.

99. Mayfield, *Puritans and Regicide,* 159–62.

100. Ibid., 190–92.

101. Samuel Rutherford, *A Free Disputation against Pretended Liberty of Conscience;* William Prynne, *The Sword of Christian Magistry Supported;* Thomas Edwards, *Gangraena: Or a Catalogue and Discovery of many of the Errours, Heresies, Blasphemies and pernicious Practices of the Sectaries of this time, vented and acted in England in these four last years;* Ann Hughes, *Gangrena and the Struggle for the English Revolution.*

102. John Owen, *A Sermon Preached to the Honorable House of Commons, in Parliament—Assembled on January 31. A Day of Solemn Humiliation: With a Discourse About Toleration, and the Duty of the Civil Magistrate About Religion, Thereunto Annexed;* John Milton, *Of Reformation in England And the Causes that have Hitherto Hindered it.*

103. Robert Baillie, *A Dissuasive from the Errors of the Time;* Rutherford, *Summe of*

Church Discipline, A Survey of the Spiritual Antichrist, and *A Free Disputation.*

104. John Goodwin, *Theomachia, Innocency and Truth Triumphing Together* and *Hagiomastix: or the Scourge of the Saints Displayed,* and *The Obstructors of Justice;* John Cotton, *The Way of the Congregational Churches Cleared;* John Cooke, *What the Independents Would Have;* John Cooke, *Redintegratio Amoris* and *Monarchy No Creature of God's Making.*

105. John Cooke, *The Vindication of the Law: so far forth as scripture and right reason may be judge, and speedy justice (which exalts a nation) may be advanced. Wherein is declared what manner of persons Christian magistrates, judges, and lawyers ought to be;* Mayfield, *Puritans and Regicide,* 165–74.

106. William Prynne, *The Substance of a Speech to the House of Commons.*

107. John Milton, *The Tenure of Kings and Magistrates.*

108. John Owen, *A Dissertation on Divine Justice.*

109. Milton, *Kings and Magistrates.*

110. Mayfield, *Puritans and Regicide,* 174.

111. Ibid., 167–68, 179–80.

112. Peters, *God's Doings,* 25, 31, cited in Mayfield, *Puritans and Regicide,* 176.

113. Cooke, *Vindication of the Law.*

114. Sterry, *Comings Forth of Christ.*

115. Mayfield, *Puritans and Regicide,* 220–21.

CHAPTER 8: THE COVENANT IN AMERICA

1. For example, when Princeton theologian Charles Hodge argued in 1839 that most of the New England Puritans were essentially Presbyterians, William Hill, a Virginia pastor, retorted, "There is no term used more vaguely, and in a more indefinite sense, than that of Presbyterian. Next to it, was the term Puritan—and these two are often so united, or blended together, that by many they are used and considered as synonymous terms, or as meaning the same thing." William W. McKinney, "Beginnings in the North," 29; Charles Hodge, *The Constitutional History of the Presbyterian Church in the United States of America, Part I;* William Hill, *A History of the Rise, Progress, Genius and Character of American Presbyterianism,* 2.

2. Alan Simpson, *Puritanism in Old and New England,* 19–38; Harry S. Stout, *The New England Soul: Preaching and Religious Culture in Colonial New England,* 29. These settlers were mainly in New England, Pennsylvania, and New Jersey. Backcountry settlements in the Middle Colonies consisted of Scots-Irish and Germans who reconstituted their churches. Frank Lambert, *Inventing the "Great Awakening,"* 36. Neither Anglicans nor Quakers had church covenants. David A. Weir, *Early New England: A Covenanted Society,* 176, 180; regarding Baptists, see 182–83, 186–87.

3. Edmund S. Morgan, *The Puritan Family: Religion & Domestic Relations in Seventeenth-Century New England,* 3–12, 90–92, 180–82; Stout, *New England Soul,* 22; Daniel J. Elazar, *Covenant and Constitutionalism: The Great Frontier and the Matrix of Federal Democracy,* 33–41.

4. Reiner Smolinski, ed., *The Threefold Paradise of Cotton Mather: An Edition of "Triparadisus";* Cotton, *Exposition,* and *The Churches Resurrection, or the Opening of the Fifth and Sixth Verses of the 20th Chap. Of the Revelation;* Stover, *Faire and Easie Way*

to Heaven, 23; Miller, *From Colony to Province,* 185–90, 213; Robert Middlekauff, *The Mathers: Three Generations of Puritan Intellectuals 1596–1728,* 179–87, 320–49; Thomas S. Kidd, *The Protestant Interest: New England after Puritanism,* 136–66; Zakai, *Exile and Kingdom.*

5. Miller, *Seventeenth Century,* 463–92; Miller, *From Colony to Province,* 3–15, 184–85, 345–66.

6. Sacvan Bercovitch, *The American Jeremiad;* Miller, *From Colony to Province,* 19–39, 184–85, 345–66; Andrew R. Murphy, *Prodigal Nation: Moral Decline and Divine Punishment from New England to 9/11,* 17–43.

7. Miller, *From Colony to Province,* 21–24, 53–67, 98–99; Edmund S. Morgan, *Visible Saints: The History of a Puritan Idea.*

8. Jamestown and the Colony of Virginia were founded in 1607 on the model of the 1606 Charter of Virginia. There is no record of a Jamestown compact or combination supplementing the 1606 charter. The Mayflower Pilgrims secured permission in 1619 from the London Company and from the Plymouth Company. The Pilgrims, who were Separatists, supplemented the 1606 Charter with the Mayflower Compact. Weir, *Early New England,* 30–31.

9. Before 1660, most covenants were established by male members of the community as either a combination or a compact. The second generation of New Englanders moved away from the communal approach and allowed a committee system to articulate the covenantal vision. Whereas the making of an ecclesiastical covenant was seen as a very solemn and significant occasion, the making of a civil covenant was a more mundane affair. Ibid., 9, 134.

10. Ibid., 85.

11. Ibid., 29–30, 103, 107, 108, 118, 158. "The Articles of Confederation of the United Colonies of New England," which established a military defense for four colonies, asserted a rare christocentric vision for New England (excluding Providence Plantation and Rhode Island).

12. Ibid., 125.

13. Ibid., 9–10, 42, 48, 57, 71, 211.

14. Ibid., 14, 148, 225.

15. Samuel Hugh Brockunier, *The Irrepressible Democrat: Roger Williams;* James E. Ernst, *The Political Thought of Roger Williams;* Alan Simpson, "How Democratic Was Roger Williams?" 54.

16. For a defense of Williams as a Reformed theologian (rather than casting Williams as someone outside the Reformed tradition), see James Calvin Davis, *The Moral Theology of Roger Williams: Christian Conviction and Public Ethics.*

17. Miller, *From Colony to Province,* 68–81.

18. Roger Williams, *The Complete Writings of Roger Williams,* 3:123–24. As James P. Byrd points out, Williams was willing and able to use the Old Testament to argue for religious liberty. He did not reject the Old Testament as some have suggested. James P. Byrd, *The Challenges of Roger Williams: Religious Liberty, Violent Persecution, and the Bible,* 53–86. For a discussion of typology, see Stout, *New England Soul,* 45.

19. Williams, *Complete Writings,* 3:244–45, 367–68. Under Williams's leadership, Rhode Island became a center for religious toleration. There were exceptions, of course. Catholics were excluded from toleration on the common Protestant justification that they swore allegiance to a foreign power. Williams allowed Quakers to worship but disarmed

them and required them to wear distinctive clothing. Williams, like many others, suspected the Quakers of incivility and contempt for authority. Morgan, *Roger Williams,* 137; Williams, *Collected Writings,* 4:313–14, 3:171. See also Morgan, *Roger Williams,* 137.

20. Williams, *Complete Writings,* 3:317, 324, 327.

21. Ibid., 343–44, 329.

22. Byrd, *Challenges of Roger Williams,* 104–27.

23. Williams, *Complete Writings,* 3:5, 131–33.

24. Ibid., 225, 353.

25. Ibid., 237–41. See also Byrd, *Challenges of Roger Williams,* 139–51.

26. Williams, *Complete Writings,* 3:153–55.

27. Ibid., 70–71, 79, 249, 353.

28. Ibid., 97–108, 4:114–30. See also John Cotton, *The Bloudy Tenent Washed, And made white in the bloud of the Lambe: being discussed and discharged of bloud-guiltinesse by just Defence,* 38–49. The debate between Cotton and Williams is nicely summarized in Lisa M. Gordis, *Opening Scripture: Bible Reading and Interpretive Authority in Puritan New England,* 128–42.

29. Williams, *Complete Writings,* 3:111.

30. Ibid., 127.

31. Ibid., 126–27.

32. Ibid., 258, 259.

33. Ibid., 138, 203, 302.

34. Ibid., 225.

35. Cotton puts the question to Williams as to whether "It is true the Lord knoweth who are his and none of his Elect shall perish. But neverthelesse, Is it not a tempting of God, to presume upon Gods Election for our salvation, and to neglect the meanes of our preservation?" Cotton, *Bloudy Tenent Washed,* 50.

36. Weir, *Early New England,* 51–54. The question of religious toleration was not related to just conscience and orthodoxy but pertained also to civil disruption and to preserving the common good. While much can be said about these matters, suffice it to say that the emphasis on public virtue through private religiosity—and on civil piety *only* through free ecclesiastical association—is a minority view of the covenant.

37. For example, Richard Baxter, though technically not a firm Presbyterian, disagreed with Independent John Owen's restrictive admission to communion. Baxter's Ministerial Associations took a more generous approach. Lamont, "Bibliographical Notes," xxx.

38. Miller, *From Colony to Province,* 78–92, 209–25.

39. Weir, *Early New England,* 183.

40. David D. Hall, ed., *Puritans in the New World: A Critical Anthology,* 7.

41. Jon Butler, *Awash in a Sea of Faith: Christianizing the American People,* 55–63.

42. Robert G. Pope, *The Half-Way Covenant: Church Membership in Puritan New England,* 13–42.

43. Miller, *From Colony to Province,* 93–104.

44. Pope, *Half-Way Covenant,* 43–72; Mark Noll, *America's God: From Jonathan Edwards to Abraham Lincoln,* 30–41; Stout, *New England Soul,* 58–61.

45. Connecticut did not send a representative to the synod, and its clergy were divided on the question, particularly given the growing Presbyterianism there. Pope, *Half-Way Covenant,* 75–131.

46. Weir, *Early New England,* 216; Miller, *From Colony to Province,* 254–55; Morgan,

Visible Saints, 148–50.

47. Mark A. Peterson, *The Price of Redemption: The Spiritual Economy of Puritan New England,* 41.

48. Pope, *Half-Way Covenant,* 132–205.

49. Ibid., 272–73.

50. Miller, *From Colony to Province,* 105–13.

51. Ibid., 234–40.

52. Peter Y. De Jong, *The Covenant Idea in New England Theology, 1620–1847,* 129. Stoddard himself did not identify as a Presbyterian, nor did he advocate anything distinctly "Presbyterian" in church polity.

53. Solomon Stoddard, *The Doctrine of Instituted Churches,* cited in Noll, *America's God,* 41. Stoddard also believed that cross-examination of conversion narratives was of dubious value. See George M. Marsden, *Jonathan Edwards: A Life,* 30–31.

54. Middlekauf, *The Mathers,* 113–38.

55. C. C. Goen, *Revivalism and Separatism in New England, 1740–1800: Strict Congregationalists and Separate Baptists in the Great Awakening,* 5–6; Miller, *From Colony to Province,* 234-40, 257-61; DeYoung, *The Covenant Idea,* 130-35.

56. Miller, *From Colony to Province,* 257–58.

57. Marsden, *Jonathan Edwards,* 31.

58. Ibid., 32.

59. Increase Mather, *The Order of the Gospel, Professed and Practised by the Churches of Christ in New-England,* cited in Miller, *From Colony to Province,* 260–61.

60. Miller, *From Colony to Province,* 283-85.

61. Solomon Stoddard, *The Inexcusableness of Neglecting the Worship of God, Under A Pretence of Being in an Unconverted Condition.*

62. Miller, *From Colony to Province,* 276–81.

63. Stout, *New England Soul,* 119; Miller, *From Colony to Province,* 119–29, 165–72.

64. Weir, *Early New England,* 65–66, 69. The move toward religious toleration, even denominational pluralism, should not be overstated. Dissenters often remained second-class citizens. Weir writes, "It should be noted, however, that freedom of worship did not entail disestablishment of religion and secularization of institutional life, nor did it prohibit each colony from making life difficult for dissenters to the established church: Baptists, Quakers, and Anglicans still had to pay the compulsory tithes, and there were no laws protecting dissenting religious groups from bias."

65. Stout, *New England Soul,* 120–21; Cotton Mather, *Optanda, Good Men Described and Good Things Propounded,* cited in ibid.; Increase Mather from Miller, *From Colony to Province,* 169.

66. Noll, *America's God,* 37.

67. Pettit, *Heart Prepared,* 48–85.

68. Leonard J. Trinterud, *The Forming of an American Tradition: A Re-examination of Colonial Presbyterianism,* 170.

69. Cotton Mather, *A Midnight Cry;* Miller, *From Colony to Province,* 115–18.

70. Thomas S. Kidd, *The Great Awakening: The Roots of Evangelical Christianity in Colonial America,* 3–4; Peterson, *The Price of Redemption,* 48–49, 131–37.

71. Kidd, *The Great Awakening,* 4–5.

72. Miller, *From Colony to Province,* 223–25.

73. This was the goal of revivalists such as Gilbert Tennent, who learned pietism from

his father (Wiliam Tennent, Sr.) and his friend Theodorus Jacobus Frelinghuysen. See Milton J. Coalter, Jr., *Gilbert Tennent, Son of Thunder: A Case Study of Continental Pietism's Impact on the First Great Awakening in the Middle Colonies,* xviii–xx, 27–54; Charles Hartshorn Maxson, *The Great Awakening in the Middle Colonies,* 11–39.

74. Revivalists in New England and New Jersey lamented the growing gap between the visible and invisible church. Lambert, *Inventing the Great Awakening,* 32.

75. Stout, *New England Soul,* 175–76.

76. Bonomi, *Under the Cope of Heaven,* 133–60.

77. Lambert, *Inventing the Great Awakening,* 139, 195.

78. Noll, *America's God,* 44.

79. For a seventeenth-century criticism of enthusiasm, and one that many educated Americans would likely have read and agreed with, see John Locke's *An Essay Concerning Human Understanding,* book 4, chapters 16, 18, 19. For a balanced reading of Locke's influence on Edwards, see Marsden, *Jonathan Edwards,* 62–64.

80. Kidd, *Great Awakening,* 153-54.

81. Lambert, *Inventing the Great Awakening,* 109–10.

82. Ibid., 186, 195-97.

83. Kidd, *Great Awakening,* 5–9.

84. Lambert, *Inventing the Great Awakening,* 39–41, 62.

85. Jonathan Edwards, *Distinguishing Marks of a Work of the Spirit of God, Lectures on the Qualifications for Full Communion in the Church of Christ, Freedom of the Will,* and *Nature of True Virtue.*

86. For a provocative discussion of Edwards on the theological covenants, including treatment of him by Perry Miller and others, see John H. Gerstner, *The Rational Biblical Theology of Jonathan Edwards,* 2:79–97.

87. For a discussion of this controversy about children and the covenant in the larger context of Reformed theology, see Gerstner, *Rational Biblical Theology of Jonathan Edwards,* 2:115–38.

88. See Marsden, *Jonathan Edwards,* 291–305, for a discussion of the controversies surrounding the conduct of youth in Northampton.

89. Gerstner provides an excerpt of Edwards's response to Williams in *Rational Biblical Theology of Jonathan Edwards,* 2:132–36.

90. Noll, *America's God,* 46–47.

91. Edwards's sermon cited in Gerstner, *Rational Biblical Theology of Jonathan Edwards,* 2:141.

92. Gerald R. McDermott, *One Happy and Holy Society: The Public Theology of Jonathan Edwards,* 128–35. McDermott misses the significance of Edwards's role when he concludes, "On this score Edwards was no innovator. Puritan tradition held that church and state were to be separate in function." While it is true that Edwards's position had become mainstream by the eighteenth century, and not inconsistent with the commonwealth thinking within Reformed political theology, coupling this position with Edwards's other opinions makes him significant in the collapse of the civil-religious covenantal political theology.

93. Ibid., 34.

94. Noll believes that Edwards discarded the national covenant; Gerstner believes he retained a form of it. Noll, *America's God,* 47–48; Gerstner, *Rational Biblical Theology of Jonathan Edwards,* 2:139–40.

95. Edwards's sermon from Gerstner, *Rational Biblical Theology of Jonathan Edwards,* 2:139–40. Proverbs 14:34 reads, "Righteousness exalts a nation, but sin is a reproach to any people."

96. One example is Edwards's interpretation of an agricultural crisis in 1736 as a judgment of God. For a discussion of this and an overview of Edwards's view of national covenant in the context of Puritan scholarship, see McDermott, *One Happy and Holy Society,* 11–36.

97. The passage in II Chronicles 23:16 reads, "Jehoiada then made a covenant that he and the people and the king would be the LORD's people." Jonathan Edwards, *A Covenant People Ought to Resolve to Be the Lord's People,* quoted in Gerstner, *Rational Biblical Theology of Jonathan Edwards,* 2:140.

98. Marsden, *Jonathan Edwards,* 260–63.

99. Ruth H. Bloch, "Religion and Ideological Change in the American Revolution," 52–54.

100. Dale S. Kuehne, *Massachusetts Congregationalist Political Thought, 1760–1790: The Design of Heaven,* 137.

101. Keith L. Griffin, *Revolution and Religion: American Revolutionary War and the Reformed Clergy,* 71–81, 85–86.

102. Garry Wills, *Inventing America,* cited in Elazar, *Covenant and Constitutionalism,* 78. For a longer (and very enthusiastic) treatment of the Presbyterian role, see W. P. Breed *Presbyterians and the Revolution.*

103. Elazar, *Covenant and Constitutionalism,* 68.

104. Donald S. Lutz, *A Preface to American Political Theory,* 136.

105. On millennialism, see Stephen A. Marini, "Uncertain Dawn: Millennialism and Political Theology in Revolutionary America," and Ruth H. Bloch, *Visionary Republic. Millennial themes in American thought, 1756–1800,* 3–94. Millennialism in America was not confined to the Reformed tradition. Lutheran revivalists, only decades before the Revolution, also included millennialists. Kidd, *Great Awakening,* 26.

106. Henry Cumings, *A Sermon Preached at Lexington on the 19th of April.*

107. Samuel Cooper, *A Sermon on the Day of the Commencement of the Constitution,* 634–35.

108. Joseph Sewall, *Nineveh's Repentance and Deliverance,* 38, 42; Samuel Dunbar, *The Presence of God With His People,* 220, 221, 229; Jacob Cushing, *Divine Judgments Upon Tyrants,* 612, 613, 618, 625–26. Both Sewall and Dunbar were orthodox in their Reformed theology. Sandoz, ed., *Political Sermons,* 26, 208.

109. Samuel Sherwood, *The Church's Flight into the Wilderness: An Address on the Times;* Abraham Keteltas, *God Arising and Pleading His People's Cause; Defensive Arms Vindicated and the Lawfulness of the American War Made Manifest.* As to the source of *Defensive Arms,* see Sandoz, ed., *Political Sermons,* 712–13.

110. Kidd, *Great Awakening,* 289–91.

111. Butler, *Awash in a Sea of Faith,* 202.

112. Jeffry H. Morrison, *John Witherspoon and the Founding of the American Republic,* 71–92; Kidd, *Great Awakening,* 291–92.

113. John Joachim Zubly, *An Humble Enquiry;* Kidd, *The Great Awakening,* 302–3.

114. Butler, *Sea of Faith,* 203–4.

115. Jonathan Mayhew, *The Snare Broken* and *A Discourse concerning Unlimited Submission and Non-Resistance to the Higher Powers: With some Reflections on the Resistance made to King Charles I. And on the Anniversary of his Death.*

116. Isaac Backus, *An Appeal to the Public for Religious Liberty.*

117. George Whitfield, *Britain's Mercies, and Britain's Duties;* Charles Chauncy, *Civil Magistrates Must be Just, Ruling in the Fear of God.*

118. Alice Baldwin, *The New England Clergy and the American Revolution.* Nathan O. Hatch does not characterize Baldwin's text fairly when he argues that she falls prey to a temptation characteristic of her era: *Locke et praeterea nihil.* It is true that most pre–World War II studies of the Revolution and Founding, influenced mainly by Carl Becker and Louis Hartz, emphasized its liberal aspects. But Hatch's charge reflects the sensitivities of his own era—against liberalism and in favor of republicanism in the Revolution and Founding. His critique of Baldwin demonstrates the influence of Bernard Bailyn, Gordon Wood, and J. G. A. Pocock. Hatch, *Sacred Cause of Liberty,* 57n.

119. Alan Heimert, *Religion and the American Mind: From the Great Awakening to the Revolution;* Kidd, *The Great Awakening,* 288–89.

120. Hatch, *Sacred Cause of Liberty,* 3, 12, 16–17, 139–75.

121. Ibid., 25–36, 11–12 (quote).

122. Stout, *New England Soul,* 7, quoted in Kuehne, *Massachusetts Congregationalist Political Thought,* 148.

123. Kuehne, *Massachusetts Congregationalist Political Thought,* 144–45.

124. Ibid., 145.

125. Griffin, *Revolution and Religion,* 18–21, 26–28.

126. Ibid., 10–13, 19–21, 37–38, 60–61.

127. Miller, *From Colony to Province,* 295–98.

128. Stoddard, *Doctrine of Instituted Churches,* 30.

129. Cotton Mather, *Magnalia Christi Americana; or, The Ecclesiastical History of New-England,* 2:248; Miller, *From Colony to Province,* 242; Weir, *Early New England,* 216–17. Weir argues that the Brattle Street Manifesto is evidence of secularization. But the use of nature by the Cambridge Association demonstrates to the contrary.

130. William Bradford, *Of Plymouth Plantation: 1620–1647,* 320, 405.

131. Griffin, *Revolution and Religion,* 52.

132. Ellis Sandoz, *A Government of Laws: Political Theory, Religion, and the American Founding,* 105–49.

133. Cooper, *Commencement of the Constitution,* 639.

134. Richard M. Gummere, *The American Colonial Mind and the Classical Tradition: Essays in Comparative Culture;* Margo Todd, *Christian Humanism and the Puritan Social Order;* Sandoz, *Government of Laws,* 83–104; Carl J. Richard, *The Founders and the Classics: Greece, Rome, and the American Enlightenment.*

135. Sandoz, *Government of Laws,* 146–51; Noll, *America's God,* 49–63; see also Ellis Sandoz, *Republicanism, Religion, And the Soul of America,* 1–52. Elazar contrasts this language as either a "republicanism of virtue" or a "republicanism of interest." See Elazar, *Covenant and Constitutionalism,* 49.

136. Steven M. Dworetz, *The Unvarnished Doctrine: Locke, Liberalism, and the American Revolution.*

CHAPTER 9: NATURAL LAW AND NATURAL RIGHT IN REFORMED POLITICAL THEOLOGY

1. Stephen J. Grabill, *Rediscovering the Natural Law in Reformed Theological Ethics,* 1, 3–5,

21–53; John D. Eusden, "Natural Law and Covenant Theology in New England, 1620-1670," 1.

2. Thomas P. Peardon, "Introduction," xi; Peter Laslett, "Appendix B: Sources of 'Two Treatises' in Locke's Reading," 135. Regarding Calvinist sources in Locke, see Herbert D. Foster, "International Calvinism through Locke and the Revolution of 1688." Peardon also asserts that Locke had contact with Huguenot thinkers when he was in exile on the Continent; Becker rejects this idea, though Amos retorts that Becker understood neither Mornay's covenant theology nor Locke's theism. See Carl Becker, *The Declaration of Independence: A Study in the History of Political Ideas,* 33–39; Gary T. Amos, *Defending the Declaration: How the Bible and Christianity Influenced the Writing of the Declaration of Independence,* 50–55.

3. Coffey, *Politics, Religion,* 12. See also Peter Judson Richards, "The Law Written in Their Hearts? Rutherford and Locke on Nature, Government and Resistance," for an extended comparison. While I agree with his essential conclusions about Rutherford and Locke and their important differences, it is harder to agree with his conclusions that Locke had an essentially minimalist or rationalist natural law theory. Seventeenth-century political theory is particularly difficult to untangle with precision, especially in categorizing arguments from nature.

4. Wilson, *Pulpit in Parliament,* 143.

5. McNeill, *History and Character of Calvinism,* 413; Lamont, *Godly Rule,* 126–27.

6. Grabill, *Rediscovering the Natural Law,* 5–7, 14–20.

7. Todd, *Christian Humanism,* 22.

8. Grabill, *Rediscovering the Natural Law,* 3, 16.

9. Richard Tuck, *Natural Rights Theories: Their Origin and Development,* 32, 43.

10. Robert Kingdon, *Geneva and the Consolidation of the French Protestant Movement 1564–1572: A Contribution to the History of Congregationalism, Presbyterianism, and Calvinist Resistance Theory,* 18.

11. John Adair, *Founding Fathers: The Puritans in England and America,* 50–51.

12. Coffey, *Politics, Religion,* 16; Alexander Taylor Innes, "Samuel Rutherford," 48, cited in ibid., 8.

13. L. S. Koetsier, *Natural Law and Calvinist Political Theory,* 47. Calvin called Erasmus "the glory and darling of literature." Todd, *Christian Humanism,* 56.

14. Koetsier, *Natural Law and Calvinist Political Theory,* 28–33, 42–49. Koetsier does not always quite get this right, however. She asserts of Zwingli, "As a humanist, Zwingli ignored natural law." Zwingli's view of natural law was not characteristic of the other reformers' views, but cannot be attributed to his humanism. Koetsier, *Calvinist Political Theory,* 31. See also Grabill, *Rediscovering the Natural Law,* 3. For a short discussion of Zwingli on the subject of secular scholarship, see G. W. Bromiley, "General Introduction," 38–39.

15. David W. Hall, *The Genevan Reformation and the American Founding,* 2–5.

16. See also Calvin, *New Testament Commentaries,* 8:29–32, *Institutes,* II.i and iii.

17. Ibid., 5:77.

18. Partee, *Calvin and Classical Philosophy,* 48–49, 97–104.

19. Grabill, *Rediscovering the Natural Law,* 87; Harro Hopfl, *The Christian Polity of John Calvin,* 181, 184.

20. Calvin, *Institutes,* II.ii.13, 234–35.

21. Ibid., IV.xx.15–16, 663–65.

22. Ibid., II.ii.15, 236.

23. Hancock, *Foundations of Modern Politics,* 82–92, 100–107, quote on p. 100.
24. Hopfl, *Christian Polity,* 179, 181.
25. Grabill, *Rediscovering the Natural Law,* 89–90, 93–94.
26. Mosse, *Holy Pretence.*
27. Goodman, *Superior Powers,* 30 (the Kessinger edition has errors that I have corrected from a reprint edition).
28. For references to the Church Fathers, see Knox, *First Blast,* 10–25; for sources outside the Bible, see 9, 11, 15, 22, 30.
29. Ibid., 9, 41; Knox, Copy of a Letter, 62.
30. Mason, "Introduction," xv.
31. Kelly, *Emergence of Liberty,* 44, 46.
32. Quentin Skinner discounts any significant connection between Mornay's political and religious covenants. George Garnett argues that Roman and canon law were fundamental, and that the Scripture is read through the lens of the categories and principles of Roman and canon law. J. Wayne Baker, in response to Skinner, notes that Mornay (like Bullinger) used *pactum* and *foedus* interchangeably as legal and biblical terms and also related piety to both religious obligation and civil justice. Anne McLaren responds to Garnett and Skinner by reasserting the significance of the individual covenant with God, which, she argues, emphasizes the critical role of theology in the development of early modern republicanism. Skinner, *Modern Political Thought* 2:331; George Garnett, "Law in the Vindiciae, Contra Tyrannos: A Vindication"; Baker, "Covenant and Community," 24–25; Anne McLaren, "Rethinking Republicanism: *Vindiciae, Contra Tyrannos* in Context."
33. Preface, in Mornay, *Vindiciae, Contra Tyrannos,* 8–13. Emphasis added.
34. Fuhrmann, "Philip Mornay," 59.
35. Mornay, *Vindiciae, Contra Tyrannos,* 52.
36. Ibid., 53.
37. Ibid., 60, 114.
38. Ibid., 62–68.
39. Ibid., 71–74.
40. Ibid., 56–59.
41. This is evident from Locke's treatment of regimes in *Second Treatise on Government,* chapters 8, 10, 19.
42. Mornay, *Vindiciae, Contra Tyrannos,* 74. Emphasis added.
43. Skinner, *Modern Political Thought,* 2:327–28.
44. Mornay, *Vindiciae, Contra Tyrannos,* 75, 93.
45. Ibid., 76; Hobbes argues in chapter 13 of his *Leviathan* that the State of Nature denies any "mine" or "thine."
46. Mornay, *Vindiciae, Contra Tyrannos,* 80.
47. Ibid., 82.
48. Ibid., 84, 86.
49. Ibid., 75.
50. Plato, *Republic,* 342e.
51. Mornay, *Vindiciae, Contra Tyrannos,* 51.
52. Ibid., 87–88.
53. Ibid., 149.
54. Ibid., 125.

55. Ibid., 142–43.

56. Coffey, *Politics, Religion,* 70.

57. Ibid., 74.

58. John Marshall, "Natural Law and the Covenant: The Place of Natural Law in the Covenantal Framework of Samuel Rutherford's *Lex, Rex,*" 148.

59. Coffey, *Politics, Religion,* 69.

60. McKay, *Ecclesiastical Republic,* 110–11, 272–73.

61. Marshall, "Natural Law and the Covenant," 101–4.

62. Richards, "The Law Written in Their Hearts?" 185.

63. Rutherford, *Lex, Rex,* 1.

64. Ibid., 30.

65. Marshall, "Natural Law and the Covenant," 143–47, 82, 98–100.

66. Ibid., 115–20.

67. Ibid., 117–19, 120; Rutherford, *Influences of the Life of Grace,* 386–87.

68. On Calvin and the cooperation of Word and Spirit, see Partee, *Calvin and Classical Philosophy,* 14.

69. Eusden, "Natural Law," 19–21.

70. Like Strauss, Tuck appears to presume that relevant natural right theory must be an essentially secular theory. He does not see any significant development of the idea of natural right between the medieval period and the seventeenth century. Reformation political theorists either earn a passing mention or else are yoked with others who "pulled the foundations out from underneath the theory" developed during the Middle Ages. Strauss, *Natural Right and History;* Tuck, *Natural Rights Theories.*

71. Rutherford, *Lex, Rex,* 1–2.

72. Also, "I conceive, by nature's light, they should incline to defend themselves and to join in one body politic for their own safety, as is most natural." Ibid., 80, 93.

73. Ibid., 2. Michael P. Zuckert argues that the Mayflower Compact, for example, asserts divine right. Zuckert, *The Natural Rights Republic: Studies in the Foundation of the American Political Tradition,* 130.

74. Rutherford, *Lex, Rex,* 51. See also 3 and 50. Rutherford's extended attack on hereditary monarchy in *Lex, Rex* reminds one of Locke's *First Treatise of Government.*

75. Rutherford, *Lex, Rex,* 201.

76. Ibid., 114.

77. Ibid., 2–3.

78. Ibid., 1.

79. Ibid., 5.

80. Ibid., 67–68. Recall Mornay's reference to "mine and thine" (*Vindiciae, Contra Tyrannos,* 76).

81. Tuck elsewhere disqualifies the Presbyterians of the 1640s and 1650s from being natural rights theorists by asserting that they "never abandoned the idea of the special, divine origin of governmental dominium" and thus "lie outside the area of natural rights theories proper." Tuck, *Natural Rights Theories,* 145.

82. Rutherford, *Lex, Rex,* 3. Also, "The king is said to be from God by way of naked approbation; God given to a people power to appoint what government they shall think good, but instituting none in special in his word."

83. Ibid., 80, 123, 126, 143.

84. Ibid., *Rex,* 81–82, 102.

85. This necessity for consent extends not only to those who rule by conquering but also to children, who cannot have their liberties traded away by their fathers. Ibid., 46–50, 53.

86. Tuck, *Natural Rights Theories,* 56–57.

87. Rutherford, *Lex, Rex,* 66, 69.

88. Ibid., 64, 69–72, 84.

89. Ibid., 16, 72–77, 99–106.

90. Ibid., 6, 26.

91. Ibid., 105.

92. Zuckert, *Natural Rights Republic,* 148–201. Zuckert's treatment of Protestant political theology in this work is particularly weak: he does not achieve a firm grasp on the tradition before he draws conclusions. He makes assertions such as "The Puritans were not, as it turns out, so 'covenantal' in their political theory as often claimed" without offering citation or evidence. More important, he works within false dichotomies that make nature and revelation incompatible.

93. Rutherford, *Lex, Rex,* 144.

94. Ibid., 34.

95. Ibid., 103.

96. Ibid., 75.

CHAPTER 10: THE REFORMATION IN RETROSPECT

1. George Selement, "The Covenant Theology of English Separatism and the Separation of Church and State."

2. Reformers believed that the Anglican-Catholic practice confused sincere piety with ritual.

3. Elazar, *Covenant and Constitutionalism,* 78–79. Elazar argues that the governments of America resemble the political systems proposed by federal theologians and implemented in church polities more than they resemble the political systems of prominent political theorists.

4. Ibid., 17–19, 124–33, 167–88. The continuity of jeremiads is the argument of Murphy in *Prodigal Nation.*

5. Morrison, *John Witherspoon,* 25.

CHAPTER 11: CONTEMPORARY PERSPECTIVES ON COVENANTING

1. Eric Voegelin, *Israel and Revelation,* 10–11.

2. Ibid., 114. This is perhaps Voegelin's most eloquent statement of the problem of not only Israel, but of all failed uses of profound political symbols.

3. Ibid., 113.

4. Ibid., 470.

5. Ibid., 187.

6. Ibid., 185.

7. Ibid., 245.

8. Voegelin adopts Martin Buber's term "theopolity." Ibid., 415.

9. Ibid., 183, 247–48.
10. Ibid., 113.
11. Ibid., 461.
12. Ibid., 10.
13. Ibid., 180.
14. Ibid., 183.
15. Ibid., 472–73.
16. Ibid., 186.
17. Ibid., 423.
18. Ibid., 425, 427.
19. Ibid., 429–30.
20. Ibid., 460.
21. Ibid., 426.
22. Ibid., 440.
23. Ibid., 446.
24. Ibid., 439.
25. Ibid., 439, 445.
26. Ibid., 481–82. This is the first time that Voegelin uses the concept anywhere in his published work.
27. Ibid., 454.
28. For a good summary of Voegelin's treatment of *metastasis,* including his treatment of Isaiah, see Glenn Hughes, "Balanced and Imbalanced Consciousness," 175–76.
29. Voegelin, *Israel and Revelation,* 465.
30. The mystical element is another reason why Voegelin has no praise for Calvin, whose approach to theology he views as Gnosticism of the first order.
31. Eric Voegelin, *The New Science of Politics: An Introduction,* 122.
32. Ibid., 123.
33. Ibid., 134.
34. Ibid., 139.
35. In addition to the summary and expansion of Hooker's critique in *The New Science of Politics,* there is also a summary in Eric Voegelin, *History of Political Ideas: Religion and the Rise of Modernity,* 88–98.
36. Voegelin, *The New Science of Politics,* 133–61.
37. Voegelin, *Religion and the Rise of Modernity,* 98.
38. Ibid., 41.
39. Eric Voegelin, *History of Political Ideas: Renaissance and Reformation,* 217.
40. Ibid., 218.
41. Voegelin, *Religion and the Rise of Modernity,* 17.
42. Ibid., 44–45.
43. Ibid., 55, 59. This is a recurring debate in studies of Althusius.
44. Ibid., 52–54.
45. Glenn A. Moots, "The Covenant Tradition of Federalism: The Pioneering Studies of Daniel J. Elazar."
46. For his discussion of modern manifestations of covenanting, see Daniel J. Elazar, *Covenant and Civil Society: The Constitutional Matrix of Modern Democracy,* 101–59.
47. Daniel J. Elazar, *Covenant and Polity in Biblical Israel: Biblical Foundations and Jewish Expressions,* 35–51.

48. Ibid., 24, 194–95.

49. Elazar, *Covenant and Civil Society,* 343. He writes, "[A]ll covenantal political understanding revolves around similar questions of obligation and consent, free will, self–government, and political order—in other words, how are the relationships of humans one to another and to this universe and its transcendent power established and maintained so as to preserve both order and freedom, equality and opportunity, neighborliness and distinctiveness, liberty and law?"

50. Daniel J. Elazar, *Covenant and Commonwealth: From Christian Separation through the Protestant Reformation,* 6–7.

51. Elazar, *Covenant and Polity in Biblical Israel,* 20.

52. Ibid., 21.

53. Elazar, *Covenant and Commonwealth,* 79.

54. Ibid., 247.

55. Elazar, *Covenant and Polity in Biblical Israel,* 2.

56. Ibid., 28, 44.

57. Ibid., 44.

58. John Winthrop, "A Little Speech on Liberty."

59. The role of the natural law in Elazar's scheme is unclear here. It is a subject addressed better by Novak, who argues that a Jewish conception of the natural law is rooted in the Noahide covenant and presumes a common moral understanding available to all persons.

60. Daniel J. Elazar, *Covenant and Constitutionalism: The Great Frontier and the Matrix of Federal Democracy,* 249.

61. Ibid., 5.

62. Elazar, *Covenant and Polity in Biblical Israel,* 30–32.

63. Elazar, *Covenant and Constitutionalism,* 43.

64. Elazar, *Covenant and Commonwealth,* 61.

65. Elazar, *Covenant and Constitutionalism,* 8.

66. Thomas Hobbes has a lengthy discussion of covenants in his *Leviathan,* Chapters 14, 15, and 16. Note also his remark at 15.8 regarding those who use political covenants for revolution (no doubt a swipe at Presbyterians).

67. Weir, *Early New England.*

68. Elazar sees John Winthrop's articulation of this distinction as very important. See Elazar, *Covenant and Constitutionalism,* 26–27.

69. Elazar, *Covenant and Polity in Biblical Israel,* 43.

70. Elazar, *Covenant and Commonwealth,* 233–34. This call for moral reformation sometimes placed great strain on the ability of covenanting to survive.

71. Elazar, *Covenant and Constitutionalism,* 250.

72. Elazar, *Covenant and Civil Society,* 7.

73. Ibid., 265.

74. Elazar, *Covenant and Constitutionalism,* 251.

75. Ibid., 253.

76. Elazar, *Covenant and Civil Society,* 359.

77. Ibid., 348.

78. Ibid., 265–66.

79. Ibid., 348.

80. Elazar, *Covenant and Constitutionalism,* 10.

81. Elazar, *Covenant and Civil Society,* 16–17.

82. Elazar, *Covenant and Constitutionalism,* 6.
83. Elazar, *Covenant and Commonwealth,* 12.
84. Ibid., 49.
85. Elazar, *Covenant and Constitutionalism,* 6–7.
86. Elazar, *Covenant and Civil Society,* 19.
87. Ibid., 242–48.
88. Ibid., 242.
89. Ibid., 247–49.
90. Ibid., 266.
91. This is what also makes covenanting anti-utopian. Ibid., 360.
92. Ibid., 344.
93. Ibid., 351.
94. Novak, *Jewish Social Contract,* 40.
95. Ibid., 34.
96. Ibid., 33–34.
97. Ibid., 48–49.
98. Ibid., 49–50. David Hume serves as a representative of the Enlightenment cosmology. He defines a miracle by its "supernatural" quality, which (as he casts it) violates the "laws" of nature. David Hume, *An Enquiry Concerning Human Understanding,* Chapter 10.
99. Novak, *Jewish Social Contract,* 45.
100. Ibid., 42.
101. Genesis 14:21–24, 18:20, 19:4–5.
102. Novak, *Jewish Social Contract,* 44.
103. Ibid., 47.
104. Novak, *Covenantal Rights,* 85; Novak, *Jewish Social Contract,* 52–53.
105. Novak, *Jewish Social Contract,* 47; Novak, *Covenantal Rights,* 84–85; Genesis 11:9.
106. Novak, *Jewish Social Contract,* 47.
107. Ibid., 47.
108. Ibid., 30, 80–81.
109. It should be noted that Novak sees no such thing as a "social contract" in Scripture or rabbinic exegesis; it lacks a direct precedent. But this does not preclude it from having an indirect precedent in private contracts that presuppose the primary social structure to be already in place. Ibid., 63.
110. Ibid., 80–81.
111. Ibid., xi.
112. By "ontological," Novak means one's identity or existence. Fundamentally, what defines one's existence determines his or her identity.
113. Novak, *Jewish Social Contract,* 11.
114. Novak, *Covenantal Rights,* 4–8.
115. Elazar, *Covenant and Constitutionalism,* 8.
116. Novak, *Jewish Social Contract,* 30–31.
117. Ibid., 182.
118. Jews originally could live under the political rule of gentiles, but they could not live under gentile law when it came to civil or criminal matters. This would be a reversion from the Sinaitic revelation to the Noahide commandments. Gentiles could, however, seek justice from the law of the Torah. Ibid., 100–102; 119–20; Novak, *Covenantal Rights,* 90.

119. Novak, *Jewish Social Contract,* 183.

120. Novak, *Covenantal Rights,* 11.

121. Novak, *Jewish Social Contract,* 182–84; David Novak, *Natural Law in Judaism,* 25–29.

122. Novak, *Covenantal Rights,* 50.

123. Ibid., 3.

124. Ibid., 7–8. Novak goes so far as to argue that a biblical theory of rights is actually a means of resuscitating and rescuing the better aspects of modern natural right from the critique of classical natural law.

125. Ibid., 27–32.

126. Ibid., 142.

127. Ibid., 145.

128. Ibid., 146.

129. Ibid., 145.

130. Ibid., 118, 131.

131. Ibid., 216–18. Seeing God as the source of all rights does not deny all autonomy-based rights, however. There is still the possibility for the exercise of human will. Ibid., 133–34.

CHAPTER 12: LESSONS FOR RELIGION AND POLITICS TODAY

1. Sandoz, *Soul of America,* 42–52.

2. Madison, Federalist Papers 10 and 51, in Alexander Hamilton, John Jay, and James Madison, *The Federalist,* 42–49, 267–72.

3. Lincoln's "Address to the Senate of New Jersey" on February 21, 1861. There were certainly millennial implications resonating throughout the nation during the American Civil War. Also see Ernest Lee Tuveson, *Redeemer Nation: The Idea of America's Millennial Role;* Conrad Cherry, ed., *God's New Israel: Religious Interpretations of American Destiny;* Richard M. Gamble, The *War for Righteousness: Progressive Christianity, the Great War, and the Rise of the Messianic Nation.*

4. Johannes Althusius, *Politica: Politics Methodically Set Forth and Illustrated with Sacred and Profane Examples.*

5. Matthew 22:21, and John 18:36.

6. Novak, *Jewish Social Contract,* 121.

7. Ibid., 120–21.

8. Ibid., 193.

9. Ibid., 5, 121.

10. Ibid., 9.

11. Ibid., 19.

12. Ibid., 18.

13. Ibid., 13, 120–23.

14. Ibid., 19–21.

15. Novak argues that Jews and Christians, for example, must make public arguments for their moral position only from the general human condition rather than from the singular experience of God speaking directly to them. Ibid., 193. See also Novak, *Natural Law in Judaism,* 16–26, 174–93.

16. David Novak, *In Defense of Religious Liberty.*
17. Aristotle, *Nicomachean Ethics,* 1139a15–20.
18. Plato, *Symposium;* Thomas Hobbes, *Leviathan,* I.6.24.
19. Emmanuel Levinas, *Otherwise Than Being, or Beyond Essence,* 161–62, 188.
20. Hosea 6:6.
21. Deuteronomy 6:5; Matthew 9:13, 12:7, 22:36–40; John 13:34–35.
22. I Corinthians 13:13.
23. John von Heyking, *Augustine and Politics as Longing in the World,* 172–221.

Works Cited

PRIMARY SOURCES

The Acts of the General Assemblies of the Church of Scotland, From the Year 1638 to the Year 1649 Inclusive. 1682.

Adams, John. *A Defense of the Constitutions of Government of the United States of America, Against the Attack of M. Turgot, in His Letter to Dr. Price, Dated the Twenty-Second Day of March, 1778.* In *The Political Writings of John Adams,* edited by George Carey, Conservative Leadership Series, 6:195–303. Washington: Regnery Publishing, Inc., 2000.

Althusius, Johannes. *Politica: Politics Methodically Set Forth and Illustrated with Sacred and Profane Examples.* Translated by Frederick S. Carney. Indianapolis: Liberty Fund, 1995.

Ames, William. *Conscience with the Power and Cases thereof: Divided into Five Books.* 1643.

———. *The Marrow of Theology.* 1629. Reprint, edited by John D. Eusden. Grand Rapids, Mich.: Baker Books, 1998.

Anonymous. *An Admonition to the Parliament.* 1572. Reprinted in Walter H. Frere and C. E. Douglas, *Puritan Manifestoes: A Study of the Origin of the Puritan Revolt* (London: Society for Promoting Christian Knowledge, 1954), 8–19.

Anonymous. *Le Reveille-matin des François.* 1574.

Aristotle. *Metaphysics.*

———. *Nicomachean Ethics.*

———. *Physics.*

———. *Politics.*

Ayre, John, ed. *The Works of John Whitgift, D.D.* 3 vols. London: Parker Society, 1851.

Backus, Isaac. *An Appeal to the Public for Religious Liberty.* 1773. In Ellis Sandoz, ed.,

Political Sermons of the American Founding Era: 1730–1805 (Indianapolis: Liberty Fund, 1991), 331–68.

Baillie, Robert. *A Dissuasive from the Errors of the Time.* London, 1645.

———. *Letters and Journals of Robert Baillie.* 3 vols. Edinburgh, 1841.

Baxter, Richard. *A Holy Commonwealth: Richard Baxter.* Edited by William Lamont. Cambridge Texts in the History of Political Thought. Cambridge, UK: Cambridge University Press, 1994.

Beza, Theodore. *De jure magistratium.* 1575.

———. *De vera excommunicatione et Christiano presbyterio.* Geneva: Jean Le Preux, 1590.

Bradford, William. *Of Plymouth Plantation: 1620–1647.* 1650. Reprint, New York: Modern Library, 1967.

Browne, Robert. *A Book which sheweth the Life and Manners of all true Christians.* Middleburg, 1582.

Buchanan, George. *De Jure Regni Apud Scotos.* 1579.

Bullinger, Heinrich. *Anklag und ernstliches ermanen Gottes Allmaechtigen.* 1528.

———. *A Brief Exposition of the One and Eternal Testament or Covenant of God.* Translated by Charles S. McCoy and J. Wayne Baker. Contained in *Fountainhead of Federalism: Heinrich Bullinger and the Covenantal Tradition. With a Translation of De testamento seu foedere unico et aeterno (1534) by Heinrich Bullinger* (Louisville: Westminster/John Knox Press, 1991), 101–38.

———. *De Origine Erroris.* 1539.

———. *Ermanung Früntliche zur Grechtigheit wider alles verfelschen rychtigen gerychtes.* 1526.

———. *Lucretia and Brutus.* 1533.

———. *A confutation of the Popes bull which was published more than two yeres agoe against Elizabeth the most gracious Queene of England, Fraunce, and Ireland, and against the noble realme of England: together with a defence of the sayd true Christian Queene, and of the whole realme of England.* London: John Day, cum privilegio Regiae Maiestatis per decennium, 1572.

———. *The Decades of Henry Bullinger.* Edited by Thomas Harding for the Parker Society, 1849–1852. 2 vols. Reprint, with new introductions by George Ella and Joel R. Beeke. Parker Society Edition. Grand Rapids, Mich.: Reformation Heritage Books, 2004.

Burges, Cornelius. *The First Sermon Preached to the Honourable House of Commons now assembled in Parliament at their Publique Fast.* London, 1641.

Calvin, John. *Calvin's Commentaries.* Translated by John King. 22 volumes. Grand Rapids, Mich.: Baker Books, 2005.

———. *Catechism 1538.* Contained in I. John Hesselink, *Calvin's First Catechism: A Commentary.* Louisville: Westminster/John Knox Press, 1997.

———. *Calvin's New Testament Commentaries.* Edited by David W. Torrence and Thomas F. Torrence. Various Translators. 12 vols. Grand Rapids, Mich.: Wm. B. Eerdmans, 1989.

———. *Concerning the Eternal Predestination of God.* Translated, with an Introduction, by J. K. S. Reid. Cambridge, UK: James Clarke and Co, 1961.

———. *The Covenant Enforced: Sermons on Deuteronomy 27 and 28.* Translated by Arthur Golding. London, 1583. Reprint, edited by James B. Jordan. Tyler, Texas: Institute for Christian Economics, 1990.

———. *Institutes of the Christian Religion.* Translated by Henry Beveridge from the 1559 edition. Grand Rapids, Mich.: Wm. B. Eerdmans Publishing Co., 1989.

———. *Theological Treatises.* Translated by J. K. S. Reid. Philadelphia: Westminster Press, 1954.

Carier, Benjamin. *A Treatise written by Mr. Doctour Carier.* Liège, 1614.

Caryl, Joseph. *The Nature, Solemnity, Grounds, Property, and Benefits of a Sacred Covenant together with the duties of those who enter into such a covenant.* London, 1643.

Chauncy, Charles. *Civil Magistrates Must be Just, Ruling in the Fear of God.* Boston 1747. In Ellis Sandoz, ed., *Political Sermons of the American Founding Era: 1730–1805* (Indianapolis: Liberty Fund, 1991), 141–77.

Commissioners of the General Assembly of the Kirk of Scotland. *A Solemn Testimony Against Toleration and the present Proceedings of Secretaries and their Abettors in England, In Reference to Religion and Government, with An Admonition and Exhortation to their Brethren there.* Edinburgh: Evan Tyler, 1649.

Cooke, John. *King Charles's case or, an appeal to all rational men, concerning his trial at the High Court of Justice.* London, 1649.

———. *Monarchy No Creature of God's Making.* London, 1651.

———. *Redintegratio Amoris.* London, 1647.

———. *The Vindication of the Law: so far forth as scripture and right reason may be judge, and speedy justice (which exalts a nation) may be advanced. Wherein is declared what manner of persons Christian Magistrates, Judges, and Lawyers ought to be.* London, 1651.

———. *What the Independents Would Have.* London, 1647.

Cooper, Samuel. *A Sermon on the Day of the Commencement of the Constitution.* Boston, 1780. Contained in Ellis Sandoz, ed., *Political Sermons of the American Founding Era: 1730–1805* (Indianapolis: Liberty Fund, 1991), 631–56.

Cotton, John. *The Bloudy Tenent, Washed, And made white in the bloud of the Lambe: being discussed and discharched of bloud-guiltinesse by just Defence.* 1647. Reprint, New York: Arno Press, Inc., 1972.

———. *The Churches Resurrection, or the Opening of the Fifth and sixth verses of the 20th Chap. Of the Revelation.* London, 1642.
———. *An Exposition Upon the Thirteenth Chapter of Revelation.* London, 1655.
———. *The Powring [sic] Out of the Seven Vials or an Exposition, of the 16 Chapter of the Revelation, with an Application of it to our times.* London, 1642.
———. *Subjection to Christ.* 1657.
———. *The Way of the Congregational Churches Cleared.* London, 1648.
Cumings, Henry. *A Sermon Preached at Lexinton on the 19th of April.* Boston, 1781. Contained in Ellis Sandoz, ed., *Political Sermons of the American Founding Era: 1730–1805* (Indianapolis: Liberty Fund, 1991), 661–81.
Cushing, Jacob. *Divine Judgment Upon Tyrants.* Boston, 1778. Contained in Ellis Sandoz, ed., *Political Sermons of the America Founding Era, 1730–1805* (Indianapolis: Liberty Fund, 1991), 611–26.
Dell, William. *The City Ministers Unmasked.* London, 1649.
Descartes, Rene. *Discourse On Method And Meditations On First Philosophy.* 4th ed. Translated by Donald Cress. Indianapolis: Hackett Publishing Company, 1998.
Dunbar, Samuel. *The Presence of God With His People.* Boston, 1760. Contained in Ellis Sandoz, ed., *Political Sermons of the American Founding Era: 1730–1805* (Indianapolis: Liberty Fund, 1991), 211–30.
Edwards, Jonathan. *A Covenant People Ought to Resolve to Be the Lord's People.* 1737.
———. *Distinguishing Marks of a Work of the Spirit of God.* 1741.
———. *Freedom of the Will.* 1754.
———. *Lectures on the Qualifications for Full Communion in the Church of Christ.* 1749.
———. *Nature of True Virtue.* 1765.
Edwards, Thomas. *Gangrena: Or a Catalogue and Discovery of many of the Errours, Heresies, Blasphemies and pernicious Practices of the Sectaries of this time, vented and acted in England in these four last years.* 1646.
Fenner, Dudley. *Sacra Theologia.* London, 1585.
Feuerbach, Ludwig. *The Essence of Christianity.* 1841. Reprint, New York: Prometheus Books, 1989.
Foxe, John. *Actes and Monuments of these Latter and Perillous Days, Touching Matters of the Church.* 1563.
Frere, W. H., and C. E. Douglas. *Puritan Manifestoes. A Study of the Origin of the Puritan Revolt. With a Reprint of the Admonition to Parliament and Kindred Documents, 1572.* London: Society for Promoting Christian Knowledge, 1907.
Gillespie, George. *Aaron's Rod Blossoming.* 1646. Reprint, Harrisonburg, Va.: Sprinkle Publications, 1985.

Goodman, Christopher. *How Superior Powers Ought to Be Obeyed.* 1558. Reprint: Whitefish, Mont.: Kessinger Publishing, 2004.
Goodwin, John. *Hagiomastix: or the Scourge of the Saints Displayed.* London, 1646.
———. *Innocency and Truth Triumphing Together.* London, 1646.
———. *The Obstructors of Justice.* London, 1649.
———. *Theomachia.* London, 1644.
Goodwin, Thomas. "Epistle to the Reader." In *Innocence and Truth Triumphing Together* (London, 1645).
———. *Works.* 1863. 12 vols. Reprint, Edinburgh: Banner of Truth Trust, 1985.
———. *A Glimpse of Zions Glory.* London, 1641. In Thomas Goodwin, *Works,* vol. 12, 61–80.
———. *Zerubbabels Encouragement to Finish the Temple.* London, 1642. In Thomas Goodwin, *Works,* vol. 12, 101–28.
Hakewill, George. *An Answere to a Treatise Written by Dr. Carier.* 1616.
Hall, Thomas. *A Confutation of the Millenarian Opinion.* London, 1657.
Hayne, Thomas. *Christs Kingdome on Earth, opened according to the Scriptures. Herein is examined what Mr. Th. Brightman, Dr. J. Alstede, Mr. I. Mede, Mr. H. Archer, The Glympse of Sions Glory, and such as concurre in opinion with them, hold concerning the thousand years of the Saints Reign with Christ, and of Satans binding.* London, 1645.
Henderson, Alexander. *A Sermon Preached to the Honorable House of Lords.* London, 1645.
Hill, Thomas. *The Trade of Truth Advanced.* London, 1642.
Hobbes, Thomas. *Leviathan, with selected variants from the Latin edition of 1668.* Edited by Edwin Curley. Indianapolis: Hackett Publishing Company, Inc., 1994.
Hooker, Thomas. *A Survey of the Summe of Church Discipline.* 1648.
Hotman, Francis. *Franco Gallia.* 1575.
Hume, David. *An Enquiry Concerning Human Understanding.* 1748. Edited by Tom L. Beauchamp. The Clarendon Works of David Hume. New York: Oxford University Press, 1999.
Johnston, Archibald. *Diary of Sir Archibald Johnston of Wariston.* 2 vols., edited from the original manuscript, with notes and introduction by David Hay Fleming. Edinburgh: Scottish History Society, 1919.
Keteltas, Abraham. *God Arising and Pleading His People's Cause.* Newbury-Port, 1777. Contained in Ellis Sandoz, ed., *Political Sermons of the American Founding Era: 1730–1805* (Indianapolis: Liberty Fund, 1991), 583–605.
Knox, John. *The Appellation of John Knox.* In *John Knox On Rebellion,* edited by Roger Mason (Cambridge, UK: Cambridge University Press, 1994), 72–114.
———. *The Copy of a Letter delivered to the Lady Mary, Regent of Scotland.* In *John Knox On Rebellion,* edited by Roger Mason (Cambridge, UK: Cambridge

University Press, 1994), 48–71.

———. *The Debate at General Assembly, June 1564.* In *John Knox On Rebellion,* edited by Roger Mason (Cambridge, UK: Cambridge University Press, 1994), 182–209.

———. *The First Blast of the Trumpet against the Monstrous Regiment of Women.* In *John Knox On Rebellion,* edited by Roger Mason (Cambridge, UK: Cambridge University Press, 1994), 3–47.

———. *Summary of the Second Blast of the Trumpet.* In *John Knox On Rebellion,* edited by Roger Mason (Cambridge, UK: Cambridge University Press, 1994), 128–29.

———. *The Works of John Knox.* 1854–1895. 6 vols. Edited by David Laing. Reprint, New York: AMS Press, 1966.

Kolfhaus, W. *"Der Verkehr Calvins mit Bullinger" in Calvinstudien, in Calvinstudien: Festschrift zum 400.* Edited by J. (Josef) Bohatec. Leipzig: Rudolf Haupt, 1909.

Lechford, Thomas. *Plain Dealing.* London, 1642.

Lightfoot, John. *A sermon preached before the honorable House of Commons.* London, 1645.

Lincoln, Abraham. "Address to the Senate of New Jersey." February 21, 1861. In Roy P. Basler, ed., *Abraham Lincoln: His Writings and Speeches* (Cambridge, Mass.: Da Capo, 2001), 574–75.

Locke, John. *An Essay Concerning Human Understanding.* The Clarendon Edition of the Works of John Locke. Edited by Peter H. Nidditch. Oxford: Oxford University Press, 1979.

———. *Political Essays.* Edited by Mark Goldie. Cambridge, UK: Cambridge University Press, 1997.

———. *Two Treatises of Government and A Letter Concerning Toleration.* Edited by Ian Shapiro. New Haven, Conn.: Yale University Press, 2003.

Marx, Karl, and Engels, Friedrich. *The Communist Manifesto.* 1848. Translated by Samuel Moore. Edited by Gareth Stedman Jones. Reprint, New York: Penguin Putnam Inc., 2002.

Mather, Cotton. *Magnalia Christi Americana; or, The Ecclesiastical History of New-England,* 2 vols. London, 1702. Reprint from the 1852 edition. Carlisle: Banner of Truth Trust, 1979.

———. *A Midnight Cry.* Boston, 1692.

———. *Optanda, Good Men Described and Good Things Propounded.* Boston, 1692.

Mather, Increase. *The Order of the Gospel, Professed and Practised by the Churches of Christ in New-England.* Boston, 1700.

Mayhew, Jonathan. *Discourse concerning Unlimited Submission and Non-Resistance to the Higher Powers: With some Reflections on the Resistance made to King Charles I. And on the Anniversary of his Death.* London, 1750.

———. *The Snare Broken.* Boston, 1766. In Ellis Sandoz, ed., *Political Sermons of the American Founding Era: 1730–1805* (Indianapolis: Liberty Fund, 1991), 235–64.

Milton, John. *Complete Prose Works.* 8 vols. Edited by Don M. Wolfe. New Haven, Conn.: Yale University Press, 1953.

———. *Of Reformation in England And the Causes that have Hitherto Hindered It.* 1641.

———. *On the New Forcers of Conscience under the Long Parliament.* 1646.

———. *The Tenure of Kings and Magistrates.* 1648. In Areopagitica *and Other Political Writings of John Milton* (Indianapolis: Liberty Fund, 1999), 52–97.

———. *Works of John Milton.* Edited by F. A. Patterson. 18 vols. New York: Columbia University Press, 1931–1938.

A Moderate Whig [pseud.]. *Defensive Arms Vindicated.* New Marlborough, 1783. In Ellis Sandoz, ed., *Political Sermons of the American Founding Era 1730–1805* (Indianapolis: Liberty Fund, 1991), 715–70.

Mornay, Philippe Du Plessis [Junius Brutus, pseud.]. *Vindiciae, Contra Tyrannos. A Defense of Liberty Against Tyrants or Of the lawful power of the Prince over the People and of the People over the Prince.* 1579. Edmonton, Alb.: Still Waters Revival Books, 1989. Reprint of 1689 translation.

Morrison, Jeffry H. *John Witherspoon and the Founding of the American Republic.* Notre Dame, Ind.: University of Notre Dame Press, 2005.

Nietzsche, Friedrich. *The Gay Science.* 1882. In *The Gay Science: With a Prelude in Rhymes and an Appendix of Songs.* Translated by Walter Kaufmann. New York: Random House, 1974.

Owen, John. *A Dissertation on Divine Justice.* In *Works,* vol. 10, 483–624.

———. *Ebenezer: A Memorial of the Deliverance Of Essex County, And Committee. In Two Sermons.* In *Works,* vol. 8, 73–127.

———. *A Sermon Preached to the Honorable House of Commons, in Parliament–Assembled on January 31. A Day of Solemn Humiliation: With a Discourse About Toleration, and the Duty of the Civil Magistrate About Religion, Thereunto Annexed.* London, 1649.

———. *The Shaking and Translating of Heaven and Earth in Works.* In *Works,* vol. 8, 245–81.

———. *The Works of John Owen.* Edited by William H. Goold. 16 vols. Johnstone and Hunter, 1850–1853. Reprint, Edinburgh: Banner of Truth Trust, 1965.

Palmer, Herbert. *The Glasse of Gods Providence.* London, 1644.

———. *The Necessity and Encouragement, of Utmost Ventureing for the Churches Help.* London, 1643.

Pascal, Blaise. *Memorial.* 1654.

Peters, Hugh. *God's Doings and Man's Duty.* London, 1646.

———. *A Word for the Army and Two Words to the Kingdom.* London, 1647.

Plato. *Euthyphro.*
———. *Republic.*
———. *Symposium.*
Ponet, John. *A Shorte Treatise of Politike Power.* 1556.
The Presbyterians Not Guilty of the Unjust Charge of being concerned in the murther [sic] of King Charles I. London, 1649.
Prynne, William. *The Substance of a Speech to the House of Commons.* London, 1648.
———. *The Sword of Christian Magistry Supported.* London, 1647.
Robinson, Hastings, ed. *Original Letters Relative to the English Reformation Written During the Reigns of King Henry VIII, King Edward VI, and Queen Mary: Chiefly from the Archives of Zurich.* 2 vols. Translated and edited by Hastings Robinson for the Parker Society, 1846. New York: Johnson Reprint Corporation, 1968.
———. *The Zurich Letters (Second Series) Comprising the Correspondence of Several English Bishops and Others with Some of the Helvetian Reformers During the Reign of Queen Elizabeth.* 2 vols. Translated and edited by Hastings Robinson for the Parker Society, 1846. New York: Johnson Reprint Corporation, 1968.
Rousseau, Jean-Jacques. *Discourse on the Sciences and Arts.* In *The Social Contract and The First and Second Discourses,* edited by Susan Dunn. Rethinking the Western Tradition Series. New Haven, Conn.: Yale University Press, 2002.
———. *Discourse on the Origin and Basis of Inequality Among Men.* In *The Social Contract and The First and Second Discourses,* edited by Susan Dunn. Rethinking the Western Tradition Series. New Haven, Conn.: Yale University Press, 2002.
———. *The Social Contract.* In *The Social Contract and The First and Second Discourses,* edited by Susan Dunn. Rethinking the Western Tradition Series. New Haven, Conn.: Yale University Press, 2002.
Rutherford, Samuel. *The Covenant of Life Opened Or, A Treatise of the Covenant of Grace.* Edinburgh, 1655.
———. *A Free Disputation Against Pretended liberty of Conscience.* London, 1649.
———. *Influences of the Life of Grace.* 1659.
———. *Lex, Rex, or The Law and the Prince.* 1644. Reprint, Harrisonburg: Sprinkle Publications, 1982.
———. *A Survey of the Spiritual Antichrist.* London, 1648.
———. *A Survey of the Summe of Church Discipline.* London, 1648.
Sandoz, Ellis, ed. *Political Sermons of the American Founding Era: 1730–1805.* Indianapolis: Liberty Fund, 1991.
Sartre, Jean Paul. *Existentialism as a Humanism.* 1946. New Haven, Conn.: Yale University Press, 1987.

The Second Peace of Cappel, 20 Nov. 1531. In *Documents Illustrative of the Continental Reformation,* edited by B. J. Kidd (Oxford, UK: Clarendon, 1967), 475–76.

Sewall, Joseph. *Nineveh's Repentance and Deliverance.* Boston, 1740. In Ellis Sandoz, ed., *Political Sermons of the American Founding Era: 1730–1805* (Indianapolis: Liberty Fund, 1991), 29–50.

Sherwood, Samuel. *The Church's Flight Into the Wilderness: An Address on the Times.* New York, 1776. In Ellis Sandoz, ed., *Political Sermons of the American Founding Era: 1730–1805* (Indianapolis: Liberty Fund, 1991), 496–527.

Shields, Alexander. *A Hind Let Loose or An Historical Representation of the Testimonies of the Church of Scotland for the Interest of Christ with the True State Thereof in All its Periods. Together with a Vindication of the Present Testimony Against Popish, Prelatical and Malignant Enemies of that Church, as it is now Stated, for the Prerogatives of Christ, Privileges of the Church, and Liberties of Mankind; and Sealed by the Sufferings of a Reproached Remnant of Presbyterians There, Witnessing against the Corruptions of the Time.* Glasgow: William Paton, 1687.

Sibbes, Richard. *Works of Richard Sibbes.* 7 vols. Edited by Alexander B. Grosart. 1862–1864. Reprint, Edinburgh: Banner of Truth Trust, 1977.

Smolinski, Reiner, ed. *The Threefold Paradise of Cotton Mather: An Edition of "Triparadisus."* Athens: University of Georgia Press, 1995.

Sterry, Peter. *The Comings Forth of Christ.* London, 1650.

Stoddard, Solomon. *The Doctrine of Instituted Churches.* London, 1700.

———. *The Inexcusableness of Neglecting the Worship of God, Under A Pretence of Being in an Unconverted Condition.* Boston, 1708.

Strickland, John. *Mercy rejoycing against Judgment.* London, 1645.

Tocqueville, Alexis de. *Democracy in America.* Translated by Harvey C. Mansfield and Delba Winthrop. Chicago: University of Chicago Press, 2000.

Vermigli, Peter Martyr. *The Oxford Treatise and Disputation on the Eucharist, 1549.* The Peter Martyr Library, vol. 7: Sixteenth Century Essays and Studies, vol. 56. Translated with an introduction by Joseph C. McLelland. Kirksville, Mo.: Truman State University Press, 2000.

———. *To the Most Renowned Princess Elizabeth, by the grace of God Queene of England, France and Ireland.* Published in *Martyr's Divine Epistles,* an appendix to the *English Edition of Common Places.* Translated by Anthony Marten, part 5, 58–61. London: Henry Denham and Henry Middleton, 1583.

Westminster Confession of Faith. 1644.

Whitefield, George. *Britain's Mercies, and Britain's Duties.* Boston, 1746. In Ellis Sandoz, ed., *Political Sermons of the American Founding Era: 1730–1805* (Indianapolis: Liberty Fund, 1991), 123–36.

Williams, Roger. *The Complete Writings of Roger Williams.* 7 vols. Edited by James Hammond Trumbull et al. New York: Russell and Russell, 1963.

Winthrop, John. "A Little Speech on Liberty." In *The Journal of John Winthrop, 1630–1649,* edited by Richard S. Dun, James Savage, and Laetitia Yeandle (Cambridge, Mass.: Harvard University Press, 1996), 584–89.

Zubly, John Joachim. *An Humble Inquiry* (1769). In Ellis Sandoz, ed., *Political Sermons of the American Founding Era: 1730–1805* (Indianapolis: Liberty Fund, 1991), 267–99.

SECONDARY SOURCES

Adair, John. *Founding Fathers: The Puritans in England and America.* Grand Rapids, Mich.: Baker Book House, 1986.

Ahlstrom, Sydney E. *A Religious History of the American People.* New Haven, Conn.: Yale University Press, 1972.

Amos, Gary T. *Defending the Declaration: How the Bible and Christianity Influenced the Writing of the Declaration of Independence.* Brentwood, Tenn.: Wolgemuth and Hyatt, Publishers, Inc., 1989.

Bailyn, Bernard. *The Ideological Origins of the American Revolution.* 1967. Cambridge, Mass.: Belknap Press, 1992.

Baker, J. Wayne. "Church, State, and Dissent: The Crisis of the Swiss Reformation, 1531–1536." *Church History* 57, no. 2, 135–52.

———. "Covenant and Community in the Thought of Heinrich Bullinger." In Daniel J. Elazar and John Kinkaid, eds., *The Covenant Connection: From Federal Theology to Modern Federalism* (New York: Lexington Books, 2000), 15–29.

———. *Heinrich Bullinger and the Covenant: The Other Reformed Tradition.* Athens: Ohio University Press, 1980.

Baldwin, Alice M. *The New England Clergy and the American Revolution.* 1928. New York: Frederick Ungar Publishing Co., 1965.

Battles, Ford Lewis. *Concordance to Calvin's Corpus Reformatorum 1559 Edition of the Institutes.* Unpublished microfilm of computer printouts.

Becker, Carl. *The Declaration of Independence: A Study in the History of Political Ideas.* 1922. New York: Vintage Books, 1958.

Bell, M. Charles. *Calvin and Scottish Theology: The Doctrine of Assurance.* Edinburgh: Handsell Press, 1985.

Bellah, Robert N. *The Broken Covenant: American Civil Religion in Time of Trial.* 2nd ed. Chicago: University of Chicago Press, 1992.

Benedict, Philip. *Christ's Churches Purely Reformed: A Social History of Calvinism.* New Haven, Conn.: Yale University Press, 2002.

Beneke, Chris. *Beyond Toleration: The Religious Origins of American Pluralism.* Oxford, UK: Oxford University Press, 2006.

Bercovitch, Sacvan. *The American Jeremiad.* Madison: University of Wisconsin Press, 1978.

Berman, Joshua. *Created Equal: How the Bible Broke with Ancient Political Thought.* Oxford, UK: Oxford University Press, 2008.

Bierma, Lyle D. "Covenant or Covenants in the Theology of Olevianus?" *Calvin Theological Journal* 22 (November 1987): 228–50.

———. "Federal Theology in the Sixteenth Century: Two Traditions?" *Westminster Theological Journal* 45 (1983): 304–21.

Bloch, Ruth H. "Religion and Ideological Change in the American Revolution." In Mark A. Noll, ed., *Religion and American Politics From the Colonial Period to the 1980s* (Oxford, UK: Oxford University Press, 1990), 47–63.

———. *Visionary Republic: Millennial themes in American thought, 1756–1800.* New York: Cambridge University Press, 1985.

Bolliger, Daniel. "Bullinger on Church Authority: The Transformation of the Prophetic Role in Christian Ministry." In Bruce Gordon and Emidio Campi, eds., *Architect of Reformation: An Introduction to Heinrich Bullinger, 1504–1575* (Grand Rapids, Mich.: Baker Academic, 2004), 159–77.

Bonomi, Patricia U. *Under the Cope of Heaven: Religion, Society, and Politics in Colonial America.* Oxford, UK: Oxford University Press, 1986.

Boughton, Lynne Courter. "Choice and Action: William Ames's Concept of the Mind's Operation in Moral Decisions." *Church History* 56, no. 2 (June 1987): 188–203.

Bozeman, Theodore Dwight. *To Live Ancient Lives: The Primitivist Dimension in Puritanism.* Chapel Hill: University of North Carolina Press, 1988.

Brachlow, Stephen. *The Communion of Saints. Radical Puritan Separatist Ecclesiology 1570–1625.* Oxford, UK: Oxford University Press, 1988.

Breed, W. P. *Presbyterians and the Revolution.* 1876. Reprint, Decatur, Miss.: Issacharian Press, 1993.

Bremer, Francis J. "The Defense of Regicide: John Cotton on the Execution of Charles I." *William and Mary Quarterly* 37 (January 1980): 103–24.

Brett, Annabel. *Liberty, Right and Nature: Individual Rights in Later Scholastic Thought* (Ideas in Context). Cambridge, UK: Cambridge University Press, 1997.

Brockunier, Samuel Hugh. *The Irrepressible Democrat: Roger Williams.* New York: Ronald Press, 1940.

Bromiley, G. W. "General Introduction" to *Zwingli and Bullinger.* Translated by G. W. Bromiley. Vol. 24 of The Library of Christian Classics. Philadelphia: Westminster Press, 1953.

Brown, P. Hume. *George Buchanan, Humanist and Reformer: A Biography.* Edinburgh: David Douglas, 1890.

Buchanan, George Wesley. *The Consequences of the Covenant.* Leiden: E. J. Brill, 1970.

Burnett, Stephen G. "Reassessing the 'Basel-Wittenberg Conflict': Dimensions of the Reformation-Era Discussion of Hebrew Scholarship." In Allison Coudert and Jeffrey S. Shoulson, eds., *Hebraica Veritas. Christian Hebraists and the Study of Judaism in Early Modern Europe* (Philadelphia: University of Pennsylvania Press, 2004), 181–201.

Burns, J. H. *The True Law of Kingship: Concepts of Monarchy in Early-Modern Scotland.* Oxford, UK: Clarendon Press, 1996.

Butler, Jon. *Awash in a Sea of Faith: Christianizing the American People.* Cambridge, Mass.: Harvard University Press, 1990.

Byrd, James P. *The Challenges of Roger Williams: Religious Liberty, Violent Persecution, and the Bible.* Macon, Ga.: Mercer University Press, 2002.

Campi, Emidio. "Bullinger's Early Political and Theological Thought: Brutus Tigurinus." In Bruce Gordon and Emidio Campi, eds., *Architect of Reformation: An Introduction to Heinrich Bullinger, 1504–1575* (Grand Rapids, Mich.: Baker Academic, 2005), 181–99.

———. "Current State and Future Directions of Bullinger Research." In *Heinrich Bullinger: Life—Thought—Influence. Zurich, August 25–29, 2004. International Congress Heinrich Bullinger (1504–1575),* vol. 1, edited by Emidio Campi and Peter Opitz (Zurich: Theologischer Verlag Zurich, 2007), 1–30.

———, and Peter Opitz, eds. *Heinrich Bullinger: Life—Thought—Influence. Zurich, August 25–29, 2004. International Congress Heinrich Bullinger (1504–1575).* 2 vols. Zurich: Theologischer Verlag Zurich, 2007.

Caputo, John D., and Michael J. Scanlon, eds. *God, the Gift, and Postmodernism.* Bloomington: Indiana University Press, 1999.

Cherry, Conrad, ed. *God's New Israel: Religious Interpretations of American Destiny.* Chapel Hill: University of North Carolina Press, 1998.

Clines, David J. A. "Predestination in the Old Testament." In *On the Way to the Postmodern: Old Testament Essays 1967–1998,* vol. 2 (Sheffield, UK: Sheffield Academic Press, 1998), 524–41.

Coalter, Milton J., Jr. *Gilbert Tennent, Son of Thunder: A Case Study of Continental Pietism's Impact on the First Great Awakening in the Middle Colonies.* Contributions to the Study of Religion, Number 18. New York: Greenwood Press, 1986.

Cochrane, Charles Norris. *Christianity and Classical Culture: A Study of Thought and Action from Augustus to Augustine.* 1940. Reprint, Indianapolis: Liberty Fund, 2003.

Coffey, John. *Politics, Religion and the British Revolutions: The Mind of Samuel Rutherford.* New York: Cambridge University Press, 1997.

Courtois, Stephane, Nicolas Werth, Jean-Louis Panné, and Andrzej Paczkowski.

The Black Book of Communism: Crimes, Terror, Repression. Translated by Jonathan Murphy and Mark Kramer. Cambridge, Mass.: Harvard University Press, 1999.

Cropsey, Joseph, and Leo Strauss, eds. *History of Political Philosophy.* 3rd ed. Chicago: University of Chicago Press, 1987.

Davies, Horton. *Worship and Theology in England, From Cranmer to Baxter and Fox, 1534–1690.* Grand Rapids, Mich.: Eerdmans Publishing Company, 1996.

Davis, James Calvin. *The Moral Theology of Roger Williams: Christian Conviction and Public Ethics.* Columbia Series in Reformed Theology. Louisville: Westminster/John Knox Press, 2004.

DeGreef, Wulfert. *The Writings of John Calvin: An Introductory Guide.* Expanded ed. Translated by Lyle D. Bierma. Louisville: Westminster/John Knox Press, 2008.

De Jong, Peter Y. *The Covenant Idea in New England Theology, 1620–1847.* Grand Rapids, Mich.: Wm. B. Eerdmans Publishing Co., 1945.

Diggins, John P. *The Lost Soul of American Politics: Virtue, Self-Interest, and the Foundations of Liberalism.* New York: Basic Books, Inc., 1984.

Donaldson, Gordon. *The Scottish Reformation.* New York: Cambridge University Press, 1960.

Dworetz, Steven M. *The Unvarnished Doctrine: Locke, Liberalism, and the American Revolution.* Durham, N.C.: Duke University Press, 1994.

Ebenstein, William, and Alan O. Ebenstein. *Introduction to Political Thinkers.* 2nd ed. Belmont: Wadsworth/Thomson Learning, 2002.

Elazar, Daniel J. *Covenant and Civil Society: The Constitutional Matrix of Modern Democracy.* The Covenant Tradition in Politics, vol. 4. New Brunswick, N.J.: Transaction Publishers, 1998.

———. *Covenant and Commonwealth: From Christian Separation Through the Protestant Reformation.* The Covenant Tradition in Politics, vol. 2. New Brunswick, N.J.: Transaction Publishers, 1996.

———. *Covenant and Constitutionalism: The Great Frontier and the Matrix of Federal Democracy.* The Covenant Tradition in Politics, vol. 3. New Brunswick, N.J.: Transaction Publishers, 1998.

———. *Covenant and Polity in Biblical Israel: Biblical Foundations and Jewish Expressions.* The Covenant Tradition in Politics, vol. 1. New Brunswick, N.J.: Transaction Publishers, 1995.

Ella, George M. *Henry Bullinger: Shepherd of the Churches.* Durham: Go Publications, 2007.

Ernst, James E. *The Political Thought of Roger Williams.* Seattle: University of Washington Press, 1929.

Eusden, John Dykstra. "Introduction." In William Ames, *The Marrow of Theology,* edited by John D. Eusden (Grand Rapids, Mich.: Baker Books, 1998), 1–66.

———. "Natural Law and Covenant Theology in New England, 1620–1670." *Natural Law Forum* 5 (1960), 1–30.

Ferguson, Everett, ed. *Backgrounds of Early Christianity.* Grand Rapids, Mich.: Eerdmans Publishing Company, 2003.

Figgis, John Neville. *The Divine Right of Kings.* 2nd ed. Cambridge, Mass.: Cambridge University Press, 1934.

Firth, Katherine. *The Apocalyptic Tradition in Reformation Britain 1530–1645.* Oxford, UK: Oxford University Press, 1979.

Forster, Greg. *John Locke's Politics of Moral Consensus.* Cambridge, UK: Cambridge University Press, 2005.

Foster, Herbert D. "International Calvinism through Locke and the Revolution of 1688." *American Historical Review* 32 (April 1927): 475–99.

Freeman, Gordon M. *The Heavenly Kingdom: Aspects of Political Thought in the Talmud and Midrash.* New York: University Press of America, Inc., 1986.

Frei, Hans W. *The Eclipse of Biblical Narrative: A Study in Eighteenth and Nineteenth Century Hermeneutics.* New Haven, Conn.: Yale University Press, 1980.

Friedman, Jerome. *The Most Ancient Testimony: Sixteenth Century Christian-Hebraica in the Age of the Renaissance Nostalgia.* Athens: Ohio University Press, 1983.

Fuhrmann, Paul T. "Philip Mornay and the Huguenot Challenge to Absolutism." In George L. Hunt and John T. McNeill, eds., *Calvinism and the Political Order: Essays Prepared for the Woodrow Wilson Lectureship of the National Presbyterian Center Washington D.C.* (Philadelphia: Westminster Press, 1965), 46–64.

Gamble, Richard M. *The War for Righteousness: Progressive Christianity, the Great War, and the Rise of the Messianic Nation.* Wilmington, Del.: ISI Books, 2003.

Gardner, E. Clinton. *Justice and Christian Ethics.* New Studies in Christian Ethics no. 7. Cambridge, UK: Cambridge University Press, 1995.

Garnett, George. "Editor's Introduction" to *Vindiciae Contra Tyrannos, or Concerning the Legitimate Power of a Prince Over the People, and of the People Over a Prince.* Edited by George Garnett. Cambridge, UK: Cambridge University Press, 1994.

———. "Law in the Vindiciae, Contra Tyrannos: A Vindication." *Historical Journal* 49, no. 3 (2006): 877–91.

Gentile, Emile. *Politics as Religion.* Translated by George Staunton. Princeton, N.J.: Princeton University Press, 2004.

Germino, Dante. *Machiavelli to Marx: Modern Western Political Thought.* Chicago: University of Chicago Press, 1972.

Gerstner, John H. *The Rational Biblical Theology of Jonathan Edwards.* 3 vols. Powhatan: Berea Publications, 1991–1993.

Gibbs, Lee W. "The Puritan Natural Law Theory of William Ames." *Harvard Theological Review* 64, no. 1 (January 1971): 37–57.

Gilson, Etienne. *God and Philosophy.* New Haven, Conn.: Yale University Press, 1941.

Goen, C. C. *Revivalism and Separatism in New England, 1740–1800: Strict Congregationalists and Separate Baptists in the Great Awakening.* New Haven, Conn.: Yale University Press, 1962.

Gooch, G. P. *The History of English Democratic Ideas in the Seventeenth Century.* Cambridge, UK: Cambridge University Press, 1898.

Gordis, Lisa M. *Opening Scripture: Bible Reading and Interpretive Authority in Puritan New England.* Chicago: University of Chicago Press, 2003.

Gordon, Bruce. "Introduction: Architect of Reformation." In Bruce Gordon and Emidio Campi, eds., *Architect of Reformation: An Introduction to Heinrich Bullinger, 1504–1575* (Grand Rapids, Mich.: Baker Academic, 2005), 17–32.

———. *The Swiss Reformation.* New York: Manchester University Press, 2002.

———, and Emidio Campi, eds. *Architect of Reformation: An Introduction to Heinrich Bullinger, 1504–1575.* Grand Rapids, Mich.: Baker Academic, 2005.

Grabill, Stephen J. *Rediscovering the Natural Law in Reformed Theological Ethics.* Emory University Studies in Law and Religion. Grand Rapids, Mich.: Wm. B. Eerdmans Publishing Company, 2006.

Greaves, Richard L. *Theology and Revolution in the Scottish Reformation: Studies in the Thought of John Knox.* Grand Rapids, Mich.: Christian University Press, 1980.

Greenslade, S. L. *The Cambridge History of the Bible: Volume 3, The West from the Reformation to the Present Day.* New York: Cambridge University Press, 1963.

Gribben, Crawford. *The Puritan Millennium: Literature and Theology, 1550–1682.* Dublin: Four Courts Press, 2000.

Griffin, Keith L. *Revolution and Religion: American Revolutionary War and the Reformed Clergy.* New York: Paragon House, 1994.

Gummere, Richard M. *The American Colonial Mind and the Classical Tradition: Essays in Comparative Culture.* Cambridge, Mass.: Harvard University Press, 1963.

Gunnell, John G. "Strauss before Straussianism: Reason, Revelation and Nature." *Review of Politics* 53, no. 1 (Winter 1991): 53–74.

Hall, David D. "Understanding the Puritans." In Stanley N. Katz, ed., *Colonial America: Essays in Political and Social Development* (Boston: Little, Brown and Co., 1971).

Hall, David W. *The Genevan Reformation and the American Founding.* Lanham, Md.: Lexington Books, 2003.

Haller, William. *The Elect Nation.* New York: Harper and Row, 1963.

Hallowell, John H., and Jene M. Porter. *Political Philosophy: The Search for Humanity and Order.* Scarborough, Ont.: Prentice Hall Canada, Inc., 1997.

Hancock, Ralph C. *Calvin and the Foundations of Modern Politics.* Ithaca, N.Y.: Cornell University Press, 1989.

Hatch, Nathan O. *The Sacred Cause of Liberty: Republican Thought and the Millennium in Revolutionary New England.* New Haven, Conn.: Yale University Press, 1977.

Heimert, Alan. *Religion and the American Mind: From the Great Awakening to the Revolution.* Cambridge, Mass.: Harvard University Press, 1966.

Hesselink, I. John. *Calvin's First Catechism: A Commentary.* Louisville: Westminster/John Knox Press, 1997.

Hill, William. *A History of the Rise, Progress, Genius, and Character of American Presbyterianism.* Washington City: J. Gideon, Jr. 1839.

Hodge, Charles. *The Constitutional History of the Presbyterian Church in the United States of America, Part I: 1705–1741.* Philadelphia: Presbyterian Board of Education, 1839.

Hollander, Paul. *From the Gulag to the Killing Fields: Personal Accounts of Political Violence and Repression in Communist States.* Wilmington, Del.: ISI Books, 2006.

Hopfl, Harro. *The Christian Polity of John Calvin.* Cambridge, UK: Cambridge University Press, 1982.

Hudson, Winthrop S. "Theological Convictions and Democratic Government." In Michael McGiffert, ed., *Puritanism and the American Experience* (Reading, Pa.: Addison-Wesley Publishing Company, 1969), 226–35.

Hughes, Ann. *Gangraena and the Struggle for the English Revolution.* New York: Oxford University Press, 2004.

Hughes, Glenn. "Balanced and Imbalanced Consciousness." In Glenn Hughes, ed., *The Politics of the Soul: Eric Voegelin on Religious Experience* (New York: Rowman and Littlefield, 1999), 163–84.

Hunt, George L., and John T. McNeill, eds. *Calvinism and the Political Order: Essays Prepared for the Woodrow Wilson Lectureship of the National Presbyterian Center Washington D.C.* Philadelphia: Westminster Press, 1965.

Innes, A. T. "Samuel Rutherford." In *Studies in Scottish History* (London: Evangelical Succession Series, 1892).

Israel, Jonathan. *The Enlightenment Contested.* Oxford, UK: Oxford University Press, 2006.

———. *The Radical Enlightenment.* Oxford, UK: Oxford University Press, 2001.

Johnson, Dale Walden. "Marginal at Best: John Knox's Contribution to the Geneva Bible, 1560." In Mack P. Holt, ed., *Adaptations of Calvinism in Reformation Europe: Essays in Honor of Brian G. Armstrong* (Burlington: Ashgate Publishing Limited, 2007), 241–48.

Johnston, Warren. "The Anglican Apocalypse in Restoration England." *Journal of Ecclesiastical History* 55, no. 3 (2004): 467–501.

Jordan, James B. "Editor's Introduction." In James B. Jordan, ed., *The Covenant Enforced: Sermons on Deuteronomy 27 and 28* (Tyler, Texas: Institute for Christian Economics, 1990) xxvii–xxxvii.

Kaminsky, Joel S. *Corporate Responsibility in the Hebrew Bible.* Journal for the Study of the Old Testament Supplement Series 196. Sheffield, UK: Sheffield Academic Press, 1995.

Kaplan, Lawrence. *Politics and Religion during the English Revolution. The Scots and the Long Parliament 1643–1645.* New York: New York University Press, 1976.

Kellar, Clarke. *Scotland, England, and the Reformation, 1534–1561.* New York: Oxford University Press, 2003.

Kelly, Douglas F. *The Emergence of Liberty in the Modern World: The Influence of Calvin on Five Governments from the 16th Through the 18th Centuries.* Phillipsburg: Presbyterian and Reformed Publishing Company, 1992.

Kendall, R. T. *Calvin and English Calvinism to 1649.* Oxford: Oxford University Press, 1979.

Kennedy, George A. *Classical Rhetoric and Its Christian and Secular Tradition from Ancient to Modern Times.* Chapel Hill: University of North Carolina Press, 1999.

Kenyon, J. P. *Stuart England.* New York: St. Martin's Press, 1978.

Kenyon, John, and Jane Ohlmeyer, eds. *The Civil Wars: A Military History of England, Scotland and Ireland 1638–1660.* New York: Oxford University Press, 1998.

Kidd, Thomas S. *The Great Awakening: The Roots of Evangelical Christianity in Colonial America.* New Haven, Conn.: Yale University Press, 2007.

———. *The Protestant Interest: New England after Puritanism.* New Haven, Conn.: Yale University Press, 2004.

Kingdon, Robert. *Geneva and the Consolidation of the French Protestant Movement 1564–1572: A Contribution to the History of Congregationalism, Presbyterianism, and Calvinist Resistance Theory.* Madison: University of Wisconsin Press, 1967.

Kirby, Torrance. *The Zurich Connection and Tudor Political Theology.* Studies in the History of Christian Traditions 131. Leiden: Brill, 2007.

Koetsier, L. S. *Natural Law and Calvinist Political Theory.* Victoria: Trafford Publishing, 2003.

Kuehne, Dale S. *Massachusetts Congregationalist Political Thought, 1760–1790: The Design of Heaven.* Columbia: University of Missouri Press, 1996.

Lake, Peter. *Anglicans and Puritans? Presbyterianism and English Conformist Thought from Whitgift to Hooker.* London: Unwin Hyman, 1988.

Lambert, Frank. *Inventing the "Great Awakening."* Princeton, N.J.: Princeton University Press, 1999.

Lamont, William. "Biographical Notes." In William Lamont, ed., *A Holy Commonwealth: Richard Baxter,* Cambridge Texts in the History of Political Thought (Cambridge: Cambridge University Press, 1994), xxvi–xxxi.

———. *Godly Rule: Politics and Religion, 1603–1660.* New York: Macmillan St. Martin's Press, 1969.

———. "Introduction." in William Lamont, ed., *A Holy Commonwealth: Richard Baxter,* Cambridge Texts in the History of Political Thought (Cambridge, UK: Cambridge University Press, 1994), ix–xxi.

———. *Puritanism and Historical Controversy.* Montreal: McGill-Queen's University Press, 1996.

———. *Richard Baxter and the Millennium: Protestant Imperialism and the English Revolution.* Totowa: Rowman and Littlefield, 1979.

Laslett, Peter., ed. "Appendix B: Sources of 'Two Treatises' in Locke's Reading." In *Two Treatises of Civil Government: A Critical Edition,* rev. ed. (New York: Mentor, 1965), 130–45.

Levinas, Emmanuel. *Otherwise Than Being, or Beyond Essence.* Trans. Alphonso Lingis. Dordrecht: Kluwer Academic Publishers, 1991.

Lillback, Peter A. *The Binding of God: Calvin's Role in the Development of Covenant Theology.* Grand Rapids, Mich.: Baker Academic, 2001.

———. "The Early Reformed Covenant Paradigm: Vermigli in the Context of Bullinger, Luther and Calvin." In Frank A. James, III, ed., *Peter Martyr Vermigi and the European Reformations: Semper Reformanda* (Boston: Brill, 2004), 70–96.

Lindberg, Carter. "Eschatology and Fanaticism in the Reformation Era: Luther and the Anabaptists." *Concordia Theological Quarterly* 64, no. 4 (October 2000): 259–78.

Liu, Tai. *Discord in Zion: The Puritan Divines and the Puritan Revolution 1640–1660.* The Hague: Martinus Nijhoff, 1973.

Lutz, Donald S. *A Preface to American Political Theory.* Lawrence: University Press of Kansas, 1992.

MacCulloch, Diarmaid. "Heinrich Bullinger and the English-speaking World." In Emidio Campi and Peter Opitz, eds., *Heinrich Bullinger: Life—Thought—Influence. Zurich, August 25–29, 2004. International Congress Heinrich Bullinger (1504–1575) Volume I* (Zurich: Theologischer Verlag Zurich, 2007), 891–934.

———. *The Later Reformation in England, 1547–1603.* 2nd ed. New York: Palgrave Press, 2000.

———. *The Reformation.* New York: Viking, 2003.

Macinnes, Allan I. *Charles I and the Making of the Covenanting Movement 1625–*

1641. Edinburgh: John Donald Publishers Ltd., 1991.

MacPherson, Hector. *The Covenanters Under Persecution: A Study of their Religious and Ethical Thought.* Edinburgh: W. F. Henderson, 1923.

Marini, Stephen A. "Uncertain Dawn: Millennialism and Political Theology in Revolutionary America." In Richard Connors and Andrew Colin Gow, eds., *Anglo-American Millennialism, from Milton to the Millerites* (Leiden: Koninklijke Brill NV, 2004), 159–76.

Marion, Jean-Luc. *God Without Being: Hors-Texte.* Chicago: University of Chicago Press, 1991.

Marsden, George M. *Jonathan Edwards: A Life.* New Haven, Conn.: Yale University Press, 2003.

Marshall, John. *John Locke, Toleration, and Early Enlightenment Culture.* Cambridge, UK: Cambridge University Press, 2006.

Marshall, John L. "Natural Law and the Covenant: The Place of Natural Law in the Covenantal Framework of Samuel Rutherford's *Lex, Rex.*" Ph.D. diss., Westminster Theological Seminary, 1995.

Marshall, Peter. *Reformation England 1480–1642.* New York: Oxford University Press, 2003.

Martinich, A. P. *A Hobbes Dictionary.* Oxford, UK: Blackwell Publishers, Inc. 1995.

Mason, Roger A. "Introduction." In *John Knox On Rebellion,* edited by Roger A. Mason (Cambridge, UK: Cambridge University Press, 1994), viii–xxiv.

———. *Kingship and the Commonweal: Political Thought in Renaissance and Reformation Scotland.* East Lothian, Scotland: Tuckwell Press, 1998.

Maxson, Charles Hartshorn. *The Great Awakening in the Middle Colonies.* Gloucester: Peter Smith, 1958.

Mayfield, Noel Henning. *Puritans and Regicide: Presbyterian-Independent Differences over the Trial and Execution of Charles (I) Stuart.* New York: University Press of America, 1988.

McCarthy, Dennis J., S. J. *Old Testament Covenant: A Survey of Current Opinions.* Richmond: John Knox Press, 1972.

McClelland, J. S. *A History of Western Political Thought.* London: Routledge/ITP, 1996.

McCoy, Charles S., and Baker, J. Wayne. *Fountainhead of Federalism: Heinrich Bullinger and the Covenantal Tradition. With a Translation of* De testamento seu foedere unico et aeterno *(1534) by Heinrich Bullinger.* Louisville: Westminster/John Knox Press, 1991.

McDermott, Gerald R. *One Holy and Happy Society: The Public Theology of Jonathan Edwards.* University Park: Pennsylvania State University Press, 1992.

McGiffert, Michael. "*The Covenant of Grace in Puritan Thought* by John von Rohr" (book review). *Journal of Religion* 68, no. 1 (January 1988): 111–12.

McKay, W. D. J. *An Ecclesiastical Republic: Church Government in the Writings of George Gillespie*. Edinburgh: Paternoster Publishing Co., 1997.

McKinney, William W. "Beginnings in the North." In Gaius Jackson Slosser, ed., *They Seek a Country. The American Presbyterians: Some Aspects* (New York: Macmillan Company, 1955), 27–59.

McLaren, Anne. "Rethinking Republicanism: Vindiciae, Contra Tyrannos in Context." *Historical Journal* 49, no. 1 (2006): 23–52.

McLelland, Joseph C. "The Second Book of Common Prayer." In Joseph C. McLelland, ed., *The Visible Words of God: An Exposition of the Sacramental Theology of Peter Martyr Vermigli, A.D. 1500–1562* (Grand Rapids. Mich.: William B. Eerdmans Publishing Company, 1957), 28–40.

———. "Translator's Introduction." In Peter Martyr Vermigli, *The Oxford Treatise and Disputation on the Eucharist, 1549,* The Peter Martyr Library Volume 7: Sixteenth Century Essays and Studies, vol. 56. Translated with an introduction by Joseph C. McLelland. Kirksville, Mo.: Truman State University Press, 2000, xvii–xlvi.

McNeill, John T. *The History and Character of Calvinism.* New York: Oxford University Press, 1954.

Meier, Heinrich. *Leo Strauss and the Theologico-Political Problem.* Cambridge, UK: Cambridge University Press, 2006.

Middlekauff, Robert. *The Mathers: Three Generations of Puritan Intellectuals 1596–1728.* New York: Oxford University Press, 1971.

Milbank, John, Catherine Pickstock, and Graham Ward, eds. *Radical Orthodoxy: A New Theology.* New York: Routledge, 1999.

Miller, Perry. *Errand into the Wilderness.* New York: Harper and Row, 1956.

———. *The New England Mind: From Colony to Province.* Cambridge, Mass.: Belknap Press of Harvard University Press, 1953.

———. *The New England Mind: The Seventeenth Century.* Cambridge, Mass.: Belknap Press of Harvard University Press, 1939.

Milligan, George. *The English Bible: A Sketch of Its History.* London, 1895.

Moots, Glenn A. "The Covenant Tradition of Federalism: The Pioneering Studies of Daniel J. Elazar." In Ann Ward and Lee Ward, eds., *The Ashgate Research Companion to Federalism* (Burlington: Ashgate Publishing Company, 2009), 391–412.

Morgan, Edmund S. *The Puritan Dilemma: The Story of John Winthrop.* Boston: Little, Brown and Company, 1958.

———. *The Puritan Family: Religion and Domestic Relations in Seventeenth-Century New England.* 1944. New York: Harper and Row, Publishers, 1966.

———. *Roger Williams: The Church and the State.* New York: W. W. Norton and Company, 1967.

———. *Visible Saints: The History of a Puritan Idea.* Ithaca, N.Y.: Cornell

University Press, 1963.

Morrill, John. "Introduction." In John Kenyon and Jane Ohlmeyer, eds., *The Civil Wars: A Military History of England, Scotland and Ireland 1638–1660* (New York: Oxford University Press, 1998), xix–xxiv.

———. "The National Covenant in its British Context." In *The Scottish National Covenant in Its British Context 1638–1651* (Edinburgh: Edinburgh University Press, 1990), 1–30.

———, ed. *The Scottish National Covenant in Its British Context, 1638–1651.* Edinburgh: Edinburgh University Press, 1990.

Mosse, George L. *The Holy Pretence: A Study in Christianity and Reason of State from William Perkins to John Winthrop.* New York: Howard Fertig, 1968.

Murphy, Andrew R. *Conscience and Community: Revisiting Toleration and Religious Dissent in Early Modern England and America.* University Park: Pennsylvania State University Press, 2001.

———. *Prodigal Nation: Moral Decline and Divine Punishment from New England to 9/11.* Oxford, UK: Oxford University Press, 2008.

Naphy, William G. "Calvin's Geneva." In Donald K. McKim, ed., *The Cambridge Companion to John Calvin* (New York: Cambridge University Press, 2004), 25–37.

Noll, Mark. *America's God: From Jonathan Edwards to Abraham Lincoln.* Oxford, UK: Oxford University Press, 2002.

———, ed. *Religion and American Politics from the Colonial Period to the 1980s.* Oxford, UK: Oxford University Press, 1990.

Novak, David. *Covenantal Rights: A Study in Jewish Political Theory.* Princeton, N.J.: Princeton University Press, 2000.

———. *In Defense of Religious Liberty.* American Ideals and Institutions. Wilmington, Del.: ISI Books, 2009.

———. *The Jewish Social Contract: An Essay in Political Theology.* Princeton, N.J.: Princeton University Press, 2005.

———. *Jewish Social Ethics.* New York: Oxford University Press, 1992.

———. *Natural Law in Judaism.* New York: Cambridge University Press, 1998.

Nuttall, Geoffrey F. *Visible Saints: The Congregational Way 1640–1660.* Oxford, UK: Basil Blackwell, 1957.

O'Donovan, Joan Lockwood. *Theology of Law and Authority in the English Reformation.* Emory University Studies in Law and Religion Number 1. Atlanta: Scholars Press, 1991.

Pahl, Gretchen Graf. "John Locke as a Literary Critic and Biblical Interpreter." In *Essays Critical and Historical Dedicated to Lily B. Campbell,* edited by the Department of English, University of California at Los Angeles (New York: Russell and Russell, 1968), 137–57.

Pak, G. Sujin. *The Judaizing Calvin: Sixteenth-Century Debates over the Messianic*

Psalms. Oxford Studies in Historical Theology. Oxford, UK: Oxford University Press, 2010.

Parker, Kim Ian. *The Biblical Politics of John Locke.* Waterloo, Ontario: Wilfred Laurier University Press, 2004.

———. "That 'Dreadful Name, *Leviathan*': Biblical Resonances in the Title to Hobbes's Famous Political Work." *Hebraic Political Studies* 2, no. 4 (2007): 424–47.

Partee, Charles. *Calvin and Classical Philosophy.* Interpretation Bible Studies. Louisville: Westminster/John Knox Press, 2005.

Peardon, Thomas P. "Introduction." In *The Second Treatise of Government* by John Locke (New York: Macmillan, 1952), vii–xxii.

Pearson, A. F. Scott. *Church and State: Political Aspects of Sixteenth Century Puritanism.* Cambridge, UK: Cambridge University Press, 1928.

Peterson, Mark A. *The Price of Redemption: The Spiritual Economy of Puritan New England.* Stanford, Calif.: Stanford University Press, 1997.

Pettegree, Andrew. *Marian Protestantism: Six Studies.* Aldershot: Scholar Press, 1996.

Pettit, Norman. *The Heart Prepared: Grace and Conversion in Puritan Spiritual Life.* 2nd ed. Middletown: Wesleyan University Press, 1989.

Pieper, Josef. *The Silence of St. Thomas.* South Bend, Ind.: St. Augustine's Press, 1999.

Pilcher, George William. *Samuel Davies, Apostle of Dissent in Colonial Virginia.* Knoxville: University of Tennessee Press, 1971.

Pipes, Richard. *Communism: A History.* New York: Modern Library, 2003.

Pocock, J. G. A. *The Machiavellian Moment: Florentine Political Thought and the Atlantic Republican Tradition.* Princeton, N.J.: Princeton University Press, 1975.

Pope, Robert G. *The Half-Way Covenant: Church Membership in Puritan New England.* Princeton, N.J.: Princeton University Press, 1969.

Puckett, David L. *John Calvin's Exegesis of the Old Testament.* Columbia Series in Reformed Theology. Louisville: Westminster/John Knox Press, 1995.

Raath, Andries, and Shaun De Freitas. "From Heinrich Bullinger to Samuel Rutherford: The Impact of Reformation Zurich on Seventeenth-Century Scottish Political Theory." In *Heinrich Bullinger: Life—Thought—Influence. Zurich, August 25–29, 2004. International Congress Heinrich Bullinger (1504–1575),* vol. 2, 852–79.

Raynal, Charles, and John Leith, eds. *Calvin Studies Colloquium.* Davidson, N.C.: Davidson College Presbyterian Church, 1982.

Reid, W. Stanford. "John Knox's Theology of Political Government." *Sixteenth Century Journal* 19, no. 4 (Winter 1988): 529–40.

Rendtorff, Rolf. *The Covenant Formula: An Exegetical and Theological Investigation.*

Translated by Margaret Kohl. Edinburgh: T&T Clark, 1998.

Reventlow, Henning Graf. *The Authority of the Bible and the Rise of the Modern World.* Translated by J. Bowden. Philadelphia: Fortress Press, 1984.

Richard, Carl J. *The Founders and the Classics: Greece, Rome, and the American Enlightenment.* Cambridge, Mass.: Harvard University Press, 1995.

Richards, Peter Judson. "The Law Written in Their Hearts? Rutherford and Locke on Nature, Government and Resistance." *Journal of Law and Religion* 18, no. 1 (2002–2003): 151–89.

Richardson, Alan. "The Rise of Modern Biblical Scholarship and Recent Discussion of the Authority of the Bible." In P. R. Ackroyd, ed., *Cambridge History of the Bible* (Cambridge: Cambridge University Press, 1963), vol. 3, 294–338.

Sandoz, Ellis. *A Government of Laws: Political Theory, Religion, and the American Founding.* Baton Rouge: Louisiana State University Press, 1990.

———. *The Politics of Truth and other Untimely Essays.* Columbia: University of Missouri Press, 1999.

———. *Republicanism, Religion, and the Soul of America.* Eric Voegelin Institute Series in Political Philosophy: Studies in Religion and Politics. Columbia: University of Missouri Press, 2006.

Schlesinger, Philip, and François Foret. "Political Roof and Sacred Canopy? Religion and the EU Constitution." *European Journal of Social Theory* 9, no. 1 (2006): 59–81.

Schmitt, Carl. *Political Theology: Four Chapters on the Concept of Sovereignty.* Translated by George Schwab. 1922. Cambridge, Mass.: MIT Press, 1985.

Selement, George. "The Covenant Theology of English Separatism and the Separation of Church and State." *Journal of the American Academy of Religion* 41, no. 1. (March 1973): 66–74.

Shain, Barry Alan. *The Myth of American Individualism: The Protestant Origins of American Political Thought.* Princeton, N.J.: Princeton University Press, 1994.

Simpson, Alan. "How Democratic Was Roger Williams?" *William and Mary Quarterly* 3rd series, vol. 13, no. 1 (January 1956): 53–67.

———. *Puritanism in Old and New England.* Chicago: University of Chicago Press, 1955.

Skinner, Quentin. *The Foundations of Modern Political Thought. Volume Two: The Age of Reformation.* New York: Cambridge University Press, 1978.

———. "The Origins of the Calvinist Theory of Revolution." In Barbara C. Malament, ed., *After the Reformation: Essays in Honor of J. H. Hexter* (Philadelphia: University of Philadelphia Press, 1980), 309–30.

Slosser, Gaius Jackson. "Origins." In Gaius Jackson Slosser, ed., *They Seek a Country. The American Presbyterians: Some Aspects* (New York: Macmillan

Company, 1955), 1–26.

Smith, James K. A. *Introducing Radical Orthodoxy: Mapping a Post-secula Theology.* Grand Rapids, Mich.: Baker Academic, 2005.

Smith, Steven B. *Reading Leo Strauss: Politics, Philosophy, Judaism.* Chicago: University of Chicago Press, 2006.

Solt, Leo F. *Saints in Arms: Puritanism and Democracy in Cromwell's Army.* Chicago: University of Chicago Press, 1959.

Steele, Margaret. "The 'Politick Christian': The Theological Background to the National Covenant." In John Morrill, ed., *The Scottish National Covenant in Its British Context 1638–1651* (Edinburgh: Edinburgh University Press, 1990), 31–67.

Steinmetz, David. *Calvin in Context.* New York: Oxford University Press, 1995.

Stephens, W. Peter. "Predestination or Election in Zwingli and Bullinger." In *Heinrich Bullinger: Life—Thought—Influence. Zurich, August 25–29, 2004. International Congress Heinrich Bullinger (1504–1575) Volume I,* 313–34.

Stevenson, David. *Revolution and Counter-Revolution in Scotland, 1644–1651.* London: Royal Historical Society, 1977.

———. *The Scottish Revolution 1637–1644: The Triumph of the Covenanters.* New York: St. Martins Press, 1973.

Stoever, William K. B. *"A Faire and Easie Way to Heaven": Covenant Theology and Antinomianism in Early Massachusetts.* Middletown, Conn.: Wesleyan University Press, 1978.

Stout, Harry S. *The New England Soul: Preaching and Religious Culture in Colonial New England.* New York: Oxford University Press, 1986.

Strauss, Leo. "Jerusalem and Athens: Preliminary Reflections." In *Faith and Political Philosophy: The Correspondence between Leo Strauss and Eric Voegelin, 1934–1964,* translated and edited by Peter Emberley and Barry Cooper (Columbia: University of Missouri Press, 2004), 109–38.

———. "The Living Issues of German Postwar Philosophy." In *Leo Strauss and the Theologico-Political Problem* (Cambridge, UK: Cambridge University Press, 2006), 115–40.

———. *Natural Right and History.* Chicago: University of Chicago Press, 1953.

———. *The Rebirth of Classical Political Rationalism: An Introduction to the Thought of Leo Strauss.* Chicago: University of Chicago Press, 1989.

———, and Joseph Cropsey, eds. *History of Political Philosophy.* 3rd ed. Chicago: University of Chicago Press, 1987.

Tanguay, Daniel, and Christopher Nadon. *Leo Strauss.* Translated by Christopher Nadon. New Haven, Conn.: Yale University Press, 2007.

Tannenbaum, Donald, and David Schultz. *Inventors of Ideas: An Introduction to Western Political Philosophy.* 2nd ed. Belmont, Calif.: Wadsworth/Thomson Learning, 2004.

ıundyil, Zacharias P. *Covenant in Anglo-Saxon Thought: The Influence of the Bible, Church Fathers, and Germanic Tradition on Anglo-Saxon Laws, History, and the Poems* The Battle of Maldon *and* Guthlac. Bombay: Macmillan Company of India Ltd., 1972.

Tierney, Brian. *The Idea of Natural Rights: Studies on Natural Rights, Natural Law and Church Law 1150–1625.* Emory University Studies in Law and Religion no. 5. Grand Rapids, Mich.: William B. Eerdmans Publishing Company, 1997.

Todd, Margo. *Christian Humanism and the Puritan Social Order.* New York: Cambridge University Press, 1987.

———. "The Problem of Scotland's Puritans." In John Coffey and Paul C. H. Lim, eds., *The Cambridge Companion to Puritanism* (New York: Cambridge University Press, 2008).

Trinterud, Leonard J. *The Forming of an American Tradition. A Re-examination of Colonial Presbyterianism.* Philadelphia: Westminster Press, 1949.

———. "The Origins of Puritanism." *Church History* 20 (1951): 37–57.

Tuck, Richard. *Natural Rights Theories: Their Origin and Development.* New York: Cambridge University Press, 1979.

Tuveson, Ernest Lee. *Redeemer Nation: The Idea of America's Millennial Role.* Chicago: University of Chicago Press, 1980.

Tyacke, Nicholas. *Anti-Calvinists: The Rise of English Arminianism c. 1590–1640.* Oxford, UK: Clarendon Press, 1987.

Van Asselt, Willem J. *The Federal Theology of Johannes Cocceius (1603–1669).* Translated by Raymond A. Blacketer. Studies in the History of Christian Thought, vol. 100. Boston: Brill, 2001.

Vanhoozer, Kevin J., ed. *The Cambridge Companion to Postmodern Theology.* Cambridge, UK: Cambridge University Press, 2003.

Venema, Cornelis P. *Heinrich Bullinger and the Doctrine of Predestination. Author of "The Other Reformed Tradition"?* Grand Rapids, Mich.: Baker Academic, 2002.

Voegelin, Eric. *History of Political Ideas: Religion and the Rise of Modernity.* Vol. 5. Edited by James L. Wiser. Vol. 23 of *The Collected Works of Eric Voegelin.* Columbia: University of Missouri Press, 1998.

———. *History of Political Ideas: Renaissance and Reformation.* Vol. 4. Edited by David L. Morse and William M. Thompson. Vol. 22 of *The Collected Works of Eric Voegelin.* Columbia: University of Missouri Press, 1998.

———. *Israel and Revelation.* Order and History. Vol. 1. Baton Rouge: Louisiana State University Press, 1956.

———. *The New Science of Politics: An Introduction.* Chicago: University of Chicago Press, 1952.

———. *Science, Politics and Gnosticism.* Washington, D.C.: Regnery Gateway

Inc., 1968.

Von Heyking, John. *Augustine and Politics as Longing in the World.* Eric Voegelin Institute Series in Political Philosophy. Columbia: University of Missouri Press, 2001.

Von Rohr, John. *The Covenant of Grace in Puritan Thought.* Atlanta: Scholars Press, 1986.

Waldron, Jeremy. *God, Locke and Equality: Christian Foundations in Locke's Political Thought.* Cambridge, UK: Cambridge University Press, 2002.

Walzer, Michael. *Exodus and Revolution.* New York: Basic Books, 1985.

———. "Where Were the Elders?" Lecture given at the University of Washington as part of the Samuel and Althea Stroum Lectures in Jewish Studies—2008. Accessible at http://www.researchchannel.org/prog/displayevent.aspx?rID=26742&fID=5630.

Ward, Graham. *Barth, Derrida and the Language of Theology.* Cambridge, UK: Cambridge University Press, 2004.

Weir, David A. *Early New England: A Covenanted Society.* Grand Rapids, Mich.: Eerdmans Publishing Company, 2005.

———. *The Origins of the Federal Theology in Sixteenth-Century Reformation Thought.* Oxford, UK: Clarendon Press, 1990.

Wills, Garry. *Inventing America.* New York: Vantage Press, 1979.

Wilson, John F. *Pulpit in Parliament: Puritanism during the English Civil Wars 1640–1648.* Princeton, N.J.: Princeton University Press, 1969.

Wright, David. "Heinrich Bullinger and the Early Church Fathers." In *Heinrich Bullinger: Life—Thought—Influence. Zurich, August 25–29, 2004. International Congress Heinrich Bullinger (1504–1575) Volume I.* Edited by Emidio Campi and Peter Opitz (Zurich: Theologischer Verlag Zurich, 2007), 357–78.

Yule, George. *Puritans in Politics: The Religious Legislation of the Long Parliament 1640–1647.* Sutton Courtenay Press, 1981.

Zakai, Avihu. *Exile and Kingdom: History and Apocalypse in the Puritan Migration to America.* Cambridge, UK: Cambridge University Press, 1992.

Ziff, Larzer. *The Career of John Cotton: Puritanism and the American Experience.* Princeton, N.J.: Princeton University Press, 1962.

Zuckert, Michael P. *The Natural Rights Republic: Studies in the Foundation of the American Political Tradition.* South Bend, Ind.: University of Notre Dame Press, 1996.

Index